D1413454

AMERICAN DRAMA
1918–1960

THE
MAGILL
BIBLIOGRAPHIES

Other Magill Bibliographies:

American Theatre History—Thomas J. Taylor
Biography—Carl Rollyson
Black American Women Novelists—Craig Werner
Classical Greek and Roman Drama—Robert J. Forman
English Romantic Poetry—Bryan Aubrey
The Modern American Novel—Steven G. Kellman
Resources for Writers—R. Baird Shuman
Shakespeare—Joseph Rosenblum
The Victorian Novel—Laurence W. Mazzeno
The Vietnam War in Literature—Philip K. Jason

AMERICAN DRAMA 1918-1960

An Annotated Bibliography

R. Baird Shuman
Professor of English
University of Illinois at Urbana-Champaign

SALEM PRESS

Pasadena, California   Englewood Cliffs, New Jersey

∞ The paper used in these volumes conforms to the
American National Standard for Permanence of Paper
for Printed Library Materials, Z39.48-1984.

Library of Congress Cataloging-in-Publication Data

Shuman, R. Baird (Robert Baird), 1929-
    American drama, 1918—1960 / R. Baird Shuman
       p.   cm.—(Magill bibliographies)
    Includes index
    ISBN 0-89356-682-9
    1. American drama—20th century—History and
criticism—Bibliography. 2. Theater—United States—
History—20th century—Bibliography. I. Title. II.
Series.
Z1231.D7S55 1992
[PS350]   91-44643
016.822'508—dc20   CIP

In memory of

GEORGE WILLIAM SHUMAN
March 6, 1904–January 2, 1951

and

ELIZABETH EVANS DAVIS
July 13, 1903–February 22, 1983

Editorial Staff

CONTENTS

AMERICAN DRAMA: 1918-1960

CONTENTS

ACKNOWLEDGMENTS

No book comes into being without the assistance of various people whose efforts enable researchers to implement their research, who smooth the way when the way needs smoothing. I must acknowledge specifically the following people who have served in such a capacity: Professor George Hendrick, Professor Zohreh T. Sullivan, Professor Richard P. Wheeler, and Professor Leon Waldoff of the University of Illinois at Urbana-Champaign; Professor James P. Davis of Denison University; Professor Denny T. Wolfe of Old Dominion University; Professor Joseph B. Trahern of the University of Tennessee; Professor Cary E. Wolfe of Indiana University; Professor Emeritus James J. Clark of San Jose State University; Professor Donald E. Hall of California State University at Northridge; Professor Rudolph C. Troike and Professor Muriel Saville-Troike of the University of Arizona; Professor Yousef Bader of Yarmouk University; and Professor Gary W. Streit of Olivet Nazarene University.

Various other friends offered help and support in their individual ways: Bao Nguyen of Boulder, Colorado; Eric Hobson and Curtis White, both of Knoxville, Tennessee; Mercy Hutchings Johnson of San Antonio, Texas; Edith Williams Horn of Tampa, Florida; Mark L. Collins and Adrian Collins, both of Melbourne, Australia; the D'Amico family of Melbourne, Australia; Clive Aspin of Auckland, New Zealand; Boyer Rickel of Tucson, Arizona; and Donna Walker, Marlyn Ehlers, and Anne Moore of Urbana, Illinois.

To librarians who helped me during my visits to the libraries of the University of Arizona at Tucson, the University of New Mexico at Albuquerque, the University of Illinois at Urbana-Champaign, the University of Nevada at Reno, the University of South Florida at Tampa, the University of Colorado at Boulder, the University of Tennessee at Knoxville, the Firestone Library of Princeton University, the Lehigh University Library, the Northern Arizona University Library, the Ohio State University Library at Columbus, and the Indiana University Library at Bloomington I express my particular gratitude. I am also grateful to personnel at the public libraries I used in proceeding with my research in the communities listed below:

Albuquerque, New Mexico
Beatty, Nevada
Blacksburg, Virginia
Boulder City, Nevada
Brinkley, Arkansas

Cairo, Illinois
Casa Grande, Arizona
Danville, Virginia
Gallup, New Mexico
Glen Rock, New Jersey

Granville, Ohio
Hawthorne, Nevada
Independence, Kansas
Kankakee, Illinois
Kingman, Arizona
Los Gatos, California
Monterey, California
Norfolk, Virginia
Paso Robles, California
Perrysburg, Ohio
Portsmouth, Virginia
Reno, Nevada
Richmond, Indiana

Roxboro, North Carolina
Sapulpa, Oklahoma
San Luis Obispo, California
Santa Barbara, California
Santa Fe, New Mexico
Santa Maria, California
Somerset, New Jersey
South Hill, Virginia
Tucumcari, New Mexico
Walton, New York
Xenia, Ohio
Zanesville, Ohio
Zephyr Cove, Nevada

Various publishers provided me with information about their publications in American drama and helped me to identify and obtain some of the more recent titles that appear in this book. Their responses were consistently prompt and efficient. I am deeply indebted to them.

The University of Illinois at Urbana-Champaign gave me a sabbatical leave to work on this and another book, *Resources for Writers: An Annotated Bibliography*, also published by Salem Press. I much appreciate having received this leave time.

Finally, John Wilson of Salem Press is a sensitive and responsive editor. He has made valuable suggestions and has been a staunch friend to me as well as an astute editor during the creation of this book. His sage advice has saved me from a number of pitfalls.

INTRODUCTION

American Drama, 1918-1960: An Annotated Bibliography is intended primarily for use by secondary school, college, and university students who are interested in pursuing research projects in American drama from the point at which Eugene O'Neill helped to establish it as a serious genre of American literature to the emergence of such mid-century American playwrights as Tennessee Williams, Arthur Miller, William Inge, and Edward Albee. Only book-length studies are included, although individual chapters in books and anthologies are sometimes cited. Because the editor realizes that many people who use this book do not have ready access to the resources in research libraries, he has checked all the sources he found in the research libraries he used against holdings in twenty-six public libraries in representative communities across the United States. These twenty-six libraries are listed under "Acknowledgments."

The scope of this bibliography is broad, and therefore its listings are selective. Every effort has been made to include in the book the major comprehensive bibliographies currently available that focus on specific playwrights or movements in modern American drama so that readers who want more extensive resources will be led to the sources that provide them.

Compiling selective bibliographies forces difficult decisions upon editors. Among these is the need to present a representative listing of works relating to the field being considered. This book is intended to be as fairly representative as it can be. The conscious exclusion of a book or anthology is not meant as a slight. Many excellent sources have, after thoughtful deliberation, been excluded because of space limitations. The editor's guiding principle has been to provide readers with the most balanced and representative bibliography he could produce.

American Drama, 1918-1960: An Annotated Bibliography begins with a section on general reference works—the sorts of books found in the reference rooms of many libraries. Such books generally do not circulate but are for library use only. The next section lists general resources, books about theater that consider it broadly rather than books that focus on individual playwrights or plays. These books usually provide useful information about individual playwrights and plays but treat them more succinctly than books with a narrower focus. Their chief aim is to reach generalizations about modern drama or modern theatrical movements. Their discussions of specific playwrights and plays are designed to relate the smaller details they present to the broad framework they have established.

The third section of the book deals with sources that present information about regional theater, Off-Broadway theater, Off-Off-Broadway theater, and little theater. It also lists sources that consider such theatrical organizations as the Group Theater, the Theater Guild, and the Actors Studio Theater.

The remainder of this bibliography presents resources that deal with twenty-seven American playwrights who were active during the period in question. For the purposes of this book, T. S. Eliot is considered an American playwright, although some might dispute this classification because Eliot spent most of his productive life in Great Britain and ultimately became a British subject.

Some of the playwrights for whom sources are provided—among them Eugene O'Neill, Tennessee Williams, Arthur Miller, and Edward Albee—have been written about so voluminously that many significant works have been excluded. Other worthwhile playwrights have received scant scholarly attention. Perhaps this book will suggest to some readers areas in which additional scholarly research is needed.

A few of the playwrights included in this bibliography were not essentially writers of plays but wrote sufficiently within this genre to justify inclusion here. Among these are Langston Hughes, known primarily as a poet, and James Baldwin, Edna Ferber, and Carson McCullers, best known as novelists. Each, however, has made notable contributions to drama.

In some cases, the general resources that deal with individual authors are followed by resources that deal with specific plays written by those authors. Generally, it can be assumed that any book about an individual playwright will deal with most of that author's plays. In some cases, however, a book has appeared that deals with only one play, or a chapter in a book about an individual playwright focuses on a specific play in such a way that separate inclusion under the title of a given play seems warranted. Finally, the editor has attempted to indicate whether the sources listed here provide such helpful features as indexes and bibliographies, both of which facilitate the use of any book that is being consulted for research purposes. The lack of such features does not suggest that a book is not worthwhile; it merely warns people that they may not be able to use such sources as efficiently as they can use sources that offer them these aids to finding research material.

It is neither desirable nor possible for a book of this sort to avoid some overlapping. Although the end date stated in the title is 1960, Edward Albee had brought only one play to the stage by that date, so the entry on him deals with his work beyond the stipulated cutoff date. Similarly, authors such as Tennessee Williams, William Inge, Arthur Miller, and Thornton Wilder continued to produce plays after the end date of this bibliography. Their later work is included without apology.

GENERAL REFERENCE WORKS

The books listed below are found in the reference rooms of many libraries. Most of them deal specifically with nearly all the playwrights for whom bibliographies are provided in this book. Because these books would appear in almost every individual bibliography of the authors covered here if they were to be listed in the individual entries, these titles will be listed only here to avoid duplication.

Bibliographic Guide to Theatre Arts: 1990. New York: New York Public Library, 1990.
This guide, which is a supplement to the *Catalogue of the Theater and Drama Collections* (see below) of the New York Public Library, lists all the materials cataloged in the collection of the New York Public Library and provides additional entries from the Library of Congress MARC (Machine-Readable Cataloging) tapes. The guide covers all aspects of the theater and lists both print and nonprint materials.

Billington, Michael. *The Guinness Book of Theatre: Facts and Feats.* Enfield, England: Guinness Superlatives, 1982.
This book covers such matters as the origins of drama, theaters, actors and actresses, plays and playwrights, musical plays, acting companies, directors, and producers. The appendices cover only three British acting companies, but the book in general covers American drama comprehensively and succinctly. There is an index.

Boardman, Gerald, ed. *The Oxford Companion to American Theatre.* New York: Oxford University Press, 1984.
Boardman's book is more specialized than the Hartnoll volume (see below). It contains brief, alphabetically arranged pieces on American plays and playwrights, performers, directors, producers, composers, lyricists, theater companies and organizations, and specific theaters. The book has more than three thousand entries and is relatively up to date to mid-1983.

Catalogue of the Theatre and Drama Collections. Boston: G. K. Hall, 1967.
This catalog lists the holdings of the theater and drama collections in all the Research Libraries of the New York Public Library. This book is updated in *Bibliographic Guide to Theatre Arts: 1990* (see above).

Concise Dictionary of American Literary Biography. Detroit: Gale Research.
The volumes of this dictionary that are particularly relevant are those dealing with the years 1917 to 1929, 1929 to 1941, and 1941 to 1968. The entries are so brief as to seem superficial. They do, however, provide basic information about

authors and their work. One can determine whether playwrights are listed in this source by checking the cumulative index of *Contemporary Authors* (see below).

Connor, Billie M., and Helene G. Mochedlover, eds. *Ottenmiller's Index to Plays in Collections: An Author and Title Index to Plays Appearing in Collections Published Between 1900 and 1985.* Rev. ed. Metuchen, N.J.: Scarecrow Press, 1988.
The author index, which lists all of an author's plays that have appeared in collections, is 231 pages long. It is followed by a 233-page listing of collections and their contents and by a key to symbols used throughout the book. This invaluable reference guide concludes with a title index, which is not quite one hundred pages long.

Contemporary Authors, Bryan Ryan, Index Coordinator. Detroit: Gale Research.
The volumes in this set, now approaching the 150 mark, appear regularly and contain biographical entries about writers in every genre. Entries are updated periodically, and obituaries are included when an author dies. Especially helpful is the cumulative index to volumes 1 through 130. It not only indexes biographies included in the volumes of *Contemporary Authors* but also lists entries in twenty-one similar volumes that Gale publishes. This index is a reasonable starting point for serious researchers. It is constantly updated and is remarkably current.

Contemporary Literary Criticism. Detroit: Gale Research.
This fifty-seven-volume set presents substantial excerpts from the relevant criticism available for the authors it lists. The amount of criticism reproduced makes the book extremely valuable as a starting point for research on a writer. Writers whose work is covered in this set are listed in the cumulative index of *Contemporary Authors* (see above).

Curley, Dorothy Nyren, Maurice Kramer, and Elaine Fialka Kramer, comps. and eds. *Modern American Literature: A Library of Criticism.* New York: Frederick Ungar, 1960, 1961, 1964, 1969, 1973.
This single-volume reference book has brief entries on most of the writers included in this bibliography. Its coverage is not extensive, but it provides a valuable overview of the authors, literary movements, and other subjects it covers. It is arranged alphabetically.

Dictionary of Literary Biography. Detroit: Gale Research.
There are now more than one hundred volumes in this set, and they are readily available in the reference collections of many libraries. The entries, written by specialists in the fields covered, are long and detailed, providing extensive biographical information as well as full bibliographies of primary and secondary sources for each author covered. The cumulative index of *Contemporary Authors*

(see above) indicates whether a given writer is included in this resource. An annual yearbook provides updated information about writers included in earlier volumes.

Durham, Weldon B., ed. *American Theatre Companies, 1931-1986*. Westport, Conn.: Greenwood Press, 1987.
Weldon's book, the most comprehensive one available on American theater companies, is especially useful for its thorough coverage of such companies as the Group Theatre and the Theatre Guild. Durham deals also with regional companies, such as the Margo Jones Theatre in Dallas, the Alley Theatre in Houston, the Actors' Workshop in San Francisco, and the Guthrie Theatre in Minneapolis.

Espmark, Kjell, ed. *The Nobel Prize in Literature*. Translated by Robin Fulton. Boston: G. K. Hall, 1991.
Espmark's work provides background for each Nobel Prize in Literature from the inception of the award in 1895. The editor attempts to show how each laureate in literature fulfilled the basic aims of the Nobel awards, according to the terms of Alfred Nobel's will. He tells how decisions were made in many controversial cases.

Esslin, Martin, ed. *The Encyclopedia of World Theatre*. New York: Charles Scribner's Sons, 1977.
The major portion of this alphabetical listing contains more than two thousand entries supplemented by 420 illustrations. The entries are generally brief and direct, but they cover a broad range of plays, playwrights, actors and actresses, directors, and other matters relating to theater. The index of play titles has more than five thousand entries.

Flora, Joseph M., and Robert Bain. *Fifty Southern Writers After 1900*. Westport, Conn.: Greenwood Press, 1987.
This volume, although it focuses largely on writers of prose fiction, contains essays on Paul Green, Lillian Hellman, Carson McCullers, and Tennessee Williams. Each essay presents a biography, a discussion of major themes in the work of the subject, a survey of criticism written about the subject, a bibliography of the subject's writing, and a section labeled "Studies of . . . ." In some cases, the latter section is quite extended and provides excellent bibliographical information.

French, Warren G., ed. *The Fifties: Fiction, Poetry, Drama*. Deland, Fla.: Edwards/Everett, 1970.
Among the fifteen essays in this collection, some of those that focus on drama are by Jordan Y. Miller (Tennessee Williams' *Camino Real*, 1953), Sy Kahn (on

Archibald MacLeish's *JB*, 1956), and Jackson R. Bryer (on Eugene O'Neill's *Long Day's Journey into Night*, wr. 1941, pr. 1956). The book has a useful index.

_____. *The Thirties: Fiction, Poetry, Drama.* Deland, Fla.: Everett/
Edwards, 1967.
French's collection of fifteen essays captures the literary spirit of the 1930's. Among the essays on drama are those by Robert J. Griffin on Clifford Odets, by Gerald Rabkin on the Federal Theatre Project, by James H. Justus on William Saroyan, and by Jordan Y. Miller on Maxwell Anderson. The book is well documented and has a useful index.

French, Warren G, and Walter E. Kidd, eds. *American Winners of the Nobel Literary Prize.* Norman, Okla.: University of Oklahoma Press, 1968.
This book lists all the American Nobel laureates in literature up to 1968, including Eugene O'Neill (the thirty-page essay is by Jordan Y. Miller), and T. S. Eliot (James V. Barr's essay is twenty-seven pages long). The coverage is succinct, accurate, and useful, especially suited to the novice, who will gain a solid overview from it.

Geisinger, Marion, ed. *Plays, Players, and Playwrights: An Illustrated History of the Theatre*, updated and revised by Peggy Marks. New York: Hart, 1975.
The revised edition of this book, although it is again in need of updating, is still serviceable. Its text and illustrations are well selected. It is reasonably comprehensive and is particularly strong on American playwrights of the period covered by this bibliography.

Hart, James D., ed. *The Oxford Companion to American Literature.* New York: Oxford University Press, 1941, 1948, 1956, 1965, 5th ed., 1983.
This single-volume reference work is frequently updated and has excellent coverage, although its entries are brief. Most writers listed in this bibliography have entries in *The Oxford Companion to the Theatre*.

Hartnoll, Phyllis, ed. *The Oxford Companion to the Theatre.* New York: Oxford University Press, 1st ed., 1951; 2d ed., 1957; 3d ed., 1967; 4th ed., 1983.
Enhanced with copious illustrations, this regularly updated companion to the theater can be found in most public libraries. It contains an alphabetical listing of plays, playwrights, actors, directors, producers, theater groups, and other related materials. Following the main text is a substantial listing of suggestions for further reading.

Hochman, Stanley, ed. *McGraw-Hill Encyclopedia of World Drama.* New York: McGraw-Hill, 1984.

This ambitious five-volume work covers the whole of drama up to the date of its publication. The clear, crisp, direct essays contain useful bibliographical details. The work also contains essays on stagecraft, directing, theories and techniques of playwrighting, approaches to acting, and other subjects relevant to the production of plays.

Keller, Dean H., ed. *Index to Plays in Periodicals*. Rev. and exp. ed. Metuchen, N.J.: Scarecrow Press, 1979.
Keller lists 267 periodicals included in this index, which has a total of 4,562 entries, 2,145 of them added since earlier editions of the work. The author index runs from page 1 to page 676; the title index runs from page 679 to page 824. A most comprehensive work.

Kullman, Colby H., and William C. Young, eds. *Theatre Companies of the World*. Westport, Conn.: Greenwood Press, 1986.
This comprehensive and dependable book, arranged for easy use, provides information about theater companies in Africa, Asia, Australia and New Zealand, Canada, Eastern Europe, Latin America, the Middle East, and Scandinavia. It does for world theater companies what Durham's book (see above) does for American theater companies.

Loney, Glenn, ed. *Twentieth Century Theatre*. New York: Facts on File, 1983.
The two volumes in this set focus on the rise of theater in the twentieth century, presenting details on playwrights, critics, performances, theaters, actors, directors, and others intimately involved with play production. The solid bibliographical information it contains makes it valuable to those pursuing research in drama.

Lovell, James, Jr., ed. *Digest of Great American Plays*. New York: Thomas Y. Crowell, 1961.
Lovell provides summaries of 102 American plays from 1766 to 1959, fifty-five of them in the 1918-to-1959 period. An appendix lists the plays and their authors along with identification by type and a notation about the time and locale of each play.

MacNicholas, John. *Twentieth-Century American Dramatists*. Detroit: Gale Research, 1981.
Volume 7 of the enormous, multivolume *Dictionary of Literary Biography* is in two volumes. It presents long, detailed biographies of most notable American playwrights and gives a full biography of the writings of each. Following each entry, some of which run to twenty or more pages, is a reasonably full bibliography of secondary sources about the playwright. The set is enhanced by a foreword by John Houseman, who reflects on theater in the United States.

Magill, Frank N., ed. *Critical Survey of Drama: English Language Series*, Englewood Cliffs, N.J.: Salem Press, 1985.
The six volumes and one supplemental volume that constitute this reference set
cover most of the significant dramatists writing in English. The essays, which
are analytical and follow a standard format, average 2,500 words. Each has a
bibliography of the work of the dramatist under discussion as well as a selected
bibliography of secondary sources. The biographies contain sections in which
dramatists are evaluated in terms of their achievements relative to the times in
which they lived.

_____, ed. *Masterplots II: Drama Series*. Englewood Cliffs, N.J.: Salem
Press, 1990.
This set offers information on individual plays. Basic information about the work
and its author is given, along with a cast of characters, at the beginning of each
entry. The work under discussion is then synopsized, after which there are
sections on themes and meanings, dramatic devices used, critical context, and
a list of sources for further reading.

_____, ed. *The Nobel Prize Winners: Literature*. Englewood Cliffs, N.J.:
Salem Press, 1987.
This comprehensive presentation in three volumes covers each winner of the
Nobel Prize in Literature since the inception of the awards. The entries average
two thousand words. Each contains an account of the presentation drawn from
the presentation speech and a similar account of the acceptance speech. The
public reception of the award is discussed in the next section, which is followed
by a biographical sketch of the recipient. The heart of each essay considers the
recipient's career and contributions. A bibliography of each subject's work is
included, and this is followed by a bibliography of secondary sources.

Mapp, Edward, ed. *Directory of Blacks in the Performing Arts*. Metuchen, N.J.:
Scarecrow Press, 1978.
Mapp's directory contains an alphabetical listing of African Americans in all the
performing arts. It gives birth and—if applicable—death dates, education, and
involvement with the performing arts, listing credits fully. The book has a solid
bibliography. Its index is extremely useful because it is a classified index with
such headings as "Musicians," "Playwrights," and "Actors."

New York Theatre Critics' Reviews. New York: Critics' Theatre Reviews.
These reviews have been appearing in small fascicles every two or three weeks
since the mid-1920's. Every year, the reviews for that year are gathered into a
compact volume. The scope is broad. Every New York newspaper review of
every play that opens on Broadway in a year is represented in this annual

volume, and the fascicles are usually available within two or three weeks of a
play's Broadway opening.

The New York Times Directory of the Theater. New York: New York Times Books,
1973.
This resource, which is essentially an index, first lists titles of plays and then
provides the most extensive personal-name index currently available in drama.
The name of each person listed is followed by a list of that person's plays. This
book, which has more than 300,000 entries, is found even in many small public
libraries and is in the reference collection of almost every institution of higher
learning.

The New York Times Theater Reviews. New York: Times Books and Garland.
This annual publication reproduces all the theater reviews that appeared in *The
New York Times* for the year the volume covers. These volumes, which have
appeared every year since 1920, are a marvelous resource for scholars who prefer
not to read the newspaper on microfilm.

The Nobel Prize Annual. Boston: G. K. Hall, published annually.
Each volume of this illustrated volume provides profiles of the Nobel Prize
laureates of a given year and enumerates their accomplishments. Each laureate's
acceptance speech is printed. Each volume also includes a retrospective look at
the Nobel Prize laureates from the beginning of the prize in 1895. A number of
the recipients of the prize in literature have been dramatists.

Robinson, Alice M., Vera Mowry Roberts, and Mills S. Barranger, eds. *Notable
Women in the American Theatre: A Biographical Dictionary.* Westport, Conn.:
Greenwood Press, 1989.
The alphabetical listings in this book focus on women who have anything to do
with theater, from actresses and playwrights to stage designers and prop people.
The book is solidly researched by an impressive selection of scholars in drama.
The first of two appendices lists by place of birth those included in the book. A
second appendix lists the same people by profession, which is especially conve-
nient for those who want to use the book as a reference tool.

Salem, James M., ed. *Drury's Guide to Best Plays.* 4th ed. Metuchen, N.J.:
Scarecrow Press, 1987.
Salem renders a considerable service to those who wish to produce plays, since
he devotes 432 pages to listing playwrights and their plays, giving a synopsis of
each play, an indication of the extent of the cast required, and information about
sets needed to mount a production and royalties charged. This lengthy section,
the heart of the book, is followed by lists of plays on special topics (the black
experience, mysteries, women's experiences), a list of prize-winning plays, a list

of the most popular plays for high school and amateur community productions, a directory of publishers of plays, a list of abbreviations used in citing collections, and an index of titles.

Schlessinger, Bernard, June Schlessinger, et al., eds. *Who's Who in Nobel Prize Winners*. Phoenix, Ariz.: Oryx Press, 1986.
The biographies in this book include all Nobel Prize winners in all fields. The individual entries are brief and direct, but they are useful in establishing the subjects' claims to the award and in leading readers to other sources about the laureates.

Slide, Anthony, ed. *Selected Theatre Criticism*. Metuchen, N.J.: Scarecrow Press, Volume 2, 1985, Volume 3, 1986.
Volume 2 of this set provides criticism for the decade 1920 to 1930. Volume 3 covers the two decades from 1931 to 1950. Slide reproduces reviews or portions of reviews for most of the significant Broadway plays produced during the periods covered in these two books. One can gain important overviews of given plays quite conveniently from these books.

Spiller, Robert E., ed. *Literary History of the United States*. New York: Macmillan, 1946, 1947, 1948, 1953, 1953, 1963.
This standard history of American literature comments on nearly all the authors covered in this bibliography. The set has a bibliographical volume that is kept reasonably up to date.

Twentieth-Century Literary Criticism. Detroit: Gale Research.
This continuing series contains extensive excerpts of critical works about the work of twentieth-century authors, much as *Contemporary Literary Criticism* (see above) does. Those whose works are listed in this series are indicated in the cumulative index of *Contemporary Authors* (see above).

Wasson, Tyler, ed. *Nobel Prize Winners*. New York: H. W. Wilson, 1987.
Wasson presents, in alphabetical order, brief sketches of each of the 566 Nobel laureates selected between 1901 and 1986. Each entry is between 1,200 and 1,500 words long. The suggestions for further reading about each candidate are quite limited, but they do pinpoint the salient sources.

Willis, Kendall J. *The Pulitzer Prizes*. New York: Simon & Schuster, annually since 1987.
This book considers only those awards given to journalists; therefore, its only relevance to those interested primarily in drama is the annual award in criticism.

Yaakov, Juliette, and John Greenfield, eds. *Play Index, 1983–1987*. 7th ed. New York: H. W. Wilson, 1988.

Each volume of this work, which has been published regularly since 1953, is extremely useful to those interested in drama. The preceding volumes are for the following periods: 1949-1952, 1953-1960, 1961-1967, 1968-1972, 1973-1977, and 1978-1982. Each volume lists plays published during the period in question, indicating whether they are essentially for children (preschool to grade 6), young people (grades 7-10), or adults. The combined author, title, and subject index is 415 pages long. It is followed by a section (pages 417-464) on cast analysis, which gives the number of characters and the number of extras in each play. This section is followed by a list of collections (pages 465-516) and a director of publishers and distributors of plays (pages 517-522).

Young, William C., ed. *Documents of American Theater History: Famous American Playhouses, 1900-1971.* Chicago: American Library Association, 1973.
In this handsomely illustrated two-volume set, readers and researchers will find information about the great American playhouses of the first seven decades of the twentieth century; ample illustrations accompany the extensive and interesting commentary. Interesting sidelights about many of the theaters and the people who played in them are provided.

GENERAL RESOURCES

Abramson, Doris E. *Negro Playwrights in the American Theatre, 1925-1959*. New York: Columbia University Press, 1969.
After a chapter surveying the beginnings of African-American drama, Abramson devotes a chapter to each of the decades that her book covers. Among those about whom she writes are Langston Hughes, Alice Childress, Richard Wright, Theodore Browne, Wallace Thurman, and Lorraine Hansberry. The book contains a lengthy bibliography and a comprehensive index.

Adler, Thomas P. *Mirror on the Stage: The Pulitzer Plays as an Approach to American Drama*. West Lafayette, Ind.: Purdue University Press, 1987.
Adler traces the history of the Pulitzer Prize in Drama since its inception in 1917, noting changes in the wording of the drama citation, which now reads, "For a distinguished play by an American author, preferably original in its source and dealing with American life." Omitted is former terminology that had to do with raising the standard of American drama. He concludes that for better or worse, "the award of the Pulitzer ordinarily reflects what is being thought by the American popular imagination." Adler provides a useful index.

Anderson, John. *Box Office*. New York: Jonathan Cape and Harrison Smith, 1929.
Despite its age—or perhaps because of it—this book is extremely interesting for its insights into the business of theater. Anderson has organized it into three general sections, one each on organization (equity, labor affiliations, road companies, the box office), complications (morals, hits, movies), and personalities (producers, dramatists). His comments on the growth of little theaters are useful.

Atkinson, Brooks. *Broadway*. New York: Macmillan, 1970; rev. ed., 1974.
Three sections of this book present a season-by-season history of American drama, focusing on the periods from 1918 to 1939, from 1939 to 1950, and from 1950 to 1970 (1974 in the revised edition). This book provides a ready reference for those who need factual information about the plays that were on Broadway during a given period.

_____. *Broadway Scrapbook*. New York: Theatre Arts, 1947.
Longtime *New York Times* theater critic Brooks Atkinson has gathered together in this scrapbook many interesting items of theatrical lore, including a report on Eugene O'Neill's receiving the Nobel Prize in 1936. Atkinson prints Eleanor Roosevelt's reactions to Thornton Wilder's *Our Town* (1938) and also responds to the First Lady's comments on his review of Katherine Drayton's *Save Me the Waltz* (1938). Atkinson's comments on the New York World's Fair and drama are interesting.

Atkinson, Brooks, and Albert Hirschfeld. *The Lively Years, 1920-1973*. New York: Association Press, 1973.
This book is a carefully selected collection of Atkinson's major theater reviews from 1920 to 1973. It includes most of his notable reviews on the plays of Eugene O'Neill, Clifford Odets, Philip Barry, John Howard Lawson, Robert E. Sherwood, Irwin Shaw, Marc Blitzstein, John Steinbeck, Thornton Wilder, Tennessee Williams, Arthur Miller, and William Inge.

Baumol, William J., and William G. Bowen. *Performing Arts: The Economic Dilemma*. New York: Twentieth Century Fund, 1966.
The escalating cost of producing legitimate theater has increased to the point of threatening the future of serious theater in the United States. This book presents the realities of the situation, supporting with hard facts its contentions and predictions.

Bentley, Eric. *The Dramatic Event*. New York: Horizon Press, 1954.
In this book, Eric Bentley provides assorted reviews of Broadway plays for the 1952-to-1954 theater seasons. This is a quick guide for anyone who wants an overview of Broadway theater for the period covered. Bentley's *What Is Theatre?* (see below) is an identical book for the 1954-to-1956 theater seasons.

_____. *In Search of Theater*. New York: Alfred A. Knopf, 1953.
Although this book contains mostly reviews and articles about continental theater, it has some excellent insights about Eugene O'Neill and somewhat less detailed ones about such playwrights as Clifford Odets, Arthur Miller, Thornton Wilder, and Tennessee Williams. Among his more perceptive statements is the following: "If one does not like O'Neill, it is not really he that one dislikes: it is our age—of which like the rest of us he is more the victim than the master." The book has thirty chapters in five subdivisions, illustrations, and an index.

_____. *What Is Theatre? A Query in Chronicle Form*. New York: Horizon Press, 1956.
Bentley has gathered, culled, and presented here representative critiques of plays that were on Broadway from 1954 to 1956. His choices represent a broad sampling of critical opinions about some extremely influential plays. Bentley's *The Dramatic Event* (see above) is an identical listing for the 1952 to 1954 Broadway seasons.

Blau, Herbert. *The Impossible Theater: A Manifesto*. New York: Macmillan, 1964.
Blau offers one of the most far-reaching accounts in print of American theater during the Cold War. He discusses the hazards of trying to have a viable theater in times of such political and social upheaval. Blau, formerly the producing director of San Francisco's Actors' Workshop, presents a history of the Actors'

Workshop and recounts his involvement in it. The book's approach is global. It is not easy reading, but it is worthwhile. The illustrations are apt. There is no index.

Bonin, Jane F. *Prize-Winning American Drama: A Bibliographical and Descriptive Guide.* Metuchen, N.J.: Scarecrow Press, 1973.
Bonin considers every play from 1917 to the 1970-1971 Broadway season that has won a Pulitzer Prize, The Critics' Circle Award, The Antoinette (Tony) Perry Award, the *Village Voice* Off-Broadway (Obie) Award, or the Players' Workshop Award. A brief act-by-act synopsis is provided for each play along with the cast of characters and the names of the actors who portrayed them. A section dealing with the play's history and reviews follows. It is followed by a section that deals with the play's critical reputation. The index is extensive and accurate. The coverage is minimal but is useful in directing readers to fuller studies.

Bricker, Herschel, ed. *Our Theatre Today.* New York: Samuel French, 1939.
Chapter 4 of this well-illustrated book deals with theater in America. The book also contains essays by Irving Pichel, "The Present Day Theatre"; Barrett H. Clark, "Playwright and Theatre"; and Brock Pemberton, "The Director." The latter is followed by three essays on directing, all entitled "My Method of Directing," by Melville Burke, Bertram Harrison, and Priestly Morrison. Part 4 of the book contains six essays on stagecraft—lighting, makeup, costuming, and so forth. The bibliography is solid but dated. A comprehensive index helps readers to pinpoint information.

Brown, John Mason. *Broadway in Review.* New York: W. W. Norton, 1940.
Mason focuses in chapter 4 on what he considers the yield of American theater: Robert E. Sherwood, Clifford Odets, William Saroyan, and Philip Barry. Chapter 4 is devoted to George P. Baker's classes in play writing at Harvard and takes a look at Thomas Wolfe as dramatist, noting that he wrote one play for Professor Koch of the Carolina Players and two plays as Baker's student, which Baker produced in Cambridge.

Brustein, Robert. *Seasons of Discontent: Dramatic Opinions, 1959-1965.* New York: Simon & Schuster, 1965.
Divided into sections entitled "Off-Broadway," "Broadway," "From Abroad," "Companies," and "General," Brustein's book is a collection of pieces he wrote during a six-year period. Most of the essays appeared originally in *New Republic*. Brustein includes his scathing pieces on William Inge, "The Men-Taming Women of William Inge" and "No Loss: *A Loss of Roses* and *Natural Affection*," as well as pieces on Edward Albee, Tennessee Williams, Arthur Miller, Paddy Chayefsky, James Baldwin, and Eugene O'Neill. He writes with a combination of

brilliance and vitriol, although the vitriol, frequently born of dogmatism, is often more noticeable than the brilliance.

Case, Sue-Ellen. *Feminism and Theatre*. New York: Routledge, 1988.
This short book, with a splendid index and useful bibliography, traces the growth of feminist interpretations of American drama and the ascendancy of plays that deal with feminist issues. Case also provides helpful information about women playwrights and about male playwrights, such as Tennessee Williams and William Inge, who were intrigued by the female psychological makeup and understood it well.

Clark, Barrett H. *An Hour of American Drama*. Philadelphia: J. B. Lippincott, 1930.
Clark devotes separate chapters to Eugene O'Neill's early work, to his plays of the 1920's, to the Provincetown Players and the Washington Square Players—he notes Susan Glaspell's enormous contribution to the founding of these theaters—to George Kelly, Elmer Rice, Sidney Howard, Laurence Stallings, Maxwell Anderson, Marc Connelly and George Kaufman, Philip Barry, Paul Green, and Lynn Riggs. Clark also has a chapter on newer writers, none of whom became established writers except Michael Gold and e. e. cummings.

Clum, John M. *Acting Gay: A History of Homosexuality in Drama*. New York: Columbia University Press, 1992.
John Clum surveys plays by and/or about homosexuals from the sixteenth century to the present. He notes that gay playwrights until recently had to write in code; they communicated things to gays that were not taken in by straight people in mom-and-pop audiences. This is the most comprehensive study of male homosexuality in drama. It is impressively thorough and offers a full bibliography and comprehensive index.

Clurman, Harold. *The Naked Image: Observations on the Modern Theatre*. New York: Macmillan, 1966.
This collection of reviews and essays by Harold Clurman deals with such playwrights as Edward Albee, Clifford Odets, James Baldwin, LeRoi Jones, Eugene O'Neill, and Tennessee Williams. The book also has essays about theater across America, theater abroad, and musical theatrical productions. The author provides an extensive index.

Cohn, Ruby. *Dialogue in American Drama*. Bloomington, Ind.: Indiana University Press, 1971.
Cohn's major focus in this book is on Eugene O'Neill, Arthur Miller, Tennessee Williams, and Edward Albee, although she also comments, sometimes quite fully, on Samuel Beckett, Leroi Jones, Archibald MacLeish, Clifford Odets, Gertrude

Stein, Thornton Wilder, and others. The book is thoughtful and provocative. Its bibliography is useful, its index comprehensive.

Dickinson, Thomas H. *Playwrights of the New American Theater.* New York: Macmillan, 1925.
Although this book is old, it is easily available in many public libraries. Its virtue lies in its insights into the rising playwrights of the early 1920's. The sixty-eight page chapter (20 percent of the total book) on Eugene O'Neill is particularly perceptive. Other developing playwrights mentioned are Marc Connelly, George S. Kaufman, Zoe Atkins, Susan Glaspell, Booth Tarkington, and George Kelly. The book has an index.

Downer, Alan S., ed. *American Drama and Its Critics: A Collection of Essays.* Chicago: University of Chicago Press, 1965.
This extensive collection contains essays by James A. Herne, W. D. Howells, Walter Prichard Eaton, James Gibbons Huneker, Robert Benchley, Stark Young, H. T. Parker, and others. The most compelling essays are George Jean Nathan's on Eugene O'Neill, John Howard Lawson's on the law of conflict in drama, and Malcolm Goldstein's "Clifford Odets and the Found Generation."

_____. *The American Theater Today.* New York: Basic Books, 1967.
Central to this book are Malcolm Goldstein's essay on Thornton Wilder, Esther M. Jackson's essay on Tennessee Williams, and Gerald Weales' essay on Arthur Miller. Bernard Hewitt, Richard Barr, John Gassner, Bernard F. Dukore, Arthur Lithgow, and Edwin Burr Pettet have also contributed valuable essays. Downer also provides transcripts of interviews with Edward Albee, Murray Schisgal, Jerry Bock, and Sheldon Harnick. The book has a reliable index.

_____. *Fifty Years of American Drama: 1900–1950.* Chicago: Henry Regnery, 1951.
Rather than presenting a chronological development of American drama during its impressive half-century, Downer deals with cogent topics such as theatricalism (chapter 1), folk drama (chapter 4), and American comedy (chapter 6) and shows their development through this period. Chapter 3, "From Romance to Reality," is perhaps the most important in the book. It reveals the breakneck pace at which realism developed in the American theater after Eugene O'Neill. The index is helpful in locating comments about individual playwrights and plays.

Frick, Constance. *The Dramatic Criticism of George Jean Nathan.* Ithaca, N.Y.: Cornell University Press, 1943.
This book, which unfortunately has no index, is divided into four chapters that deal with Nathan's life and works, his critical credo regarding the art of drama, his critical credo regarding the art of criticizing drama, and his Nathan influence.

Nathan wrote the foreword. Frick, who presents a bibliography of Nathan's books, seeks to generalize about Nathan's attitudes toward drama and criticism. Her study reproduces extensive excerpts from Nathan's books and reviews.

Gardner, R. H. *The Splintered Stage: The Decline of the American Theater.* New York: Macmillan, 1965.
Gardner's is one of many polemics that point to what some critics have called the moral sickness of the modern American theater. Gardner specifically cites Arthur Miller, Tennessee Williams, Lillian Hellman, Elmer Rice, William Inge, Clifford Odets, Paddy Chayefsky, and Arthur Laurents as those who are at least partially responsible. Gardner decries the common hero of American drama. His knowledge of modern theater is encyclopedic even though his reasoning is significantly flawed and shockingly reactionary. The book has twelve chapters, a postscript, and no index.

Gassner, John. *Directions in Modern American Theatre and Drama.* New York: Holt, Rinehart and Winston, 1966.
Initially, Gassner writes about the realistic phase of American drama, but in part 2 he discusses the move from realism to expressionism. Especially interesting is part 5, which consists of essays by Bertram Joseph, August Strindberg, Henry Adler, Marvin Rosenberg, and Edward Albee, whose "Which Theatre Is the Absurd One?" has been much reprinted. The chronology of the modern theater runs for thirty-one pages. A bibliographical note and a dependable index are useful features.

_____. *Dramatic Soundings: Evaluations and Retractions Culled from Thirty Years of Dramatic Criticism.* New York: Crown, 1968.
This large volume contains a quite complete collection of John Gassner's essays and theatrical reviews for the period from 1935 to 1965 and deals with most of the influential playwrights of that period: Edward Albee, Maxwell Anderson, James Baldwin, Philip Barry, T. S. Eliot, Paul Green, Lorraine Hansberry, William Inge, Arthur Miller, Clifford Odets, Eugene O'Neill, Robert E. Sherwood, and Tennessee Williams. Gassner also reviews the plays of a number of minor authors and provides valuable information about such theater groups as the Group Theater, the Theater Guild, and the Actors Studio. The book has a comprehensive index and a detailed table of contents. An introduction is provided by Glenn Loney, who edited the book after Gassner's death.

_____. *Theatre at the Crossroads: Plays and Playwrights of the Mid-Century American Stage.* New York: Holt, Rinehart and Winston, 1960.
In this retrospective look at American drama of the first half of the twentieth century, Gassner examines the plays, playwrights, and social forces that motivated dramatic writing during that period. Gassner devotes full chapters to both

Eugene O'Neill and Tennessee Williams. In other chapters, he considers in some detail Clifford Odets, Philip Barry, Robert E. Sherwood, Lillian Hellman, Sidney Kingsley, William Saroyan, William Inge, Arthur Miller, Robert Anderson, Archibald MacLeish, and others. He devotes one chapter to revivals of classic plays and one to European drama. The book has a brief bibliographical note and a full index.

Goldman, Michael. *The Actor's Freedom: Toward a Theory of Drama*. New York: Viking Press, 1975.
Goldman's book has interesting comments about ritual parallels in modern drama and about the role of aggression in drama generally. The section on the double impulse of drama is thought-provoking. Several American playwrights are mentioned in passing: Eugene O'Neill, T. S. Eliot, Tennessee Williams, Clifford Odets, and Arthur Miller.

Goldman, William. *The Season: A Candid Look at Broadway*. New York: Harcourt, Brace & World, 1969.
This book is essentially a chatty, gossipy review of Broadway plays produced in the late 1960's. It is a good resource for statistics that have to do with the cost of staging plays. The book is extensive (35 chapters in 432 pages). It has a helpful index.

Greenfield, Thomas Allen. *Work and the Work Ethic in American Drama, 1920–1970*. Columbia, Mo.: University of Missouri Press, 1982.
Greenfield traces the question of the work ethic from nineteenth century American drama. He examines it in a full chapter devoted to Elmer Rice, another that concentrates on the drama of the 1920's and 1930's, and one that focuses on the decade of World War II, which is followed by a chapter that analyzes *Death of a Salesman* (1949), *All My Sons* (1947), and *The Glass Menagerie* (1944). Chapter 6 is entitled "The 1960's"; it is followed by a conclusion, a bibliography, and an index.

Flexner, Eleanor. *American Playwrights, 1918–1938: The Theatre Retreats from Reality*. New York: Simon & Schuster, 1938.
Flexner's book is divided into two parts, the first of which considers the retreat from realism and associates that movement with Sidney Howard, S. N. Behrman, Maxwell Anderson, and Eugene O'Neill, to each of whom she devotes a chapter. Part 1 concludes with a chapter on comedy and treats George S. Kaufman, George Kelly, Rachel Crothers, Philip Barry, and Robert E. Sherwood. The second part deals with what Flexner labels "Counter-Attack," and deals with such practitioners as Elmer Rice, Susan Glaspell, John Howard Lawson, Paul Green, John Wexley, Sophie Treadwell, and Arthur Richman. The book has a good index.

Herron, Ima Honaker. *The Small Town in American Drama*. Dallas, Tex.: Southern Methodist University Press, 1969.
In her remarkably comprehensive book, Herron demonstrates how regional American drama is. She moves geographically from small towns in New England to small towns in the Midwest, the far West, and the South, always finding strong elements of these places in the broad range of drama that she examines. She devotes one chapter to Eugene O'Neill and less space to other playwrights. No significant American playwright is neglected, however, in this book of impressive scope. The documentation is profuse, the bibliographies (a separate one for each chapter) are extensive, and the index is comprehensive.

Hill, Linda M. *Language As Aggression: Studies in Postwar Drama*. Bonn, Germany: Bouvier Verlag Herbert Grundmann, 1976.
Although Hill concentrates largely on European playwrights in this study, her extensive chapter on Edward Albee's *The American Dream* (1961) is of interest to those studying American drama. Hill's observations about language as aggression in all the playwrights she considers besides Albee—Eugene Ionesco, Peter Handke, Wolfgang Hildesheimer, Martin Walser, and Jochen Ziem—suggest fresh ways of viewing dialogue in modern drama. The book has an excellent bibliography and a useful index.

Isaacs, Edith J. R. *The Negro in American Theatre*. New York: Theatre Arts, 1947.
In this pioneering book, Isaacs treats African Americans who were involved with American theater, including Paul Robeson, Florence Mills, Josephine Baker, Bill Robinson, Charles Gilpin, DuBose and Dorothy Heyward, and Katherine Dunham. She also deals with plays by white writers that depict African-American life. Among these are Marc Connelly's *The Green Pastures* (1929), Paul Green's *In Abraham's Bosom* (1926), and Eugene O'Neill's *The Emperor Jones* (1920). The book is illustrated. Isaacs gives special attention to DuBose and Dorothy Heyward's dramatized version of DuBose Heyward's novel *Porgy* (1927), from which *Porgy and Bess* (1935)—Isaacs calls it the first native American folk opera—was made. Chapter 7 of this book makes interesting observations about the Federal Theatre Project.

Kauffmann, Stanley. *Persons of the Drama: Theater Criticism and Comment*. New York: Harper & Row, 1976.
The most compelling of this book's five parts are part 3, "Notes on Music"; part 4, "Stages of Discussion: Homosexuality, People, Themes"; and part 5, "On Criticism." Kauffmann, whose book is performance-oriented, also presents insightful comments on revivals of the work of Edward Albee (focusing largely on *Tiny Alice*, 1964), Arthur Miller (focusing particularly on *Death of a Salesman*, 1949), and Tennessee Williams (with special attention to *Cat on a Hot Tin Roof*, 1955).

Kernan, Alvin, ed. *American Theater: A Collection of Critical Essays*. Englewood Cliffs, N.J.: Prentice-Hall, 1967.
Divided into three sections—"The Background," "The Playwrights," and "The Theaters"—this collection in its thirteen essays presents two essays on Edward Albee (as well as one by Edward Albee), two on Thornton Wilder, one on William Inge, and one on Arthur Miller and Tennessee Williams. Kernan's introductory essay on modern theater is balanced and perceptive. The essays on Broadway and Off-Off-Broadway ("The Pass-the Hat-Circuit") are excellent. There is no essay on Off-Broadway, but Kernan, in an editor's note, suggests two sources that report on it. Among the contributors to the collection are Edward Albee, Francis Fergusson, Richard Gilman, Kenneth Tynan, Tyrone Guthrie, Robert Brustein, and Tom Driver. Most of the essays in the collection originally appeared elsewhere.

Kerr, Walter. *How Not to Write a Play*. New York: Simon & Schuster, 1955.
Kerr surveys American drama quite extensively in this book, focusing on some of the factors that limit playwrights' effectiveness—some intrinsic, some extrinsic. The book has a useful index and is well documented.

_____. *Journey to the Center of the Theater*. New York: Alfred A. Knopf, 1979.
Besides reprinting most of Walter Kerr's major theatrical reviews from *The New York Times*, this book, in ten chapters, covers a variety of theatrical topics, with essays on the actresses and actors who played on Broadway in the postwar United States. The book has a useful index.

_____. *Thirty Plays Hath November: Pain and Pleasure in the Contemporary Theater*. New York: Simon & Schuster, 1969.
This collection of essays written by Walter Kerr is particularly interesting for its chapter on repertory theater and for its chapter entitled "Albee, Miller, Williams," which also contains some valuable material on William Inge and his *Natural Affection* (1963). The book is spirited and lively. It has a useful index.

Keyssar, Helene. *The Curtain and the Veil: Strategies in Black Drama*. New York: Burt Franklin, 1981.
This book, besides presenting a comprehensive list of African-American playwrights and their plays, has extensive chapters on the plays of Langston Hughes, Lorraine Hansberry, and Imamu Amiri Baraka (LeRoi Jones). The bibliography is exhaustive, the index comprehensive and accurate.

Kitchen, Laurence. *Mid-Century Drama*. London: Faber & Faber, 1960.
This performance-oriented book is concerned largely with British and continental drama. Kitchen, however, makes substantial comments on Arthur Miller, Eugene

O'Neill, Tennessee Williams, and Clifford Odets. The book has a section of interviews with theater people and a comprehensive index.

Krutch, Joseph Wood. *The American Drama Since 1918*. New York: Random House, 1939; New York: George Braziller, 1957.
In the six chapters of this book, Krutch considers the effect European theater had on recent American drama, then goes on to discuss three new realists: Sidney Howard, Laurence Stallings, and George Kelly. His chapter on tragedy is almost exclusively about Eugene O'Neill, but the following chapter on comedy discusses George S. Kaufman, Marc Connelly, S. N. Behrman, Philip Barry, and Arthur Kober. The chapter on the drama of social criticism focuses on Marc Blitzstein, Elmer Rice, John Howard Lawson, and Clifford Odets. The final chapter on the poetic drama treats Maxwell Anderson quite extensively. Krutch's bibliography is suggestive, his index comprehensive.

Lewis, Allan. *American Plays and Playwrights of the Contemporary Theatre*. New York: Crown, 1965.
Lewis provides extensive discussions of such playwrights as Eugene O'Neill, Arthur Miller, Tennessee Williams, Thornton Wilder, William Saroyan, Edward Albee, Lillian Hellman, Clifford Odets, Elmer Rice, S. N. Behrman, Sidney Kingsley, William Inge, and Archibald MacLeish. This book provides a comprehensive overview of several decades of American drama. It has a useful index but no bibliography.

McCrindle, Joseph F., ed. *Behind the Scenes: Theater and Film Interviews from the Transatlantic Review*. New York: Holt, Rinehart and Winston, 1971.
The thirty-three interviews in this book all have to do with theater and film. Each interview is conducted by someone who has a particular interest in the interviewee. Among the interviewers are John Lahr, Giles Gordon, Brendan Hennessy, Digby Diehl, and Robert Rubens. Among the interviewees are Arthur Kopit, Tom Stoppard, William Inge, Joe Orton, Kenneth Tynan, Richard Barr, Harold Clurman, Robert Bolt, Peter Shaffer, Harold Pinter, Jose Quintero, and Gore Vidal. The book has no index, but its thorough table of contents makes using it relatively easy to use.

Madden, David, ed. *American Dreams, American Nightmares*. Carbondale, Ill.: Southern Illinois University Press, 1970.
Even though this collection focuses largely on prose fiction, Frederic I. Carpenter's essay, "Focus on Eugene O'Neill's *The Iceman Cometh*: The Iceman Hath Come," and Chester E. Eisingers' essay, "Focus on Arthur Miller's *Death of a Salesman*: The Wrong Dreams," are of interest to those in American drama. This collection has a selective but quite extensive bibliography and a fine index.

Mantle, Burns. *Contemporary American Playwrights*. New York: Dodd, Mead, 1938.
In nine unnumbered sections, Mantle lists playwrights in various categories, including Pulitzer Prize winners, potential Pulitzer Prize winners, new writers, and all playwrights who have had two or more plays produced since the 1919-1920 theatrical season. There are separate indexes for playwrights and plays. This quite extensive book (357 pages) is interesting in retrospect for the predictions it makes.

Miller, J. William. *Modern Playwrights at Work*. New York: Samuel French, 1968.
Although this book is concerned primarily with British and continental playwrights, it devotes one chapter to Eugene O'Neill and one to Tennessee Williams. The final three chapters of the book, which essentially address the working methods, the collaborations, and the lives of playwrights, also touch on Edward Albee, Maxwell Anderson, Robert Anderson, James Baldwin, S. N. Behrman, Marc Connelly, T. S. Eliot, Edna Ferber, Susan Glaspell, Paul Green, Lorraine Hansberry, Moss Hart, Lillian Hellman, William Inge, George S. Kaufman, Sidney Kingsley, Jerome Lawrence, Robert E. Lee, Archibald MacLeish, Carson McCullers, Arthur Miller, Clifford Odets, Elmer Rice, Lynn Riggs, William Saroyan, Robert E. Sherwood, and Thornton Wilder. Eight appendices suggest such things as a formula for analyzing plays, further readings, long runs on and off Broadway, and play-writing endowments. The index is thorough.

Morris, Lloyd. *Curtain Time: The Story of the American Theater*. New York: Random House, 1953.
This book is essentially historical, and only chapter 12, "The Glorious Years," and the epilogue are relevant to the time frame covered in this bibliography. In these sections of the book, Morris deals with such playwrights as Tennessee Williams, Arthur Miller, William Inge, Carson McCullers, Sidney Kingsley, and Clifford Odets. The book is illustrated and has a usable index.

Moses, Montrose J., and John Mason Brown. *The American Theatre as Seen by Its Critics, 1752-1934*. New York: W. W. Norton, 1934.
Montrose Moses died shortly before he finished this book, and John Mason Brown completed it. It is interesting for its numerous reviews of the early works of such playwrights as Eugene O'Neill, Elmer Rice, Sidney Kingsley, S. N. Behrman, Maxwell Anderson, Susan Glaspell, Lynn Riggs, e. e. cummings, Philip Barry, and George Kelly. The volume contains biographical notes on both actors and critics.

Nathan, George Jean. *Encyclopaedia of the Theatre*. New York: Alfred A. Knopf, 1940.
In 449 pages, Nathan offers an alphabetical listing of terms related to theater and

uses them as points of departure for his frequently puckish comments on the topic under discussion and life in general. Some comments go on at great length. "Irish Petard" gets more than six pages, and "Selling the Theatre" goes on for almost eleven, becoming a fascinating essay on the economics of show business. This book is fun to dip into at random.

_____. *Passing Judgments*. New York: Alfred A. Knopf, 1935.
Chapter 2 offers a valuable assessment of theater during the Great Depression of the 1930's. Chapters 5 and 6 identify critical presumptions, both theatrical and general. In chapter 8, Nathan writes a thoughtful essay on the humor found in Eugene O'Neill's tragedies. Chapter 9 is devoted to summer theaters. Chapter 10 is important because it notes Gertrude Stein's experimental use of language and dialogue and the impact it had upon such playwrights as George S. Kaufman, Ben Hecht, Elmer Rice, and John Howard Lawson.

Newquist, Roy. *Counterpoint*. Chicago: Rand McNally, 1964.
This book of sixty-three interviews with writers includes a number of playwrights and writers in other fields who have written some plays or who have some association with theater. Particularly relevant are the interviews with Truman Capote, Tyrone Guthrie, Ben Hecht, William Inge, Basil Rathbone, Elmer Rice, and Irwin Shaw. The book does not have an index, but it is alphabetically arranged for ease in locating materials.

O'Hara, Frank Hurburt. *Today in American Drama*. Chicago: University of Chicago Press, 1939.
O'Hara essentially focuses on the 1930's and the drama they produced, although he discusses some earlier plays. Among the plays he discusses extensively in his five chapters are Eugene O'Neill's *Anna Christie* (1921), *The Hairy Ape* (1922), and *Ah, Wilderness!* (1933), Clifford Odets' *Awake and Sing!* (1935), Lillian Hellman's *The Little Foxes* (1939), John Steinbeck's *Of Mice and Men* (1937), Maxwell Anderson's *Winterset* (1935), Robert E. Sherwood's *Abe Lincoln in Illinois* (1938), and George S. Kaufman's *You Can't Take It with You* (1936). His focus is chiefly on the social and political implications of drama during the Great Depression. The book has a useful bibliography and a reliable index.

Rabkin, Gerald. *Drama and Commitment: Politics in the American Theatre of the Thirties*. Bloomington, Ind.: Indiana University Press, 1964.
After a prologue and a chapter that sets the context, this book is divided into two parts: "Commitment and the Idea of a Theatre" and "Commitment and the Playwright." The first section deals with the Theatre Union, the Group Theatre, and the Federal Theatre. The second section has individual chapters on John Howard Lawson, Clifford Odets, S. N. Behrman, Elmer Rice, and Maxwell Anderson. The book has a selected bibliography and a serviceable index.

Reed, Joseph Verner. *The Curtain Falls.* New York: Harcourt, Brace, 1935.
Reed tells how, as a brash twenty-seven year old, he became a producer who lost a substantial amount of money but recognized the talent of and essentially discovered Katharine Hepburn. In chapter 5, Reed says that it is impossible to predict the success of a play until it has played before audiences. This book is illustrated.

Sanders, Leslie Catherine. *The Development of Black Theatre in America: From Shadows to Selves.* Baton Rouge, La.: Louisiana State University Press, 1988.
Sanders identifies as America's five most prominent African-American playwrights Willis Richardson, Randolph Edmonds, Langston Hughes, Le Roi Jones (Imamu Amiri Baraka), and Ed Bullins. Sanders suggests that the culture in which these playwrights matured directly affected their writing and shows how these writers absorbed the European-American dramatic tradition without imitating it. She also shows how these playwrights relate to such playwrights as James Baldwin and Lorraine Hansberry and how they paved the way for a playwright such as Ntozake Shange. The book has an indispensable bibliography and a fine index.

Sievers, W. David. *Freud on Broadway: A History of Psychoanalysis and the American Drama.* New York: Hermitage House, 1955.
This book presents interesting psychoanalytical perspectives on American theater from Clyde Fitch to the playwrights of the early 1950's, including Arthur Miller, Tennessee Williams, William Inge, and others. His chapter on O'Neill is excellent, and it leads to a chapter called "O'Neill's Allies in Analysis" that has interesting comments to make about Elmer Rice, Sidney Howard, Maxwell Anderson, and Robert E. Sherwood. Sievers devotes a chapter to the psychodramas of Philip Barry. The insights Sievers presents are fresh and compelling. The book's index is complete and accurate.

Stott, William, with Jane Stott. *On Broadway.* Austin, Tex.: University of Texas Press, 1978.
Rich with performance photographs by Fred Fehl, this spirited book offers extensive comments on major Broadway playwrights by such commentators as William Gibson, Harold Clurman, Marc Connelly, Walter Kerr, and Gore Vidal. One derives an authentic feeling of the atmosphere of Broadway theater from reading this book.

Von Szeliski, John. *Tragedy and Fear: Why Modern Tragic Drama Fails.* Chapel Hill, N.C.: University of North Carolina Press, 1962, 1971.
The controlling idea in this book is "that pessimism and tragedy do not mix and that this is the prime error committed in twentieth-century tragic writing." The author tests this thesis in extensive discussions of the major tragic plays of

modern American drama from 1920 to 1959, ranging from Eugene O'Neill's *Strange Interlude* (1928), *Mourning Becomes Electra* (1931), *Long Day's Journey into Night* (wr. 1941, pr. 1956), and other plays to Arthur Miller's *Death of a Salesman* (1949) and Tennessee Williams' *Glass Menagerie* (1944) and *A Streetcar Named Desire* (1947). In an appendix that lists all the tragedies von Szeliski considers in his study—he calls them "high melodramas"—the author has a checklist of six characteristics that he deems necessary in tragedy. He subjects each of the plays to this checklist. The bibliography is limited but useful; the index lists only play titles and themes discussed—no names.

Weales, Gerald. *American Drama Since World War II*. New York: Harcourt, Brace & World, 1962.
Weales' overview of theater in America since World War II is a comprehensive extension of Joseph Wood Krutch's *The American Drama Since 1918*. The book is broad in its coverage, and its insights are penetrating. Weales' grasp of his subject is phenomenally inclusive and analytically critical. This book, along with Krutch's, provides a good starting point for anyone who seeks to understand American theater from World War I to the 1960's.

Williams, Jay. *Stage Left*. New York: Charles Scribner's Sons, 1974.
The emphasis of this book is on the social drama of the 1930's. In its way, it is an informal history of the Group Theatre. Williams claims that "it may seem that between the two great wars a new kind of American theatre, with its eye on social realities rather than on the refined taste of the carriage trade, rose, flourished, and then dismally failed." This illustrated volume, with its comprehensive, accurate index, makes insightful comments about Clifford Odets, Paul Green, Sidney Kingsley, and other rising writers of the Depression era.

LITTLE THEATER, THEATER GROUPS, AND REGIONAL THEATER

Anderson, John. *Box Office*. New York: Jonathan Cape and Harrison Smith, 1929.
Anderson's early study of the business of theater is extremely interesting because the author traces the early steps of theater as it is currently known in the United States. In an apparent afterthought, Anderson added material about the growth of little theaters, which, with the founding of the Provincetown Playhouse in 1916, began to flourish in many parts of the country.

Atkinson, Brooks. *Broadway Scrapbook*. New York: Theatre Arts, 1947.
In this book, with its sixty-nine reviews and articles, Atkinson, longtime drama critic of *The New York Times*, devotes chapter 37 to small-town drama, showing its status in the postwar United States.

Blau, Herbert. *The Impossible Theater: A Manifesto*. New York: Macmillan, 1964.
Blau, former producing director of the Actors' Workshop in San Francisco, tells how the workshop grew largely as a result of Blau's awareness of what was happening outside theater. He gauged public tastes and focused his theater on them, which has made the Actors' Workshop a commercially viable enterprise. The book has excellent illustrations but no index.

Clurman, Harold. *The Fervent Years: The Story of the Group Theatre and the Thirties*. New York: Alfred A. Knopf, 1945; New York: Hill and Wang, 1957, 1975 (with new epilogue); New York: Harcourt, Brace Jovanovich, 1975.
This lively account of the founding and functioning of the Group Theatre by one of its three founders provides extremely interesting insights into the philosophy of the Group and into the accomplishments of many of its members, such as Clifford Odets, Franchot Tone, Elia Kazan, Cheryl Crawford, and Stella and Luther Adler. Chapter 12 focuses on Odets' *Awake and Sing!* (1935), and chapter 18 tells how Odets brought new life to the faltering Group Theatre with the production of *Golden Boy* (1937), which was produced for a total expenditure of $19,000.

_____. *The Naked Image: Observations on the Modern Theatre*. New York: Macmillan, 1966.
Clurman devotes thirty-eight pages of this book to a section entitled "Theatre Across America." He begins with the crisis in Broadway theater, then writes about how theater is flourishing in Minneapolis and San Francisco. He writes about the challenges of the new theaters and gives a brief history of them.

Coleman, Janet. *The Compass*. New York: Alfred A. Knopf, 1990.
Coleman traces the history of the Compass Theater from David Gwynne Shep-

herd's initiative following his arrival in Chicago in 1956 at the age of twenty-six through its demise in the late 1960's. In this well-illustrated book, she gives considerable credit to Viola Spolin and her work in improvisational drama. The bibliography is solid, the index dependable.

Dauphin, Sue. *Houston by Stages*. Burnet, Tex.: Eakin Press, 1981.
This book, which is not quite five hundred pages long, is illustrated. It has three major sections. The first treats the early history of theater in Houston. The second section, which is the longest, deals with the little-theater movement and with regional theaters in Houston, including the Federal Theatre Project, Margo Jones and the Houston Community Players, the Alley Theatre, the Houston Players, and the Playhouse. Section 3 deals with local theater, ranging from the Rice University Dramatic Club to various small theaters such as the Clear Creek Country Theatre and the Baytown Little Theatre. The author discusses musical theater in the area as well as dinner theaters. She also mentions the emerging ethnic theaters, notably African-American, Hispanic, and Jewish.

Dent, Thomas C., Richard Schechner, and Gilbert Moses, eds. *The Free Southern Theater by the Free Southern Theater*. Indianapolis, Ind.: Bobbs-Merrill, 1969.
Part 5 of this book, entitled "Departures," is Thomas Dent's journal of the development of the Free Southern Theater. The editors have compiled and collated a collection of materials that chronicle the history of the theater. The book is well illustrated, but its lack of an index makes it difficult to use for research purposes.

Diehl, Digby. "Harold Clurman." In *Behind the Scenes: Theater and Film Interviews from the Transatlantic Review*, edited by Joseph F. McCrindle. New York: Holt, Rinehart and Winston, 1971.
In this interview, conducted in 1964, Digby Diehl gives much information about the founding of the Group Theater in 1931 and the people associated with it. He discusses the economics of producing plays and points to Off-Broadway and Off-Off-Broadway theaters and regional theaters as the most encouraging signs for theater in the United States.

Deutsch, Helen, and Stella Hanau. *The Provincetown: A Story of the Theatre*. New York: Farrar and Rinehart, 1931.
This history gives full credit to Eugene O'Neill and Susan Glaspell for their pioneering efforts in establishing the Provincetown Players. The authors devote one chapter to the triumvirate that was highly influential in the theater's history: Kenneth Macgowan, Robert E. Sherwood, and Eugene O'Neill. One appendix lists all the programs from 1916 to 1929. A second appendix contains program articles by O'Neill and Glaspell.

Eaton, Walter Prichard, ed. *The Theatre Guild: The First Ten Years*. New York: Brentano's, 1929.
This book begins with Eaton's history of the Theatre Guild, then moves to a chapter by its executive director, Theresa Helburn, that takes one behind the scenes. Phillip Moeller's contribution has to do with production, Maurice Wertheim's with how to run an art theater without an endowment, Helen Westley's with the relationship of the actor to an art theater and vice versa, Lee Simonson's with staging, and Lawrence Langner's with how a little theater becomes a mature theater. An appendix lists the casts of all the Theatre Guild productions from its founding to 1929. The book is illustrated.

Flanagan, Hallie. *Arena*. New York: Duell, Sloan, and Pearce, 1940.
This large, well-illustrated volume deals with the development of the Federal Theatre Project during the Great Depression of the 1930's. Part 1 outlines the problems associated with rampant unemployment. Part 2, which is three hundred pages long, surveys the Project's activities throughout the United States. Part 3 is entitled "Blasting: Work Suspended." A sixty-one-page appendix provides a financial overview of the Project, which in 1936 employed 12,372 people. The labor costs over the life of the Project were $42,000,000, and nonlabor costs were $4,200,000. The Project gave 63,728 performances throughout the country, often in places where a play had never been produced. It played in three years to a total audience of 30,398,726. This book has an excellent index.

Flory, Julia McCune. *The Cleveland Play House: How It Began*. Cleveland, Ohio: Press of Western Reserve University, 1965.
The Cleveland Play House, one of the oldest community theaters in the United States, is located in a community that has more theaters per capita than any other U.S. city except New York. The Play House began in 1916 and was directed from 1921 to 1962 by Frederic McConnell. It was sufficiently successful that its mortgage was burned in the 1925-1926 season. It did mostly European drama, Shakespeare, and the classics, although occasionally it presented contemporary, indigenous plays.

Gard, Robert E., and Gertrude S. Burley, eds. *Community Theater: Idea and Achievement*. New York: Duell, Sloan, and Pearce, 1959; Westport, Conn.: Greenwood Press, 1975.
After a twenty-three-page overview, this book records interviews with community theater directors and/or founders in thirteen locales (in Texas, California, Illinois, Oklahoma, Pennsylvania, Ohio, Indiana, and Great Britain). Each interview is preceded by a biographical sketch. The editors provide a thirty-two-page list of community theaters.

Guthrie, Sir Tyrone. *A New Theatre.* New York: McGraw-Hill, 1964.
Guthrie tells how the Guthrie Theatre became a reality in Minneapolis in 1963. He gives details about how Oliver Rea approached him and Peter Zeisler in 1959 with the plan for a theater and how they assessed the need, cost, and possibilities. This volume has excellent illustrations and a useful index.

Houghton, Norris. *Advance from Broadway: Nineteen Thousand Miles of American Theatre.* New York: Harcourt, Brace, 1941.
Norris Houghton visited seventy regional theaters in 1940. His book provides the most comprehensive view available of regional theater in prewar America. The scope of the book encompasses summer stock and collegiate theater as well as other regional theaters.

Isaacs, Edith J. R. *The Negro in American Theatre.* New York: Theatre Arts, 1947.
In chapter 7 of this book, Isaacs offers a penetrating discussion of the Federal Theatre Project and its impact on African-American playwrights, actors, and theater people. She also notes how successful it was in bringing theater to isolated communities, including African-American communities that had never been exposed to theater until the Project arrived. This book is well illustrated.

Kanellos, Nicolas. *Mexican-American Theater: Legacy and Reality.* Pittsburgh, Penn.: Latin American Literature Review Press, 1982.
The book, which has seven unnumbered chapters, begins with a consideration of Chicano theater in the 1970's. It goes on to consider folklore in Chicano theater and Chicano theater as folklore. It traces fifty years of Chicano theater in northwest Indiana, then gives a brief overview of the Mexican-American circus in the Southwest, followed by a discussion of the origins and development of Hispanic theater in the Southwest. In his most political chapter, Kanellos considers the Mexican stage in the Southwest as a sounding board for cultural affairs.

Kerr, Walter. "Repertory in Labor." In *Thirty Plays Hath November: Pain and Pleasure in the Contemporary Theater,* edited by Walter Kerr. New York: Simon & Schuster, 1969.
Kerr discusses the problems repertory theaters face but notes the service they render not only in providing performances of well-known theatrical classics to far-flung audiences but also in bringing less-well-known playwrights to people in remote areas. It is the outreach services of repertory theater that speak most eloquently for its existence and continuance.

Lester, Eleanor. "The Pass-the-Hat Circuit." In *American Theater: A Collection of Critical Essays,* edited by Alvin Kernan. Englewood Cliffs, N.J.: Prentice-Hall, 1967.
The distinction Lester makes between Off-Broadway and, as she calls it, "Double Off-Broadway," is that Off-Broadway is required to pay rent, hire technicians,

pay actors Equity minimum wages, and incur other expenses that make it a substantial financial venture. Because Double Off-Broadway is exempted from such requirements, it attracts experimental authors whose work would not be likely to appeal to audiences sufficiently to cover expenses in any other venue. She gives special attention to New York's Open Theater Workshop.

Little, Stuart W. *Off-Broadway: The Prophetic Theater.* New York: Coward, McCann & Geoghegan, 1972.

Little provides much practical information about the financing of Off-Broadway theater, largely from contributions. He notes the moral mission of such theater and shows that it can attract contributions because it meets a social need. The book has illustrations and an index.

Morison, Bradley G., and Kay Fliehr. *In Search of an Audience: How an Audience Was Found for the Tyrone Guthrie Theatre.* New York: Pitman, 1968.

This book gives a fascinating account of how the Minnesota Theatre, which began performing in the Tyrone Guthrie Theatre in Minneapolis in 1963, created its audience. Using the best techniques of market research, the Minnesota Theatre made community surveys to determine what its audience would respond to best, then proceeded to offer what the surveys suggested. The results were such that the Guthrie began on a firm footing and has remained a viable enterprise ever since.

Newquist, Roy. *Counterpoint.* Chicago: Rand McNally, 1964.

The interviews with Tyrone Guthrie and with Elmer Rice offer useful information about regional theater and Off-Broadway theater. The Guthrie interview has an afterword by Bradley Morison, Public Relations Director of the Tyrone Guthrie Theater. Guthrie explains his objectives as Director of the Tyrone Guthrie Theater. Bradley, in the afterword interview, tells how the Guthrie Theater moved from dream to reality. Rice discusses the economics of play production, noting that productions that a decade before his 1963 interview would have cost $3,000 or $4,000 to bring to the stage by 1963 would cost $15,000.

Norton, Elliott. *Broadway Down East: An Informal Account of the Plays, Players, and Playhouses of Boston from Puritan Times to the Present.* Boston: Boston Public Library, 1978.

This informal history of Boston theater bemoans the loss of theaters in Boston and attributes it to competition from such sources as the Kennedy Center in Washington, D.C.—an apparently oversimplified explanation. Appendix A lists all the theaters that have existed in Boston since 1792 and provides maps. Appendix B lists plays that have enjoyed long runs in the city. The second half of the book emphasizes American drama from O'Neill to the date of publication. The bibliography is extensive, the index ample. The book is illustrated.

Rabkin, Gerald. *Drama and Commitment: Politics in the American Theatre of the Thirties.* Bloomington, Ind.: Indiana University Press, 1964.
The first section of this study has to do with the political postures of three major theater groups in the 1930's. Rabkin studies analytically the growth of the Theatre Union, the Group Theatre, and the Federal Theatre. Writing of the Federal Theatre's contribution, he concludes that "The project's main contribution was theatrical, not dramatic." He saw the main problem of the Theatre Union as the conflict between "the desire to do plays which would be afraid of nothing and the knowledge that such productions would be lambasted by the critics and avoided by the moneyed patrons."

_____. "The Federal Theatre Project." In *The Thirties: Fiction, Poetry, Drama*, edited by Warren G. French. Deland, Fla.: Everett/Edwards, 1967.
Rabkin's essay provides the best succinct overview in print of the Federal Theatre Project and its implications for drama in the United States. The statistics quoted are accurate, and the essay is spirited.

Ryzuk, Mary S. *The Circle Repertory Company: The First Fifteen Years.* Ames, Iowa: Iowa State University Press, 1989.
Although Ryzuk's book falls somewhat outside the time boundaries of this bibliography, it is mentioned here because the Circle Repertory Company has intimate connections with such other little-theater movements in Greenwich Village as the Washington Square Players. Ryzuk's book has eleven chapters, an epilogue, and an afterword by Marshall W. Mason, long a director in and of the Company. Chapter 6 identifies the turning point of the Company as the production of Lanford Wilson's *Hot L Baltimore* (1973). Chapter 11 presents the philosophy of the Company. Ryzuk provides extended biographical sketches of the founders: Marshall W. Mason, Lanford Wilson, Tanya Berezin, and Rob Thirkield. The bibliography is useful, as is the comprehensive index.

Smith, Wendy. *Real Life Drama: The Group Theatre and America, 1931-1940.* New York: Alfred A. Knopf, 1990.
Smith's is the most comprehensive history of the Group Theater since Harold Clurman's *The Fervent Years* (1945). It is illustrated and extremely well documented. It contains a list of the plays produced by the Group and lists the names of cast members. She tells how, as the Group was beginning to dissolve, the members felt as though they had lost their homes, as though their family was gone. She writes, "For ten years this diverse and often ill-assorted group of people found their differences less important than the vision they shared: of a theatre that spoke powerfully and truthfully to a broad audience about the moral and social concerns of their times." There is an extensive bibliography and a comprehensive index.

Spearman, Walter, assisted by Samuel Selden. *The Carolina Playmakers: The First
Fifty Years*. Chapel Hill, N.C.: University of North Carolina Press, 1970.
This book tells of the founding of the Carolina Playmakers in 1918 by Professor
Frederick Koch and traces its history, including its tours to the North. Chapter
3 deals with outdoor drama, tracing Paul Green's interest in this dramatic vehicle
to his association as a student with the Playmakers. Koch took a great interest
in Green, whose *Raleigh, The Shepherd of the Ocean* (1920), written for the
Playmakers, is the precursor of *The Lost Colony* (1937). This illustrated volume
has a useful index.

Weales, Gerald. *American Drama Since World War II*. New York: Harcourt, Brace
& World, 1962.
Chapter 10, "Off-Broadway," of Weales' comprehensive study of American
drama of the 1940's, 1950's, and early 1960's provides a fine history of Off-
Broadway theater. Weales' approach is chronological. It covers the whole of the
Off-Broadway movement up to the early 1960's, showing how the movement has
contributed to keeping serious drama alive in the United States.

Zeigler, Joseph Wesley. *Regional Theatre: The Revolutionary Stage*. Minneapolis,
Minn.: University of Minnesota Press, 1973.
Two of this book's fourteen chapters are particularly compelling. Chapter 3 is
about Margo Jones and her legacy as founder of her regional theater in Dallas
and as a moving force behind the Houston Community Players. Chapter 4,
entitled "Acorns: Theater before 1960," provides a splendid overview of the
regional theater movements out of which many more recent regional theaters
grew or on which they were modeled. The book has fine illustrations and a
serviceable index.

EDWARD ALBEE

General Studies

Amracher, Richard E. *Edward Albee*. New York: Twayne, 1969; rev. ed., Boston: Twayne, 1982.

The original edition of Armacher's study of Edward Albee deals with Albee's plays up to but not including *Box, and Quotations from Chairman Mao Tse-Tung* (1968). The revised edition deals additionally in a new chapter with six of the eight plays Albee produced between 1968 and 1982. The two other new plays are discussed in the chapter dealing with adaptations. Albee is considered from a naturalistic and absurdist point of view. Both books follow the usual format of Twayne's United States Authors Series, beginning with a chronology, proceeding to a biographical chapter, and then moving to chapters in which the playwright's dramas are viewed analytically. Both volumes have annotated bibliographies and comprehensive indexes.

Amracher, Richard E., and Margaret Rule, eds. *Edward Albee at Home and Abroad: A Bibliography*. New York: AMS, 1973.

This annotated bibliography, which covers a decade of Albee research (1958-1968), contains more than a thousand entries and, although it is dated, is still of considerable use. The secondary literature reviewed extends to European criticism, including a section on criticism from Germany, Austria, and Switzerland and another section on criticism from other countries.

Baxandall, Lee. "The Theater of Edward Albee." In *American Theater: A Collection of Critical Essays*, edited by Edward Albee. Englewood Cliffs, N.J.: Prentice-Hall, 1967.

Baxandall notes the interrelation of Edward Albee's characters from play to play and points out that in most of his plays the archetypal family is composed of three generations, although, as in *Who's Afraid of Virginia Woolf?* (1962), only one generation actually appears on stage. The essay contends, "The form of an Albee play derives from some characters' imaginative power to force events, not toward historically viable solutions, but at least into channels which are telling and satisfying symbolically."

Bigsby, C. W. E. *Albee*. Edinburgh, Scotland: Oliver & Boyd, 1969.

Bigsby provides an overview of Albee's life up to the time that he wrote *The Zoo Story* (1959). He analyzes Albee's plays through *A Delicate Balance* (1966), showing how the absurdism that was popular in European theater became a part of Albee's work, claiming that he intermingled it with "American tradition." He comments on Albee's sharp and devastating wit.

34

_____, ed. *Edward Albee: A Collection of Critical Essays*. Englewood Cliffs, N.J.: Prentice-Hall, 1975.
The twenty-one essays in this book are contributed by such scholars, directors, reviewers, and critics as Gerald Weales, Martin Esslin, Alan Schneider, Harold Clurman, Diana Trilling, Michael E. Rutenberg, Henry Hewes, Philip Roth, and Robert Brustein. The essays present a comprehensive overview of Edward Albee and his work. Some are general ("Edward Albee: Don't Make Waves" by Weales), but most focus on one or two individual plays or on topics such as Albee's naturalism, symbolism, or absurdism. Following the essays, the editor provides a detailed chronology and a selected bibliography, both of which enhance the volume's usefulness.

Blau, Herbert. *The Impossible Theater*. New York: Macmillan, 1964.
Blau makes some incisive observations about *Who's Afraid of Virginia Woolf?* (1962) and about Edward Albee in general in this book. His comments are limited to four pages but are worth noting.

Brustein, Robert. *The Theatre of Revolt: An Approach to Modern Drama*. Boston: Little, Brown, 1964.
In his comments on Edward Albee, Brustein shows how Albee uses the Pirandellian concern with the tensions that exist between illusion and reality in his plays, particularly in *Who's Afraid of Virginia Woolf?* (1962). Brustein relates Albee to the revolt of the existentialist playwrights and ties him to the theater of cruelty.

Cohn, Ruby. *Currents in Contemporary Drama*. Bloomington, Ind.: Indiana University Press, 1969.
Cohn examines *The Zoo Story* (1959), *Who's Afraid of Virginia Woolf?* (1962), *Tiny Alice* (1964), and *Box, and Quotations from Chairman Mao Tse-Tung* (1968). She demonstrates the influence such European playwrights as Luigi Pirandello had on Albee's form but calls his dialogue unique. She writes, "Under a veneer of realism, Albee had been shifting his emphasis from America's social illusion to man's metaphysical illusion."

_____. *Dialogue in American Drama*. Bloomington, Ind.: Indiana University Press, 1971.
In the fifth chapter of this book, entitled "The Verbal Murders of Edward Albee" (pages 130-169), Cohn calls Albee's idiom "intensely American yet original." She considers Albee the "most skillful composer of dialogue that America has produced." She points to his ability to combine monologue with sparkling repartee to achieve an effect that "dramatizes human situations." Cohn credits Albee with having been able to handle dialogue at the highest level since his emergence as a playwright at age thirty. She admires the lack of abstraction in his dialogue, which keeps it from being puffy and impersonal.

_____. *Edward Albee*. Minneapolis, Minn.: University of Minnesota Press, 1969.

Cohn's contribution to Minnesota's Pamphlets on American Writers surveys Albee's plays through *A Delicate Balance* (1966), showing Albee's use of European absurdism in his writing. The selected bibliography is remarkably complete, given the brevity of the book.

Debusscher, Gilbert, translated by Anne D. Williams. *Edward Albee: Tradition and Renewal*. Brussels, Belgium: Center for American Studies, 1969.

This slim volume is designed essentially to introduce Europeans to the plays of Edward Albee. It is, however, a good starting point for Americans as well. It discusses Albee in relation to Eugene O'Neill and then goes on to analyze the major plays through *Tiny Alice* (1964), considering pervasive themes, the structure of each work, and the use of symbols and images. The plays are also considered in terms of the theatrical qualities that make them satisfactory to perform. There is an extensive bibliography but no index.

Diehl, Digby. "Edward Albee." In *Behind the Scenes: Theater and Film Interviews from the Transatlantic Review*, edited by Joseph F. McCrindle. New York: Holt, Rinehart and Winston, 1971.

At twenty pages, the Edward Albee interview, conducted in 1963, is one of the longest in this book. It is the first major interview that Albee granted after *Who's Afraid of Virginia Woolf?* (1962). A great deal of interesting fencing occurs in this interview, in which Albee gives his generalized perceptions of audiences. Addressing the subject of his newly achieved fame and how he will use it, Albee says, "One of the few values that the idiotic 'success bit' brings to a man is that he is placed in a better position to try to change the situation that brought him his idiotic recognition in the first place."

Driver, Tom F. "What's the Matter with Edward Albee?" In *American Theater: A Collection of Critical Essays*, edited by Alvin Kernan. Englewood Cliffs, N.J.: Prentice-Hall, 1967.

Driver calls Edward Albee a bad playwright, a mediocre talent that has been puffed up into excellence by critics who wanted a new "gifted young playwright" to appear on the American scene. He calls *Who's Afraid of Virginia Woolf?* (1962) the most pretentious play since *Mourning Becomes Electra* (1931). Driver thinks that Albee's characters fail because "they are but surrogates for more authentic ones." Driver compares Albee to an angry child who "tears up his toys," a grown man in a tantrum "who looks as if he dreamed of evil but is actually mild as a dove and wants to be loved." He claims that this is what endears Albee to American audiences and critics.

Frenz, Horst, ed. *Playwrights on Drama*. New York: Hill & Wang, 1965.
This small volume of twenty-two essays contains excerpts from various sources
of playwrights speaking publicly about drama and their craft. The excerpt from
Edward Albee is enigmatic but quite revealing. Written when he was an emerging
but highly successful playwright, it expresses an interesting vision of theater.

Gardner, R. H. *The Splintered Stage: The Decline of the American Theater*. New
York: Macmillan, 1965.
This book presents brief discussions of *The Zoo Story* (1959), *The Death of
Bessie Smith* (1960), *The American Dream* (1961), *Who's Afraid of Virginia
Woolf?* (1962), and *The Ballad of the Sad Café* (1963). The entries on each play
are essentially brief summaries.

Gould, Jean. *Modern American Playwrights*. New York: Dodd, Mead, 1966.
Gould devotes chapter 14 of this book to Edward Albee, showing how his social
conscience developed from *The Zoo Story* (1959) up to *Who's Afraid of Virginia
Woolf* (1962) and how it faltered somewhat with *Tiny Alice* (1964). Like many
other critics, Gould marvels at Albee's use of simple, direct language and at the
emotional alternations he is able to achieve in his work, which often depends
upon placing a small cast of characters in a constricted place in which all the
action occurs.

Gottfried, Martin. *Opening Nights: Theater Criticism of the Sixties*. New York:
G. P. Putnam's Sons, 1969.
Gottfried devotes a section of this random collection of his own writings about
the theater to Edward Albee, presenting his reviews of *The Ballad of the Sad
Café* (1963), *Tiny Alice* (1964), and *Box-Mao-Box* (1968). He also offers an essay
on how Edward Albee would develop as a playwright, centered largely on
Albee's overtly homosexual play, *Malcolm* (1966).

Green, Charles Lee. *Edward Albee: An Annotated Bibliography, 1968–1977*. New
York: AMS Press, 1980.
Green's bibliography takes up where the Amacher-Rule bibliography (see above)
left off, and it is comprehensive. It contains 579 entries, most of which have
pithy annotations. The list of library sources consulted will lead readers to
additional sources of information about Albee and suggest resources that will help
scholars to find Albee manuscripts. Green also provides a contributing-authors'
index and a play-title index.

Hayman, Ronald. *Edward Albee*. New York: Frederick Ungar, 1973.
Hayman's contribution to Ungar's World Dramatists Series adheres to the
prescribed format, beginning with a chronology and then discussing each play,
from *The Zoo Story* (1959) to *All Over* (1971). A useful list of stage productions

of the plays follows, as do a bibliography and index. Hayman's comments on Albee's adaptation of Carson McCullers' *The Ballad of the Sad Café* (1963) seem especially perceptive; they show Albee working on material that did not originate with him, leaving on it his indelible mark while remaining faithful to the original author's text.

Hilfer, Anthony C. "George and Martha: Sad, Sad, Sad." In *Seven Contemporary Authors*, edited by T. W. Whitbread. Austin, Tex.: University of Texas Press, 1966.
In this eighteen-page essay, Hilfer traces some of Edward Albee's most important influences. He notes the playwright's dependence on August Strindberg, as many previous scholars have, but also notes the ways in which Eugene O'Neill's influence affected the structure of *Who's Afraid of Virginia Woolf?* (1962).

Kerr, Walter. *The Theatre in Spite of Itself*. New York: Simon & Schuster, 1963.
The chapter that deals specifically with Albee is "The Ambiguity of the Theater of the Absurd." Kerr focuses special attention on *Who's Afraid of Virginia Woolf?* (1962) in a four-page analysis of that play.

——————. "Albee, Miller, Williams." In *Thirty Plays Hath November: Pain and Pleasure in the Contemporary Theater*, edited by Walter Kerr. New York: Simon & Schuster, 1969.
In his sprightly essay, Kerr identifies two Edward Albees and contends that both are in his two-character one-act play *The Zoo Story* (1959). The first Albee is the invader, the brash bully who invades other people's space (minds), forcing his energy upon them. The second Albee is "the passive reader on the bench, the man who doesn't want to be bothered looking into other people's lives, the creature of the cut and-dried."

Kolin, Philip C., ed. *Conversations with Edward Albee*. Jackson, Miss.: University Press of Mississippi, 1988.
In this collection, Kolin has brought together some of the most significant interviews with Edward Albee in a compact, easily usable form. The selection of interviews is such that one gets a balanced view of an enigmatic playwright. Among the contributors are Digby Diehl, Irving Wardle, Paul Zindel, Alan Rich, and Terrence McNally. The collection also includes a piece from *The Choate News* in which Albee comments on his feelings upon returning to his preparatory school to view its 1968 production of *The Zoo Story* (1959).

Kolin, Philip C., and J. Madison Davis. *Critical Essays on Edward Albee*. Boston: G. K. Hall, 1986.
Following a pithy introduction by the editors, this book presents in sequence significant reviews of Edward Albee's plays (twenty-one pages), essays on Albee

. and his international standing (fifty-three pages), critical essays on Albee's plays (seventy-five pages), and a section entitled "Albee on Albee," a seven-page interview with Matthew C. Roudane. This is followed by an annotated bibliography of interviews with Albee, which includes an index of names, concepts, and places. Among the contributors to this volume are Gilbert Debusscher, Martin Esslin, Bernard F. Dukore, Michael Rutenberg, Ruby Cohn, John Kenneth Galbraith, Thomas P. Adler, Henry Hewes, Tom Driver, Robert Brustein, Clive Barnes, and Walter Kerr. The book has a serviceable index.

Lewis, Allan. *American Plays and Playwrights of the Contemporary Theatre*. New York: Crown, 1965.
In the essay "The Fun and Games of Edward Albee," Lewis looks closely at *Who's Afraid of Virginia Woolf?* (1962). He also comments incisively on Albee's other work up to 1964.

Loeffler, Donald L. *An Analysis of the Treatment of the Homosexual Character in Dramas Produced in the New York Theatre from 1950 to 1968*. New York: Arno Press, 1975.
In this published doctoral dissertation, Loeffler notes the homosexual overtones and allusions in *The Zoo Story* (1959), *The American Dream* (1961), *The Ballad of the Sad Café* (1963), *Tiny Alice* (1964), and *Malcolm* (1966). It is unfortunate that the author did not probe into this question in *Who's Afraid of Virginia Woolf?* (1962), in which the homosexual overtones, while not overt, are significant.

Paolucci, Anne. *From Tension to Tonic: The Plays of Edward Albee*. Carbondale, Ill.: Southern Illinois University Press, 1972.
Calling Albee's view of life existential, which some critics might disagree with, Paolucci identifies Albee as the first playwright since O'Neill to do something really new in American theater. She considers his plays less didactic than most of those on Broadway from the 1930's to the 1960's. Paolucci's selective bibliography is useful, as is her index.

Roudane, Matthew. *Understanding Edward Albee*. Columbia, S.C.: University of South Carolina Press, 1990.
Roudane's contribution to the Understanding Contemporary American Literature Series provides a useful chronology of Edward Albee's life and productions up to 1989 and provides a useful biographical overview. Albee's plays are analyzed in their social and historical contexts, and information is provided about their critical reception. The book has a selected bibliography and a dependable index.

Rutenberg, Michael E. *Edward Albee: Playwright in Protest*. New York: Drama Book Specialists Publications, 1969.
The most valuable feature of this book, which has chapters on each Albee play

from *The Zoo Story* (1959) to the *Box-Mao-Box* duo (1968), is the two interviews with Edward Albee that it gives in full. These trenchant interviews run from page 229 to page 260. The analyses of the plays are thoughtful, as is Rutenberg's statement that one purpose of modern experimental plays is to "create a form of cognitive dissonance in the viewer because they produce cognitions that do not correspond to a learned rationality-set." Chapter 9, which focuses on Albee's adaptations, is well done. A chronological list of the premieres of Albee's plays is followed by a selected bibliography. The book has no index.

Stenz, Anita Maria. *Edward Albee: The Poet of Loss*. The Hague: Mouton, 1978.
This reworked doctoral dissertation presents, after a brief introduction, critical analyses of Albee's plays from *The Zoo Story* (1959) to *Seascape* (1975). Accepting earlier contentions that Albee is a defeatist and a pessimist, Stenz denies that he is a nihilist. Rather, she views him as "a stern moralist who believes that there are right values and wrong values." She claims that one of Albee's chief concerns is how people waste their lives. It is in this light that she interprets—and at times misinterprets—his work. Despite some misinterpretations, however, Stenz's thesis is well supported in her study. The book has a bibliography but no index.

Tyce, Richard. *Edward Albee: A Bibliography*. Metuchen, N.J.: Scarecrow Press, 1986.
Tyce's contribution to Scarecrow Press's Author Bibliographies Series lists 2,711 sources. It is more up to date and more comprehensive than the Amacher-Rule bibliography (see above) or the Green bibliography (see above), as strong as both of those resources are. This book includes a chronology of the initial productions of Albee's plays. A section devoted to Albee's early works is followed by a section that deals with his other writings. The next section (thirty-nine pages long), which lists general works about him, is followed by a section that lists theses and dissertations about him. The final section (at 132 pages, the longest) lists critical articles and reviews. The index is comprehensive and reliable.

Vos, Melvin. *Eugene Ionesco and Edward Albee: A Critical Essay*. Grand Rapids, Mich.: Eerdmans, 1968.
Vos examines the dramatic motifs of the two playwrights he is considering and uses this examination to show how both playwrights moved inevitably toward absurdism, progressing from satire to confrontation with the absurd, and finally "dramatized the tragic futility of living within the absurd, of living without hope." He looks at Albee's plays from *The Zoo Story* (1959) through *A Delicate Balance* (1966), excluding the adaptations and *Tiny Alice* (1964).

Wasserman, Julian N., Joy L. Linsley, and Jerome A. Kramer, eds. *Edward Albee: An Interview and Essays*. Houston, Tex.: The University of St. Thomas, 1983.
The heart of this book is the interview that Julian Wasserman and Charles S.

Krohn had with Edward Albee on March 18, 1981. It is interesting because in it Albee honestly approaches the question of his own limitations. The book contains seven chapters on six Albee plays: *A Delicate Balance* (1966), *The Lady from Dubuque* (1980), *Tiny Alice* (1964), *The Zoo Story* (1959), *Counting the Ways* (1977), and *Seascape* (1975). Among the contributors are Philip C. Kolin, Thomas P. Adler, and Virginia I. Perry. The index is comprehensive.

The American Dream

Clurman, Harold. *The Naked Image: Observations on the Modern Theatre*. New York: Macmillan, 1966.
Although he points out the absurdist elements in Edward Albee's one-act play *The American Dream* (1961), Clurman contends that "Albee's talent—as with most Americans—lies closer to realism than he perhaps knows." He goes on to say that "abstraction becomes decoration when it loses touch with its roots in concrete individual experience."

Hill, Linda M. *Language as Aggression: Studies in Postwar Drama*. Bonn, Germany: Bouvier Verlag Herbert Grundmann, 1976.
Linda Hill has selected Edward Albee's *The American Dream* (1961) as the focus of her essay on language as aggression, a topic that applies to most of Albee's other plays as well. Hill recognizes that in this play, Albee "avoids details of actual American speech and customs," instead constructing "simple, uniform speech patterns of his own." Hill writes: "the slow progress of the dialogue as commonplace statements are made again and again contrasts with the abruptness with which the characters move among various senses of their words and alter conventional phrases."

The Ballad of the Sad Café

Gottfried, Martin. *Opening Nights: Theater Criticism of the Sixties*. New York: G. P. Putnam's Sons, 1969.
Gottfried's opening-night review of Edward Albee's adaptation of Carson McCullers' *The Ballad of the Sad Café* (1963) notes that Albee to date has produced only one full-length play and several one-act plays. Gottfried accuses Albee of showing "a complete unawareness of the female personality" in his plays. He calls his dialogue commonplace and feels that any judgments about his future as a playwright "must be held in abeyance."

Rutenberg, Michael E. *Edward Albee: Playwright in Protest*. New York: Drama Book Specialists Publications, 1969.
Commenting on Edward Albee's fidelity to Carson McCullers' novella in his

adaptation, *The Ballad of the Sad Café* (1963), Rutenberg provides useful insights into Albee's experimental use of a stage narrator who presented the lyrical passages of the novella, much as the narrator in Thornton Wilder's *Our Town* (1937) acts as a unifying thread in that play. Rutenberg concludes that Albee's narrator was not used successfully because Albee provided him with no compelling reason to tell his story.

A Delicate Balance

Hull, Elizabeth Anne. "A Popular Psychology Illuminates an 'Elite' Art Medium: A Look at Albee's *A Delicate Balance* through Transactional Analysis." In *Proceedings of the Sixth National Convention of the Popular Culture Association*, edited by Michael T. Marsden. Bowling Green, Ohio: Bowling Green University Popular Press, 1976.
Hull does not attempt to make a direct connection between Edward Albee and the transactional psychology movement of the 1960's. Instead, she interprets *A Delicate Balance* (1966) in the light of this movement.

Rutenberg, Michael E. *Edward Albee: Playwright in Protest*. New York: Drama Book Specialists Publications, 1969.
Calling Edward Albee's Pulitzer Prize-winning play *A Delicate Balance* (1966) the playwright's most underrated play since *Tiny Alice* (1964), Rutenberg says that most of the critics agreed that the play's theme is humankind's responsibility to humankind. He contends that the play "examines more levels of our existence than the need for truer friendship among men." He then goes on to relate this play thematically to Albee's earlier plays, reinterpreting it as he does so.

The Lady from Dubuque

Adler, Thomas P. "The Pirandello in Albee: The Problem of Knowing in *The Lady from Dubuque*." In *Edward Albee: An Interview and Essays*, edited by Julian N. Wasserman et al. Houston, Tex.: The University of St. Thomas, 1983.
Acknowledging the dramatic inferiority of *The Lady from Dubuque* (1980) when it is measured against some of Albee's other work, Adler goes on to say, "Even a cursory examination of *Dubuque*'s language reveals Albee's interest in—almost obsession with—the problem of knowing." He goes on to explore this theme in relation to Pirandello's concern with similar problems.

Tiny Alice

Clurman, Harold. *The Naked Image: Observations on the Modern Theatre*. New York: Macmillan, 1966.
In his review of Edward Albee's *Tiny Alice* (1965), Clurman tends to scold Albee for not taking the advice to "eschew the abstract" that Clurman offered gratuitously in his review of *The American Dream* (see above, 1961). He contends

that in *Tiny Alice*, "all his [Albee's] artful devices leave one impassive." Clurman further laments, "the more tightly one argues the futility of our life's struggle, the more futile the point becomes."

Debusscher, Gilbert. *Edward Albee: Tradition and Renewal*. Translated by Anne D. Williams. Brussels, Belgium: Center for American Studies, 1969.
Contending that there is no discernible plot in *Tiny Alice* (1964), Debusscher (see above) claims that the play "may be the first truly modern tragedy, in which man's fatal flaw is nothing other than his humanity." He comments also on Albee's calculated use of language.

Gottfried, Martin. *Opening Nights: Theater Criticism of the Sixties*. New York: G. P. Putnam's Sons, 1969.
Gottfried reproduces here his original review of Edward Albee's *Tiny Alice* (1964). He calls the play "at once extraordinary and ridiculous." He snipes at Albee's philosophical pretensions, calling them disorganized. He objects to the play's "intellectual preciosity and sexual justification," and also berates it for "its High English [which] is self-conscious and irritatingly inconsistent."

Kauffmann, Stanley. *Persons of the Drama: Theater Criticism and Comment*. New York: Harper & Row, 1976.
Kauffmann's comments about Edward Albee's *Tiny Alice* (1964) are among the harshest written about the play. Writing in 1969 after the San Francisco American Conservatory Theater's production of *Tiny Alice* in New York, Kauffmann says of the play, "Five years ago it seemed to me a piece of arrogant, pseudo-literary pretentiousness, flung in our faces with the usual blather of a desperate author that those who don't appreciate it are either stupid or malevolent. Five years later it [the play] seems worse."

Rutenberg, Michael E. *Edward Albee: Playwright in Protest*. New York: Drama Book Specialists Publications, 1969.
Rutenberg interprets Edward Albee's *Tiny Alice* (1964) as a play that concentrates on "the overpowering feeling of abandonment experienced by modern man." He comments extensively on the theme of betrayal that underlies the play and demonstrates how Albee uses this controlling theme to sustain his basic premise.

Who's Afraid of Virginia Woolf?

Clurman, Harold. *The Naked Image: Observations on the Modern Theatre*. New York: Macmillan, 1966.
In his review of Edward Albee's *Who's Afraid of Virginia Woolf?* (1962), reproduced in this book, Harold Clurman begins by saying that the play is packed with talent. He comments on the impotence, at least during the play's time frame,

of the four characters in it. He calls Albee's dialogue "superbly virile and pliant"; he commends the playwright's ability to keep his audience engrossed throughout the play. Nevertheless, Clurman calls this play "a minor work within the prospect of Albee's further development."

Debusscher, Gilbert. *Edward Albee: Tradition and Renewal.* Translated by Anne D. Williams. Brussels, Belgium: Center for American Studies, 1969.
Debusscher (see above) calls *Who's Afraid of Virginia Woolf?* (1962) "the logical successor of the four preceding ones" and says that it succeeds because of its "skillful blending of tradition and avant-garde, of naturalism and symbolism." He identifies the play as the first great work of the American stage in years.

Finkelstein, Sidney. *Existentialism and Alienation in American Literature.* New York: International, 1965.
Finkelstein gives only passing attention to *Who's Afraid of Virginia Woolf?* (1962), but he is well aware of the trap in which Albee has placed his characters and realizes that there is no exit for them. Alienation occurs because communication is difficult between the principals. The youthful hope exemplified by Nick and Honey is soon dashed, and it is clear that they will end up like George and Martha.

Halperen, Max. "What Happens in *Who's Afraid* . . . ?" In *Modern American Drama: Essays in Criticism,* edited by William E. Taylor. Deland, Fla.: Everett/ Edwards, 1968.
Halperen calls *Who's Afraid of Virginia Woolf?* (1962) Edward Albee's best play to date. He contends that one cannot understand it fully unless one does so within the context of Albee's earlier plays. His essay, therefore, seeks to relate this play to *The Zoo Story* (1959), *The Death of Bessie Smith* (1960), and *The American Dream* (1961). He comments appreciatively on Albee's ability to "reveal his perceptions in the give-and-take of flat, ordinary conversation."

Herron, Ima Honaker. *The Small Town in American Drama.* Dallas, Tex.: Southern Methodist University Press, 1969.
Herron compares Edward Albee in *Who's Afraid of Virginia Woolf?* (1962) to Walt Whitman and T. S. Eliot in his setting of a chronological context, noting especially Whitman's "filaments of time" and Eliot's concern with continuity. She also compares it to the European hate play, of which August Strindberg was the master, in "texture, technique, [and] shock potential."

Porter, Thomas E. *Myth and Modern American Drama.* Detroit: Wayne State University Press, 1969.
Porter pinpoints the essence of Edward Albee's *Who's Afraid of Virginia Woolf?*

(1962) in his statement that the play "demands that the spectator recognize that society standards can become defenses that the individual uses to avoid the pain of facing reality." He bases his interpretation on the mythological notion of the Void, the fear of which holds George and Martha together in a union that Porter calls "isolationist, sterile, dependent upon a mutual need."

Roudane, Matthew. *Who's Afraid of Virginia Woolf? Necessary Fictions, Terrifying Realities.* Boston: Twayne, 1990.
Following the format of Twayne's Masterwork Studies Series, Roudane provides a chronology of Edward Albee's life and sets the historical context for the play. He then offers information about the play's critical reception, followed by a list of primary sources and a list of secondary sources. There is a comprehensive index.

Rutenberg, Michael E. *Edward Albee: Playwright in Protest.* New York: Drama Book Specialists Publications, 1969.
Rutenberg claims that Edward Albee in *Who's Afraid of Virginia Woolf?* (1962) turns his "social microscope on the very essence of our civilization, revealing immorality, opportunism, cruelty, hypocrisy, and sterility in the private lives of those whose job it is to shape and guide the tastes and morals of this country's next generation." He examines the play in an attempt to determine whether it transcends the individual trials of its characters and makes a valid social statement about life in the United States and about the future of Western Civilization.

The Zoo Story

Anderson, Mary Castiglie. "Ritual and Initiation in *The Zoo Story.*" In *Edward Albee: An Interview and Essays*, edited by Julian N. Wasserman et al. Houston, Tex.: The University of St. Thomas, 1983.
Anderson considers the ritualistic elements in *The Zoo Story* (1959) and views the play as a coming-of-age drama. The author is resourceful in establishing and defending her thesis.

Clurman, Harold. *The Naked Image: Observations on the Modern Theatre.* New York: Macmillan, 1966.
Clurman reviews Edward Albee's *The Zoo Story* (1959) along with *Krapp's Last Tape* (1960) by Samuel Beckett. He considers Albee's play "flawed by improbabilities and perhaps needless notes [stage directions] to provoke, shock or outrage" but goes on to commend the play for its genuine feeling for and intimate knowledge of "certain aspects of American society, especially of our metropolitan area." Clurman says the play interested him more than any new play of the year and hopes that Albee will fulfill his promise.

Debusscher, Gilbert. In *Edward Albee: Tradition and Renewal*. Translated by
Anne D. Williams. Brussels, Belgium: Center for American Studies, 1969.
Albee's first play, *The Zoo Story* (1959), established him as a serious playwright.
Debusscher (see above) considers the Christian symbolism in the play and does
a fine job of analyzing the Jerry-dog parable that is central to its meaning.

Weales, Gerald. *The Jumping-off Place: American Drama in the 1960's: From
Broadway to Off-Off-Broadway to Happenings*. New York: Macmillan, 1969.
In the first chapter of this book, Weales has some interesting insights into a
possible homosexual interpretation of *The Zoo Story* (1959). He finds it somewhat
more plausible than the hackneyed Christian interpretations that have been
propounded.

MAXWELL ANDERSON

General Studies

Avery, Lawrence G. *Maxwell Anderson: An Analytic Catalogue*. Austin, Tex.:
University of Texas, 1968.
Avery has made a full catalog of every Maxwell Anderson item held in the
University of Texas Library. The collection is large, and this catalog is indispens-
able to serious Maxwell Anderson scholars.

Bailey, Mabel Driscoll. *The Playwright as Prophet*. New York: Abelard-Schuman,
1957.
Bailey attempts to define Maxwell Anderson's aesthetic through understanding
his collection of essays, *Off-Broadway: Essays About the Theatre* (1947). In the
sixth chapter of this book, Bailey, writing of Anderson and others of his time,
comments, "It is in the war plays of the last 30 years that the reader will find
the sharpest and truest image of the mind of our time." The book has ten chapters and a helpful index.

Cox, Martha Heasley. *Maxwell Anderson: A Bibliography*. Charlottesville, Va.:
University of Virginia Bibliographical Society, 1958.
Cox lists all of Anderson's work through 1956. She also provides information
about all the pertinent secondary sources relating to Anderson, including newspaper and magazine reviews. The coverage is reasonably comprehensive up to
1957. Although the book is now badly outdated, it is still useful for the period
of writing and research it covers.

Gassner, John. *Dramatic Soundings*. New York: Crown, 1968.
Anderson's showmanship appeals to Gassner, who thinks that it accounts for his
effectiveness more than does his use of language, which Gassner describes as
"decorative" and colorful. Gassner is one of Anderson's more sympathetic
critics.

Gerstenberger, Donna. "Three Verse Playwrights and the American Fifties." In
Modern American Drama: Essays in Criticism, edited by William E. Taylor.
Deland, Fla.: Everett/Edwards, 1968.
In this essay, which deals with Maxwell Anderson, Richard Eberhart, and
Archibald MacLeish, and which mentions Djuna Barnes in passing, Gerstenberger
credits Maxwell Anderson with creating verse plays that audiences viewed as
something more than romantic aberrations. Anderson's verse plays were "successful with conventional audiences." Anderson is close enough to the main-
stream of American theater to be able to produce verse plays that audiences can
accept.

Gould, Jean. *Modern American Playwrights*. New York: Dodd, Mead, 1966.
Chapter 6 of Gould's fourteen-chapter book is devoted to Maxwell Anderson, concentrating particularly upon his use of history in many of his plays. Gould points out Anderson's social consciousness, which was somewhat ill-defined. This volume has illustrations. Its index is full and dependable.

Klink, William R. *Maxwell Anderson and S. N. Behrman: A Reference Guide*. Boston: G. K. Hall, 1977.
Although the arrangement of this bibliography by years is somewhat cumbersome, the material it contains on Maxwell Anderson is detailed and extensive. It lists all of Anderson's published work and offers forty-eight pages of bibliography, presenting secondary sources about Anderson and his work, including major reviews of his plays. Klink provides an index for Behrman but, surprisingly, none for Anderson.

Krutch, Joseph Wood. *American Drama Since 1918*. New York: Random House, 1938; New York: George Braziller, 1957.
Krutch devotes one chapter of this seven-chapter book to the poetic drama of Maxwell Anderson. Krutch contrasts Anderson and Eugene O'Neill, to whom a chapter of this book is devoted. He considers the two opposites, although he says of Anderson, "like O'Neill he aspires with some measure of success to reach beyond realism into tragedy." Krutch claims that Anderson adapted his writing to the modern stage, whereas O'Neill demanded that the existing stage adapt to the sometimes strenuous demands of his plays. He warns against searching for rigid symbolism in Anderson's plays, claiming that they are playful fantasies. He comments also on Anderson's blank verse.

Mersand, Joseph. *The American Drama Since 1930*. New York: Kennikat Press, 1968.
Mersand, writing largely for a secondary school audience, is effective in showing the uses Anderson makes of biography in his plays, many of which are historical. This book gives special attention to *Elizabeth the Queen* (1930), *Mary of Scotland* (1933), *Joan of Lorraine* (1946), *Anne of the Thousand Days* (1948), and *Barefoot in Athens* (1951).

Miller, Jordan Y. "Maxwell Anderson: Gifted Technician." In *The Thirties: Fiction, Poetry, Drama*, edited by Warren G. French. Deland, Fla.: Everett/Edwards, 1967.
In his brief essay, Miller acknowledges the artistry, the political impact, and the philosophical content of Maxwell Anderson's plays. His chief emphasis, however, is on Miller as a playwright who experimented with structure and with the technical matters of play production that all good playwrights have to be keenly aware of if they are to produce stageworthy vehicles for their ideas.

Rabkin, Gerald. *Drama and Commitment: Politics in the American Theatre of the Thirties*. Bloomington, Ind.: Indiana University Press, 1964.
Rabkin devotes a full chapter, "The Political Paradox of Maxwell Anderson," to Maxwell Anderson. Although he compares the playwright favorably with Eugene O'Neill and does not question the integrity with which he practiced his art, Rabkin concludes that Anderson was more derivative than experimental in his writing. Anderson, according to Rabkin, had no ear for language, and his political philosophy was so confused that the political plays present no really consistent attitude toward the human condition. Although Anderson has a considerable interest in freedom, human dignity, types of authority, and rebellion against authority, his plays present no clear-cut vision of how society can be reformulated.

Sahu, N. S. *Theatre of Protest and Anger: Studies in the Dramatic Works of Maxwell Anderson and Robert E. Sherwood*. Delhi, India: Amar Prakashan, 1988.
Sahu uses Maxwell Anderson's *What Price Glory?* (1924) to make his point, interweaving his argument with Anderson's historical plays. Sahu mentions that Anderson reached the crossroads of realizing that good people "are helpless beings, the men of no actions." He calls the theater of protest and anger an offshoot of the theater of revolt. He differentiates between the two by saying that in the theater of protest and anger, "the rebel dramatist proceeds by dialogue, and implies debate and conflict," whereas in the theater of revolt, "the rebel playwright takes protest as his central theme." The author's thesis is interesting although it is only marginally defended in this book, which has a selective bibliography and a very limited index.

Shivers, Alfred S. *Maxwell Anderson*. Boston: Twayne, 1976.
A useful chronology precedes the body of this book, which essentially presents a biographical chapter followed by chapters that analyze Anderson's work. Chapter 2 treats Anderson's war plays of the late 1930's and early 1940's. These plays gave him the reputation of being a war dramatist. Chapter 3 deals with the historical plays that focus on the corruption that often accompanies political power. Chapter 4 deals with nonhistorical works, and chapter 5 reaches generalizations about Anderson as a dramatist. The discussions are limited to twenty-three of Anderson's most significant plays, half of his published output. The annotated bibliography and index are assets.

Taylor, William E. "Maxwell Anderson: Traditionalist in a Theatre of Change." In *Modern American Drama; Essays in Criticism*, edited by William E. Taylor. Deland, Fla.: Edwards/Everett Press, 1968.
Taylor supports well his thesis that Anderson spent much of his creative life trying to employ his theory of dramatic poetry, a tradition going back to Shake-

speare and beyond. Anderson, unfortunately for him, was living in an age when the theater respected—indeed, demanded—innovation, so his traditionalism resulted in his work's being undervalued.

Key Largo

Brown, John Mason. *Broadway in Review*. New York: W. W. Norton, 1940.
In his five-page review of *Key Largo* (1939), Brown contends that Anderson's reach was greater than his grasp. The elements of *Key Largo* that he finds weak are those relating to Anderson's control of the language and his conclusion, which Brown finds unconvincing and irresolute.

Winterset

Block, Anita. *The Changing World in Plays and Theatre*. Boston: Little, Brown, 1939.
In her assessment of *Winterset* (1935), Block objects to the way the play, as she says, "vaporizes" over a phantom theme. She calls Anderson an escapist and suggests that his pessimism and defeatism in regard to the Sacco and Vanzetti case found their way into the play and destroyed much of its impact.

Heilman, Robert. *Tragedy and Melodrama*. Seattle, Wash.: University of Washington Press, 1968.
Heilman considers *Winterset* (1935) more melodramatic than tragic. He particularly objects to the ending, which he dubs operatic. The general differentiations Heilman makes between tragedy and melodrama are extremely interesting in assessing modern playwrights generally.

ROBERT ANDERSON

Adler, Thomas P. *Robert Anderson*. Boston: Twayne, 1978.
In this only book-length assessment of the plays of Robert Anderson, Adler follows the usual format of the Twayne United States Authors Series, providing a detailed chronology, an initial biographical chapter, six chapters that analyze Anderson's works (including, in chapter 4, his writing for films), a concluding chapter, a selected bibliography with annotations, and a comprehensive index. Adler writes, "What causes the loneliness and disillusionment that pervade the world of Anderson's plays is, put simply, the tendency of American society not only to undervalue sensitivity but, whenever possible, to destroy it, as part of perpetuating a distorted notion of manliness."

Bentley, Eric. *The Dramatic Event: An American Chronicle*. New York: Horizon Press, 1954.
Bentley discusses *Tea and Sympathy* (1953) in detail. He considers it a fine exemplar of what he calls "the theatre of 'realist' escape." He identifies the basic theme of the play convincingly and discusses its development well.

Bigsby, C. W. E. In *Contemporary Dramatists*, edited by James Vinson. London: St. James Press, 1973.
In his untitled comments about Robert Anderson, Bigsby offers some of the most penetrating insights in print into Anderson's writing. He calls him "a writer of genuine power and considerable subtlety." He acknowledges Anderson's tendency to dramatic hyperbole but feels that his virtues outweigh this slight fault.

Gassner, John. *Theatre at the Crossroads: Plays and Playwrights of the Mid-Century American Stage*. New York: Holt, Rinehart and Winston, 1960.
Focusing on Robert Anderson's *All Summer Long* (1954; an adaptation of David Wetzel's novel *A Wreath and a Curse*) and *Tea and Sympathy* (1953), Gassner, who always appreciated Robert Anderson's work, mentions the playwright's restraint and good dramatic judgment. In commenting on Anderson's *Silent Night, Lonely Night* (1960), Gassner says that it would have been a better play had it been a one-act play in two or three scenes. He laments the pressure on playwrights to observe conventional lengths in their plays to conform to the demands of Broadway commercialism.

Herron, Ima Honaker. *The Small Town in American Drama*. Dallas, Tex.: Southern Methodist University Press, 1969.
Herron writes about Robert Anderson's *Tea and Sympathy* (1953), *All Summer Long* (1955), *Silent Night, Lonely Night* (1960), and *The Days Between* (1965), paying particular attention to his characterization and his thematic development

in these four plays. She values "Anderson's talent for dramatizing lonely towns-people."

Kerr, Walter. *How Not to Write a Play.* New York: Simon & Schuster, 1955.
Kerr acknowledges the commercial success of Robert Anderson's *Tea and Sympathy* (1953) but attributes this success to his writing according to a formula. Kerr considers the play to be lacking somewhat in honesty and accuracy.

Meserve, Walter J. *An Outline History of American Drama.* Totowa, N.J.: Littlefield, Adams, 1965.
This book is quite abbreviated, hence the comments on Robert Anderson and his plays are quite brief and not always penetrating. Meserve comments on the plays' slow movement and regrets the playwright's sentimentality. He also objects to Anderson's facile resolution of the plays' dilemmas through illicit sex.

Miller, J. William. *Modern Playwrights at Work.* New York: Samuel French, 1968.
Miller quotes Robert Anderson, who for four years taught play writing, as saying that he thinks the skill can be taught, although "that certain quality which lifts a play—making it particular—this you cannot teach." Miller has little to say directly about specific plays of Anderson.

Sievers, W. David. *Freud on Broadway: A History of Psychoanalysis and the American Drama.* New York: Hermitage House, 1955.
Sievers presents one of the best psychological analyses of Robert Anderson's *Tea and Sympathy* (1953). The oedipal overtones in the play are obvious, and Sievers goes far beyond the obvious in his discussion.

Weales, Gerald. *American Drama Since World War II.* New York: Harcourt, Brace & World, 1962.
Weales' seven-page commentary on Robert Anderson and his plays is scathing. Weales calls Anderson's work sentimental and melodramatic. He accuses Anderson of establishing his "reputation for seriousness" on specious grounds.

Wharton, James F. *Life Among the Playwrights: Being Mostly the Story of The Playwrights Producing Company.* New York: New York Times Books, 1974.
In his fourteen-page section on Robert Anderson, Wharton tells about his association with the playwright as a theatrical producer. This performance-oriented book focuses on production aspects of Anderson's work.

JAMES BALDWIN

General Studies

Bigsby, C. W. E., ed. *Confrontation and Commitment: A Study of Contemporary American Drama, 1959-1966.* Columbia, Mo.: University of Missouri Press, 1968.
Bigsby's eight-page essay on James Baldwin deals with both of his plays. Bigsby calls *Blues for Mr. Charlie* (1964) overwritten but captivating. He contends that Baldwin seethes with the spirit of revolt that was abroad in the 1960's. Bigsby notes that criticism of the play has been quite mixed, with favorable criticism more likely to come from black commentators than from white critics.

Eckman, Fern Marja. *The Furious Passage of James Baldwin.* New York: M. Evans, 1966.
This slender volume examines the causes and some of the effects, including the artistic ones, of James Baldwin's racial anger. The emphasis is on the novels, although some reference is made to the dramas.

Keyssar, Helene. *The Curtain and the Veil: Strategies in Black Drama.* New York: Burt Franklin, 1981.
Although Keyssar does not devote a great deal of space to the dramas of James Baldwin, she presents a significant bibliographical entry on him as dramatist. This entry, which contains information about his plays and about his articles that touch on drama, is brief but valuable. It presents more than two pages of secondary sources, including reviews, and will lead readers to the most important sources for Baldwin research.

Kinnamon, Keneth, ed. *James Baldwin: A Collection of Critical Essays.* Englewood Cliffs, N.J.: Prentice-Hall, 1974.
Although this collection of thirteen essays by Langston Hughes, F. W. Dupee, Eldridge Cleaver, Irving Howe, Michel Fabré, and Benjamin DeMott among others focuses on Baldwin's prose writing, Kinnamon mentions *The Amen Corner* (1955) in his introduction, and it is mentioned again in Michel Fabré's essay. *Blues for Mr. Charlie* (1964) is mentioned in Calvin C. Hernton's "A Fiery Baptism" and more fully by Sherley Anne Williams in "The Black Musician."

Macebuh, Stanley. *James Baldwin: A Critical Study.* New York: The Third Press, 1973.
Macebuh is essentially concerned with Baldwin's search for identity. He seeks to relate Baldwin to the Civil Rights Movement, and he addresses somewhat indirectly the pressing matter of Baldwin's sexuality and the way in which it affected his writing. This book seems marginal at best.

O'Daniel, Therman B., ed. *James Baldwin: A Critical Evaluation.* Washington, D.C.: Howard University Press, 1977.
This collection contains three essays on James Baldwin as playwright. Their primary focus is on *Blues for Mr. Charlie* (1964). Carlton W. Mollette discusses *The Amen Corner* (1955) in his brief essay but devotes twice as much space to Baldwin's other play. Darwin Turner writes about the dilemma of black playwrights who, if they are to succeed, must write for white audiences, as Baldwin obviously did. Waters E. Turpin's contribution is brief—only two pages—and is concerned exclusively with *Blues for Mr. Charlie.*

Phillips, Louis. "The Novelist as Playwright: Baldwin, McCullers, and Bellow." In *Modern American Drama: Essays in Criticism*, edited by William E. Taylor. Deland, Fla.: Everett/Edwards, 1968.
Phillips shows how many novelists have been intrigued by drama and reminds his readers that James Baldwin once prepared a dramatic version of *Giovanni's Room* (1956) for performance by an Actors Studio workshop. Baldwin is, however, of the three novelists-turned-playwrights about whom Phillips writes, the one least attracted to drama. He has expressed himself on the subject, and Phillips quotes him. He comments on Baldwin's conclusion to *Blues for Mr. Charlie* (1964), in which the Bible and the gun are brought together, leaving the impression that they go hand in hand.

Pratt, Louis H. *James Baldwin.* Boston: Twayne, 1978.
Following the prescribed format of the Twayne United States Authors Series, this critical biography has a chronology, an initial biographical chapter, and subsequent chapters that analyze the work of James Baldwin. Pratt deals with Baldwin's dramatic writing in a brief section (pages 83-96). He believes that *The Amen Corner* (1955) has better artistic qualifications than *Blues for Mr. Charlie* (1964), which is what most critics believe. This book has an annotated bibliography and a comprehensive index.

Rosset, Lisa. *James Baldwin.* New York: Chelsea House, 1989.
Rosset's book is aimed essentially at high school students. It is well illustrated and contains a chronology, a limited bibliography, and an index. It identifies *The Amen Corner* (1955) as "a morality tale about a minister whose life is ruined by her fanatical devotion to spiritual purity and by her lack of compassion for human feelings." It calls *Blues for Mr. Charlie* (1964), a play inspired by the murder of Medgar Evers, a "bitter story about a down-and-out jazz musician who returns to his birthplace in the South and is murdered."

Standley, Fred L., and Nancy V. Burt. *Critical Essays on James Baldwin.* Boston: G. K. Hall, 1988.
One brief section (pages 295-302) of this collection, which consists of thirty-five

essays by such contributors as Stephen Spender, Mario Puzo, Harold Clurman, Houston A. Baker, and Leslie Fiedler, focuses on Baldwin's drama. Of the essays concerned with drama, Fred Standley's "James Baldwin as Dramatist" is the most comprehensive. Martha Bayle's article is about an adaptation of Baldwin's *Go Tell It on the Mountain* (1953) for television. Clurman's contribution is essentially a review of *The Amen Corner* (1955), which he says is "marred by many blemishes but the total effect is touching and valuable." He likes it for its genuineness and for the level of writing in the play's most crucial passages. Tom F. Driver's contribution is an in-depth review of *Blues for Mr. Charlie* (1964), in which Driver contends that Baldwin succeeds because of neither sophisticated plot development nor the psychological penetration of his characterization, but rather because of his ability to preach a good sermon, to speak didactically to audiences who accept his didacticism.

Blues for Mr. Charlie

Brustein, Robert. *Seasons of Discontent: Dramatic Opinions, 1959-1965.* New York: Simon & Schuster, 1965.
Entitled "Everybody's Protest Play," Brustein's review of the Actors Studio Theatre's presentation of *Blues for Mr. Charlie* (1964) calls the play "the embodiment of everything [Baldwin] once professed to deplore." Brustein calls the play aesthetically flat, but finds more distressing than that flatness deficiencies in its moral and intellectual tone. He cites Baldwin's early statement that he wanted only to be an honest man and a good writer, claiming that the playwright has, in this play, ceased to be both.

Margolis, Edward. "The Negro Church: James Baldwin and the Christian Vision." In *James Baldwin*, edited by Harold Bloom. New York: Chelsea House, 1986.
Margolis shows how Baldwin advances the cause of the church militant in *The Fire Next Time* (1963) and in *Blues for Mr. Charlie* (1964). He contends that in the latter, "Baldwin translates his apocalypse into concrete social terms," presaging the racial upheavals that occurred later in the 1960's.

Phillips, Louis. "The Novelist as Playwright: Baldwin, McCullers, and Bellow." In *Modern American Drama*, edited by William E. Taylor. Deland, Fla.: Everett/Edwards, 1968.
Phillips says that "what is amazing [in *Blues for Mr. Charlie*, 1964] is Baldwin's ability to see the white community of a small southern town through its own eyes and his ability to portray the wider issues involved in a racial matter: The terrible self-deceptions that racial murderers must live by." He points out that in Baldwin's notes for the play, the author calls race a plague, and contends that his play reflects this attitude.

Roth, Philip. *"Blues for Mr. Charlie."* In *James Baldwin*, edited by Harold Bloom. New York: Chelsea House, 1986.

Roth notes that in *Blues for Mr. Charlie* (1964), "being dutiful to the murderer is not Baldwin's overriding impulse." He goes on to explain the subconscious overtones in the play that led him to reinterpret it. He concludes that neither Lyle nor Richard is essentially a wretched character; both simply behave wretchedly.

PHILIP BARRY

Brown, John Mason. *Upstage: The American Theatre in Performance*. New York: W. W. Norton, 1930.
Brown offered in this book one of the most extended discussions of the young Barry. The playwright had gained considerable celebrity with his collaboration with Elmer Rice, *Cock Robin* (1928), and with his *Holiday* (1928) and *Hotel Universe* (1930). Brown appreciates Barry's upbeat approach to theater.

Downer, Alan S. *Fifty Years of American Drama, 1900-1950*. Chicago: Henry Regnery, 1951.
In his brief survey of more than half a century of American drama, Downer claims that Philip Barry, as the author of serious plays such as *Hotel Universe* (1930) and *Here Come the Clowns* (1938), emerges as an "O'Neill *in petto*. His great technical skill is evident in his social comedies." The author alludes briefly to half a dozen of Barry's more important plays.

Flexner, Eleanor. *American Playwrights: 1918-1938*. New York: Simon & Schuster, 1938.
In a substantial section on Philip Barry, Flexner comments adversely on his refusal to join the progressive theater movement of the early 1930's. She also feels that he is naïve for not approaching his material with a greater awareness of the socioeconomic climate of his day.

Gassner, John. *Theatre at the Crossroads: Plays and Playwrights of the Mid-Century American Stage*. New York: Holt, Rinehart and Winston, 1960.
Gassner, discussing Philip Barry in a section that also considers Robert E. Sherwood, mentions Barry's "success in the diminishing genre of American comedy of manners" as well as his "disappointment in most of his endeavors at writing symbolic morality plays." He contends that Barry's successful comedies presented a "unified attitude and development."

Gould, Jean. *Modern American Playwrights*. New York: Dodd, Mead, 1966.
Jean Gould devotes one chapter of this fourteen-chapter book to a discussion of Philip Barry, commenting on his relationship to his times and his uniqueness in maintaining his optimism and producing plays that rose above the immediate socioeconomic problems with which many of the playwrights of his time were concerning themselves.

Krutch, Joseph Wood. *American Drama Since 1918*. New York: Random House, 1938; New York: George Braziller, 1957.
Comparing Philip Barry to S. N. Behrman, Krutch says that with the two of them, "more abstract high comedy" came to American drama. He says that both

are cosmopolitan in their outlooks. He notes that Barry depends on neither the wisecrack nor the epigram for his humor, saying that Barry's dialogue is not the sort that can be quoted meaningfully in snippets. He says that Barry's dialogue "is almost too insubstantial to be subject to analysis." He calls *Here Come the Clowns* (1938) Barry's best play.

Mersand, Joseph. *The Play's the Thing: Enjoying Plays Today.* New York: The Modern Chapbooks, 1941.
This book is aimed largely at the high school students whom Mersand taught. He deals generously with Philip Barry, pointing to the commercial success that his plays enjoyed, certainly one—if not the most important—indicator of a playwright's acceptance.

Quinn, Arthur Hobson. *A History of the American Drama from the Civil War to the Present Day.* New York: Appleton-Century Crofts, 1936.
In the second volume of this compendious two-volume history that surveys the development of American drama, Quinn refers frequently to Philip Barry, showing him as a significant force in American drama during the 1920's. In one seven-page assessment of Barry, Quinn shows admiration for his psychological insights and for his creation of realistic characters who have verisimilitude. This treatment is valuable for placing Barry in his times and in contrast to his fellow playwrights.

Roppolo, Joseph Patrick. *Philip Barry.* New York: Twayne, 1965.
Roppolo's is the first full critical biography of Philip Barry. This book, according to the usual format of Twayne's United States Authors Series, has a chronology, an initial biographical chapter, and analyses of the plays in the next four chapters, which are followed by an annotated bibliography and a reliable index. Roppolo portrays Barry as a playwright who remained optimistic and hopeful in his plays, a man who was in great "awe of the unrealized potentialities of the human individual."

Sievers, W. David. *Freud on Broadway: A History of Psychoanalysis and the American Dream.* New York: Hermitage House, 1955.
In a twenty-four-page consideration of Barry's dramatic writing from *You and I* (1923) to *Second Threshold* (1951), Sievers shows how Barry employs his knowledge of modern psychology and psychoanalytical techniques in his writing. He identifies *In a Garden* (1925), *Hotel Universe* (1930), and *Here Come the Clowns* (1938) as Barry's most notable psychodramas, noting that they confused the critics. According to Sievers, Barry deserves to be recognized as one of the earliest writers of psychodrama.

S. N. BEHRMAN

Agate, James. *The Contemporary Theatre*. London: George G. Harrap, 1946.
Agate accuses Behrman of being patronizing and condescending to his audience in *Jacobowsky and the Colonel* (1944), his adaptation of the Franz Werfel play. He also contends that the Broadway production was badly miscast, intensifying the problems inherent in the adaptation.

Behrman, S. N. "Query: What Makes Comedy High?" In *The Passionate Playgoer: A Personal Scrapbook*, edited by George Oppenheimer. New York: Viking Press, 1958.
Behrman answers the question posed to him by saying that high comedy depends on the articulateness of its characters, on the "plane on which they talk, the intellectual and moral climate in which they live." This is a succinct statement of Behrman's philosophy of writing comedies.

Brown, John Mason. *Two on the Aisle*. New York: W. W. Norton, 1938.
Brown comments rather superficially on Behrman's way of depicting characters whose society is changing more rapidly than they can adapt. He praises Behrman's wit and his "validity of irresolution."

Downer, Alan S. *Fifty Years of American Drama: 1900-1950*. Chicago: Henry Regnery, 1951.
Although Downer mentions Behrman only twice in this book—and briefly both times—his comments in regard to *The Second Man* (1927) and *Biography* (1932) are worth noting. He writes that the manners these plays reflect are neither American nor universal. They are the conventional manners of high comedy. It is high comedy that Behrman best succeeded in writing.

Flexner, Eleanor. *American Playwrights, 1918-1938*. New York: Simon & Schuster, 1938; New York: Books for Libraries Press, 1969.
According to Flexner, Behrman's most remarkable dramatic assets initially were his detachment and his tolerance. She claims that in his early plays, he was willing "to examine and express every point of view." She complains that in his later work, he deviated from this detachment.

Gassner, John. *Masters of Drama*. New York: Dover Publishers, 1940; rev. ed., 1954.
Gassner admits that Behrman writes appealingly and entertainingly, but he contends that he does not provide satisfactory resolutions for the situations he creates. He calls Behrman a master of "self-revealing" dialogue.

Klink, William R. *Maxwell Anderson and S. N. Behrman: A Reference Guide.*
Boston: G. K. Hall, 1977.
Klink's bibliography is arranged by years, which makes it somewhat difficult to
use. It provides, nevertheless, the most complete listing of Behrman's own
writing, including letters and reviews, and of secondary sources that deal with
him and his work, including major reviews of his plays. Klink offers twenty-eight
pages of secondary sources that deal with S. N. Behrman. Klink provides an
index for Behrman but not for Anderson.

_____. *S. N. Behrman: The Major Plays.* Amsterdam: Editions Rodopi,
1978.
Klink's study appears to be an unrevised doctoral dissertation. It deals with the
major plays from *The Second Man* (1927) to *But for Whom Charlie* (1964) and
is generally quite pedestrian. The final chapter, however, which deals with
Behrman's language, is well worth reading. It compares Behrman's nonhumorous
language with his humorous language, showing, sometimes by mathematical
computation, how Behrman controls his language in both of these forms. Klink
shows how Behrman depends largely on epigrammatic humor, which he uses
well, up to *End of Summer* (1936). With that play, however, he adds several
other forms of humor to his writing. Slim bibliography, no index.

Krutch, Joseph Wood. *The American Drama Since 1918.* New York: Random
House, 1939; New York: George Braziller, 1957.
Krutch admires Behrman's critical detachment in his comedies. This book deals
briefly with Behrman's plays up to *Wine of Choice* (1938). He is impressed by
the clarity of Behrman's writing.

_____. "The Comic Wisdom of S. N. Behrman." In *The American Theatre
as Seen by Its Critics*, edited by Montrose J. Moses and John Mason Brown.
New York: W. W. Norton, 1934.
Krutch's article, which originally appeared in *The Nation*, is reprinted in this
collection. Krutch calls Behrman witty, gifted, urbane, and intellectual in the way
he presents ideas. The most important point Krutch makes is that Behrman's
measure of people is their intelligence and articulateness, not their heroism. The
result is, according to Krutch, a high level of comedy.

Lewis, Allan. *American Plays and Playwrights of the Contemporary Theatre.* New
York: Crown, 1965.
Lewis identifies S. N. Behrman, along with Elmer Rice, as one of the "respected
but tired elder statesmen of the Broadway stage." In his comments on Behrman,
Lewis deals in some detail with *The Second Man* (1927), *Lord Pengo* (1962), *The
Cold Wind and the Warm* (1958), and *Rain from Heaven* (1934). Lewis calls
Behrman the William Congreve of the American stage.

Millett, Fred B. *Contemporary American Authors*. New York: Harcourt, Brace, 1940.
Millett takes Behrman to task for the lack of moral conviction and intellectual commitment in his plays. He contends that they do not have a fundamental concern with the meaning of life, which, in Millett's view, great drama must consider centrally.

Moses, Montrose J., ed. *Representative American Dramas: National and Local*. Rev. ed. Boston: Little, Brown, 1933.
The introduction Moses wrote to *Second Man* (1927) points out that the play has a minimal plot and depends for its impact upon the convoluted characterization of the protagonist, Storey, who has a dual personality. Moses comments favorably on Behrman's wit and his mastery of satire.

Nathan, George Jean. *The Entertainment of a Nation: Or, Three Sheets in the Wind*. New York: Alfred A. Knopf, 1942.
Nathan criticizes *The Talley Method* (1941) for focusing too much on the concerns of the world. He wishes Behrman would lighten up, overcoming an attitude perhaps attributable to the recent entry of the United States into World War II.

Rabkin, Gerald. *Drama and Commitment: Politics in the American Theatre of the Thirties*. Bloomington, Ind.: Indiana University Press, 1964.
In his chapter "S. N. Behrman: No Time for Comedy," Rabkin considers Behrman's plays an intermixture of the comic and the serious. He calls the plays high comedy because of Behrman's adherence to the conventions of such comedy as it has evolved through the ages. He contends that Behrman "uses serious problems as vehicles for his wit." He indicates that like Elmer Rice, Behrman was intellectually interested in Marxism but found it too dogmatic for his taste.

Skinner, Richard Dana. *Our Changing Theatre*. New York: L. McVeagh, Dial Press, 1931; Toronto: Longmans, Green, 1931.
Skinner, drama critic for *Commonweal*, comments incisively on S. N. Behrman's *The Second Man* (1927). He thinks that the dual personality of the protagonist is telling, concluding that the less skeptical, less cynical of his two personalities is the real basis for the character as Behrman develops him.

MARC CONNELLY

General Studies

Connelly, Marc. *Voices Offstage: A Book of Memoirs*. Chicago: Holt, Rinehart and Winston, 1968.
This book is valuable for Connelly's memories of his association with Kaufman when he collaborated with him in the early 1920's. He verifies their continuing friendship and association during the years after their collaboration ended in 1924. Connelly goes on to note his involvement in the founding of *The New Yorker* and to recall the halcyon years during which *The Green Pastures* (1930) earned for him a Pulitzer Prize and one of his short stories won an O. Henry Award. Although he is not always accurate in remembering details, this book has overall merit.

Miller, J. William. *Modern Playwrights at Work*. New York: Samuel French, 1968.
Miller cites quotations from Marc Connelly's interviews and articles about his collaborative efforts. Connelly notes that things that seemed acceptable to one member of the collaboration sometimes seemed "overwritten or underwritten or cloudy" to the other; therefore, collaboration had a corrective effect upon the writing of both collaborators.

Nolan, Paul T. *Marc Connelly*. New York: Twayne, 1969.
Following the prescribed format of Twayne's United States Authors Series, this compact volume begins with a chronology and ends with an annotated bibliography and index. Although Nolan covers all of Connelly's dramas, he gives special attention to *The Green Pastures* (1930), to which he devotes the entire fourth chapter. Chapter 2 focuses on Connelly's collaboration with George S. Kaufman, which lasted from 1920 until 1924 and resulted in nine plays, several of them highly successful (see Pollack below). Chapter 3 focuses on Connelly's role in beginning the *New Yorker* and provides valuable insights into the frequenters of the Algonquin "Round Table."

Pollack, Rhoda-Gale. *George S. Kaufman*. Boston: Twayne, 1988.
Chapter 2 of this book is about the Marc Connelly-George S. Kaufman collaboration of the early 1920's, which began with *Dulcy* (1921) and ended with *Be Yourself* (1924). The two collaborated on a total of nine plays, the most artistically successful of which was *Beggar on Horseback* (1924), the best-received expressionistic play of its day in the United States. It had a run of 224 Broadway performances. Their greatest commercial success was *Merton of the Movies* (1922), which ran for 398 Broadway performances. The collaboration ended amicably, and the two playwrights remained friends for life.

The Green Pastures

Herron, Ima Honaker. *The Small Town in American Drama*. Dallas, Tex.: Southern
Methodist University Press, 1969.

In her assessment of *The Green Pastures* (1930), Herron praises Connelly for
his "photographically clear stage directions, folk psychology, and colloquial
dialogue," which she claims captures the essence of what it is like to be African-
American in a small Louisiana town. She notes that African-American life in such
a setting often revolves around the church, and Connelly depicts this atmosphere
deftly and convincingly. Herron thinks the play succeeded because it allowed
audiences to accept the spirit of the Bible in terms of "earthly familiarity."

T. S. ELIOT

General Studies

Ackroyd, Peter. *T. S. Eliot: A Life.* New York: Simon & Schuster, 1984.
Although this chronologically arranged biography emphasizes Eliot's life rather than his work, the two are so inextricably entwined that one cannot be discussed without the other. Each of the seven Eliot plays is discussed here and there throughout this book, and in the case of *The Cocktail Party* (1949), quite a bit is said about the critical reception of the play. The material on *Sweeney Agonistes* (1926) is particularly interesting for what it has to say about the play's declamatory style and its music-hall qualities. This illustrated volume is comprehensive. It offers an extensive bibliography and a well-constructed index.

Baker, James V. "T. S. Eliot." In *American Winners of the Nobel Literary Prize*, edited by Warren G. French and Walter E. Kidd. Norman, Okla.: University of Oklahoma Press, 1968.
Although Baker considers T. S. Eliot primarily as the writer of the poetry for which he was awarded the prize, he discusses all of his plays, giving special attention to *Murder in the Cathedral* (1935) and *The Cocktail Party* (1947).

Browne, E. Martin. *The Making of T. S. Eliot's Plays.* Cambridge, England: Cambridge University Press, 1969.
Browne, who directed Eliot's plays from 1933 until 1958, focuses on Eliot as playwright, not losing sight of the fact that it was his career as a poet that motivated a great deal of his dramatic writing. This study traces how the plays came to be written and suggests the connections between Eliot's plays and his poetry. It also demonstrates that events in Eliot's personal life account for much that is in the plays and for the fact that the plays were written at all.

Canary, Robert H. *T. S. Eliot: The Poet and His Critics.* Chicago: American Library Association, 1982.
A comprehensive consideration of Eliot's critical standing based on fifty years of criticism. Canary presents opposing points of view fairly. His approach reflects Eliot's dictum that the writer must be objective.

Chiari, Joseph. *T. S. Eliot: Poet and Dramatist.* London: Vision Press, 1972.
Chiari's main concern is with T. S. Eliot as a poet, but he devotes considerable space to discussing the plays, showing how closely related they are philosophically to the poetry. Chiari is especially helpful in identifying pervasive themes and variations on those themes.

Davidson, Harriet. *T. S. Eliot and Hermeneutics*. Baton Rouge, La.: Louisiana State University Press, 1985.
Although Davidson focuses on T. S. Eliot's poetry, specifically on *The Waste Land* (1922), her approach suggests interesting new ways of interpreting the poet. Such approaches might be used productively in assessing Eliot's verse dramas.

Donoghue, Denis. *The Third Voice: Modern British and American Verse Drama*. Princeton, N.J.: Princeton University Press, 1959.
Donoghue devotes six of the sixteen chapters in this book to T. S. Eliot's plays, including *Murder in the Cathedral* (1935), *The Family Reunion* (1939), *The Cocktail Party* (1949), *The Confidential Clerk* (1953), and *The Elder Statesman* (1958). Donoghue also devotes a chapter to analyzing Eliot's verse line. The book has an index but no bibliography.

Freed, Lewis. *T. S. Eliot: The Critic as Philosopher*. West Lafayette, Ind.: Purdue University Press, 1979.
In this book, Freed examines some of the philosophical influences upon T. S. Eliot, including Francis Herbert Bradley and his phenomenological thinking. Although this book does not treat the plays specifically, it provides a solid background for understanding the philosophical antecedents of most of them. The book has a serviceable index but no bibliography.

Gardner, Helen. *The Art of T. S. Eliot*. New York: E. P. Dutton, 1949, 1950, 1959; new ed., 1968.
Because Gardner's book is concerned essentially with T. S. Eliot's poetry, notably *Four Quartets* (1940-1942), the author says little about his dramas. Her sixth chapter, however, which is entitled "The Language of Drama," offers worthwhile insights into Eliot's verse plays, particularly *Sweeney Agonistes* (1926-1927), *Murder in the Cathedral* (1935), and *The Family Reunion* (1939). She notes that *The Family Reunion*, unlike the other plays, anticipates important poems that follow it, noting, "It is in *Four Quartets* that the subject of *The Family Reunion* finds completely satisfying artistic expression." This book has no index.

Gordon, Lyndall. *Eliot's Early Years*. New York: Oxford University Press, 1977.
Although this book focuses largely on T. S. Eliot's early poetry, it comments on some of the plays, most notably *Sweeney Agonistes* (1926-1927) and *The Family Reunion* (1939). Surprisingly, it does not mention *Murder in the Cathedral* (1935), despite the book's religious slant. Gordon offers both a bibliography and a reasonably comprehensive index.

Headings, Philip R. *T. S. Eliot*. New York: Twayne, 1964; rev. ed., Boston: Twayne, 1982.

Both of these volumes follow the usual format of Twayne's United States Authors Series, beginning with a detailed chronology and an initial biographical treatment followed by chapters that analyze T. S. Eliot's major works, including his dramas. The book has a selected bibliography and a comprehensive index.

Hinchliffe, Arnold P., ed. *T. S. Eliot: Plays*. London: Macmillan, 1985.
The whole of T. S. Eliot's dramatic production is considered in this casebook that draws its contributions from such scholars and artists as Northrop Frye, Helen Gardner, Carol H. Smith, Conrad Aiken, Hugh Kenner, Francis Fergusson, Stephen Spender, and Michael Goldman. The plays are discussed individually in chronological order with between three and eight essays being presented on each play and, in several cases, Eliot's own comments on the play under discussion. The book has a very limited bibliography and a useful index.

Howarth, Herbert. *Notes on Some Figures Behind T. S. Eliot*. Boston: Houghton Mifflin, 1964.
Howarth provides a careful analysis of the background of much of Eliot's writing, including his dramas. He assesses the cultural and social milieux of the works he discusses and answers many of the questions that have lingered about Eliot's sources and motivations. The book has an index and a useful bibliography.

Jones, David E. *The Plays of T. S. Eliot*. London: Routledge & Kegan Paul, 1960; Toronto: University of Toronto Press, 1971.
Jones's much-reprinted book begins with a chapter on poetry in the theater. It moves on to Eliot's experimental plays, focusing on *Sweeney Agonistes* (1926) and *The Rock* (1934) in the second chapter. The next chapter is devoted to *Murder in the Cathedral* (1935), and four succeeding chapters deal with "Plays in a Contemporary Setting," focusing on the rest of Eliot's dramatic canon. Jones designed his book for the beginner, to whom it is easily accessible. His extensive bibliography will lead readers to writings about the plays. An appendix of criticism of *Murder in the Cathedral* and an accurate index further enhance the book.

Kenner, Hugh. *The Invisible Poet: T. S. Eliot*. New York: McDowell, Obolensky, 1959, 1965.
In this intellectually lively book, Kenner reviews T. S. Eliot's major works, including the plays. He demonstrates ways in which Eliot consistently pursued philosophical stands revealed in his poetry and prose that are also pursued in his dramatic writing, most of which have to do with finding one's personal salvation.

Litz, A. Walton, ed. *Eliot in His Time*. Princeton, N.J.: Princeton University Press, 1973.
This collection of essays covers most of T. S. Eliot's major works, including his dramas, which it covers in considerable detail.

Matthews, T. S. *Great Tom: Notes Towards the Definition of T. S. Eliot*. New York: Harper & Row, 1974.
Matthews focuses largely on the biography of T. S. Eliot, but in doing so, he mentions all of his drama at least in passing, and he includes extended passages about some of the plays, having the most to say about *The Cocktail Party* (1949).

Porter, Thomas E. *Myth and Modern American Drama*. Detroit: Wayne State University Press, 1969.
Porter devotes twenty-three pages to the plays of T. S. Eliot, focusing essentially on *The Cocktail Party* (1949). Showing the uses Eliot makes of ancient forms and mythology in this play, Porter claims that "by presenting the modern audience with ancient forms wrapped in a modern disguise, Eliot hopes to re-create, with all its archetypal resonance, a model for this community of all men." Eliot's acquaintance with ancient mythology was, of course, extensive, as was his familiarity with Jessie Weston's influential *From Ritual to Romance* (1920), which he read shortly before writing *The Waste Land* (1922).

Sarkar, Subhas. *T. S. Eliot the Dramatist*. Calcutta, India: The Minerva Associates, 1972.
Sarkar presents separate analytical chapters on *Murder in the Cathedral* (1935), *The Family Reunion* (1939), *The Cocktail Party* (1949), *The Confidential Clerk* (1953), and *The Elder Statesman* (1958). She discusses Eliot's theory of drama in a thirty-five-page chapter that precedes the discussion of individual plays. Her early chapter on poetry and drama is thoughtful and well presented. Using it as a base, Sarkar seeks to discuss Eliot's development as a dramatist in the light of his development as a poet. A full bibliography and comprehensive index enhance the book's usefulness.

Schneider, Elisabeth. *T. S. Eliot: The Pattern in the Carpet*. Berkeley: University of California Press, 1975.
Schneider succeeds in her attempt to demonstrate that Eliot's work seen collectively represents a consistent and coherent philosophical statement. This book, which gives more attention to Eliot's poetry than to his plays and criticism, shows the development of his thought and the conscious building of his philosophical and aesthetic viewpoints.

Smith, Carol H. *T. S. Eliot's Dramatic Theory and Practice*. Princeton, N.J.: Princeton University Press, 1963.
T. S. Eliot thought deeply and often about what and how literature means. He published significant theoretical books about literature, some addressing specifically matters pertaining to drama. Among these are *John Dryden: The Poet, the Dramatist, the Critic* (1932), *Poetry and Drama* (1951), and *Religious Drama: Medieval and Modern* (1952), in all of which he addresses drama directly. In

many of his other books, he touches on the subject. Smith examines Eliot's plays in the light of his dramatic theory in an attempt to show correspondences and deviations. Her book is enticing though quite intricate. Smith traces Eliot's vicissitudes during his career, contending that such dramas as *The Rock* (1934) and *Murder in the Cathedral* (1935) seemed hardly to be works of the same hand that produced *The Cocktail Party* (1949). This is not a book for the beginner by any means.

Smith, Grover, Jr. *T. S. Eliot's Poetry and Plays: A Study in Sources and Meaning.* Chicago: University of Chicago Press, 1956.
This early assessment of T. S. Eliot's work remains one of the most satisfying. The work is comprehensive and discusses the plays exhaustively with sharp critical acumen and with clear indications of their sources. Unlike many of the books on Eliot, this one does not allow Eliot's drama to be overshadowed by his poetry. Instead, it shows linkages between the two forms in his work and provides some of the best analyses in print of the plays. The book has a solid bibliography and a reliable index.

The Cocktail Party

Browne, E. Martin. *The Making of T. S. Eliot's Plays.* Cambridge, England: Cambridge University Press, 1969.
Browne's treatment of T. S. Eliot's *The Cocktail Party* (1949) occupies seventy-seven pages of his book. Considerable space is devoted to the correspondence between Eliot and Browne, who directed the first performances of all of Eliot's plays from 1933 until 1958. Browne's book is production oriented and gives running accounts of changes that took place in the scripts as the plays were rehearsed and afterward.

Donoghue, Denis. *The Third Voice: Modern British and American Verse Drama.* Princeton, N.J.: Princeton University Press, 1959.
Donoghue discusses the question of alienation in T. S. Eliot's *The Cocktail Party* (1949). He quotes Eliot as saying that we live in a society that is essentially negative but is positive insofar as it is Christian. It is in this light that Donoghue assesses and analyzes *The Cocktail Party*.

Goldman, Michael. "Fear in the Way: The Design of Eliot's Drama." In *Eliot in His Time*, edited by A. Walton Litz. Princeton, N.J.: Princeton University Press, 1973.
Commenting that in *The Cocktail Party* (1949) T. S. Eliot deals with much that is haunting in modern life in light comedy, Goldman goes on to commend this play as Eliot's best. He contends that Eliot responds line by line to every theatrical opportunity in two ways: the interaction of the characters and "the use of all

the elements in the *mise en scène* to advance the action and to intensify and render more subtle our experience of it."

Headings, Philip R. *T. S. Eliot*. New York: Twayne, 1964; rev. ed., Boston: Twayne, 1982.
Headings traces T. S. Eliot's *The Cocktail Party* (1949) to the *Alcestis* of Euripides, the plot and many significant details of which it uses. He identifies the theme as being a husband's self-discovery and the restoration of his marriage. The play concentrates on the question of self-deception among most of its seven characters, who move toward self-discovery in their own ways with the help of the saint (psychiatrist), Sir Henry Harcourt-Reilly, and the guardians, on whom Headings has a cogent section.

Howarth, Herbert. "The Supreme Result." In *T. S. Eliot: Plays*, edited by Arnold P. Hinchliffe. London: Macmillan, 1985.
Howarth contends that T. S. Eliot perfected his dramatic method in *The Family Reunion* (1939), without which *The Cocktail Party* (1949) would have been impossible. In the latter play, according to Howarth, "Instead of alternating between tragedy and comedy, he interfuses them." Howarth goes on to commend Eliot for his use of poetic language in the play and for his ability to lead "into the rites without suspending the action."

Jones, David E. *The Plays of T. S. Eliot*. London: Routledge & Kegan Paul, 1960; Toronto: University of Toronto Press, 1971.
Jones sees T. S. Eliot in *The Cocktail Party* (1949) as being less concerned with the saintly person in isolation than with the relationship of that person to the community and the people in it. Jones sees an intermixture of spiritual and social concerns in this play, but he concludes that Eliot has moved more toward the social than the spiritual, which dominated his earlier plays.

Kenner, Hugh. "Something Happens at Last." In *T. S. Eliot: Plays*, edited by Arnold P. Hinchliffe. London: Macmillan, 1985.
Kenner comments on T. S. Eliot's attempt in *The Cocktail Party* (1949) "to devise a stage verse that shall *set the characters free* [Kenner's italics], and enable him to construct his plots around a theme of liberation." He notes the unusually clear discourse in the play, attributing it to Eliot's "using only those components of poetry which can enhance the defining powers of colloquial speech."

Kojecky, Roger. "The Role of the Guardians." In *T. S. Eliot: Plays*, edited by Arnold P. Hinchliffe. London: Macmillan, 1985.
Kojecky notes the "critical unease" that has ensued because of the vagueness of the roles of the guardians. The author recognizes that they are in the play to

"offer illumination and render help." He calls Sir Henry Harcourt-Reilly "the Saint in the desert," who invokes the protection of the higher powers for his patients.

Smith, Carol H. *T. S. Eliot's Dramatic Theory and Practice*. Princeton, N.J.: Princeton University Press, 1963.
Smith views T. S. Eliot's *The Cocktail Party* (1949) as part of a progression that begins with *Murder in the Cathedral* (1935) and is a part of *The Family Reunion* (1939). That the play is labeled a comedy should not deceive anyone. Smith warns that "the same motive determined his [Eliot's] use of a comic surface in *The Cocktail Party* as that which lay behind his disruption of the expectations of his audience in *The Family Reunion*: the desire to destroy and clear away conventional modes of thought and interpretation . . ."

Spender, Stephen. "The Search for Religious Vocation." In *T. S. Eliot: Plays*, edited by Arnold P. Hinchliffe. London: Macmillan, 1985.
Spender points to Sir Henry Harcourt-Reilly in T. S. Eliot's *The Cocktail Party* (1949) as a priest figure intimately involved in helping Celia Coplestone fulfill her spiritual quest, which results in her martyrdom. Spender comments on the meaning of the guardians and on the ritualistic elements in the play. He sees as a problem "for Eliot as a playwright that for him the choice of eternity is so obviously preferable to life on this earth that it is difficult for him not to make actual living seem second-rate."

Williams, Raymond. "A Theatrical Compromise." In *T. S. Eliot: Plays*, edited by Arnold P. Hinchliffe. London: Macmillan, 1985.
Williams recognizes the dramatic kinship between T. S. Eliot's *The Family Reunion* (1939) and *The Cocktail Party* (1949), both of which use verse conversationally. Williams notes that by the time he wrote *The Cocktail Party*, Eliot had virtually abandoned the formality—linguistic and ritualistic—of *Murder in the Cathedral* (1935).

The Confidential Clerk

Donoghue, Denis. *The Third Voice: Modern British and American Verse Drama*. Princeton, N.J.: Princeton University Press, 1959.
Donoghue concludes in his twenty-page essay on T. S. Eliot's *The Confidential Clerk* (1954) that it is in some ways like *The Waste Land* (1922) in that "each work represents the end of a certain stage of experiment and the point of departure for new work in the same mode." Donoghue also points to the play as an example of Eliot's dictum that one of the functions of literature is to keep language from changing too fast.

Frye, Northrop. *T. S. Eliot: An Introduction.* Chicago: University of Chicago Press, 1981.

In T. S. Eliot's *The Confidential Clerk* (1954), Northrop Frye notes the ancient, classical-Greek device of the recognition of long-lost parents by the protagonist. Frye goes on to note that the play sustains an "atmosphere of demure farce" throughout, commenting on Eliot's respect for farce in his essays on drama, speaking of it as "the creation of a distorted by self-consistent world."

Headings, Philip R. *T. S. Eliot.* New York: Twayne, 1964; rev. ed., Boston: Twayne, 1982.

Searching for classical antecedents, Headings finds striking similarities between the *Ion* of Euripides and T. S. Eliot's *The Confidential Clerk* (1954). He shows a significant number of specific parallels between the two plays. Headings also finds "various echoes of the *Bhagavad-Gita*" throughout the play. He identifies some of the play's themes: the interrelatedness of human lives, the hazards of trying to direct the lives of others, the need to make decisions and accept the consequences of those decisions, the need to find one's mission or vocation in life, and the discovery of a tougher self.

Smith, Carol H. *T. S. Eliot's Dramatic Theory and Practice.* Princeton, N.J.: Princeton University Press, 1963.

Smith begins by commenting on the deceptive comedy of T. S. Eliot's *The Confidential Clerk* (1954), which seemed designed to entertain rather than to puzzle audiences. Underlying this surface comedy, however, Smith finds Eliot's usual seriousness. She points out that Eliot, responding to audiences "insulated against both religious meaning and poetic method, . . . has gradually evolved a new kind of religious drama which could introduce both religion and poetry without either being immediately obvious."

The Family Reunion

Headings, Philip R. *T. S. Eliot.* New York: Twayne, 1964; rev. ed., Boston: Twayne, 1982.

The family curse of the biblical era is a fundamental part of T. S. Eliot's *The Family Reunion* (1939), according to Philip Headings, who notes that in this play, Eliot has scrupulously avoided Christian symbols to prevent audiences from falling into any "facile acceptance of the reality of the supernatural." Headings comments positively on the use of the Eumenides in the play, a convention that has been disputed by various scholars and that left audiences confused.

Jones, David E. *The Plays of T. S. Eliot.* London: Routledge & Kegan Paul, 1960; Toronto: University of Toronto Press, 1971.

Jones's forty-page essay on T. S. Eliot's *The Family Reunion* (1939) makes many valuable points, but is strongest perhaps in its discussion of Eliot's use and control of language in the play and of his inventions in versification, of his devising "a line of varying length but a fixed number of stresses, normally three, with a caesura coming after the first or the second stress." Jones comments on the gap that Eliot was unable to bridge between the intellectual aloofness of the play's characters and the audience. He sought to have the chorus bridge that gap, but the attempt was not successful.

Kenner, Hugh. *The Invisible Poet: T. S. Eliot*. New York: McDowell, Obolensky, 1959, 1965.
Like Helen Gardner, Hugh Kenner relates T. S. Eliot's *The Family Reunion* (1939) to *Four Quartets* (1940-1942), focusing specifically on "Burnt Norton," claiming that the play is Eliot's "next poem after 'Burnt Norton'" rather than his first play for the commercial stage. Kenner notes Eliot's concern with time in *The Family Reunion*, with the "artificial timeless moment," as in the opening lines of "Burnt Norton."

Smith, Carol H. *T. S. Eliot's Dramatic Theory and Practice*. Princeton, N.J.: Princeton University Press, 1963.
A major point in Smith's thirty-four-page essay on T. S. Eliot's *The Family Reunion* (1939) is that the play is hard to classify because it is unlike other dramas of its time. She recognizes that "his theme of spiritual election and its effects on the secular world was, as before, the starting point of his dramatic ideal." Smith points out the mythic antecedents of this play and notes that this is the last play in which Eliot employs the chorus.

Murder in the Cathedral

Aiken, Conrad. *Collected Criticism*. New York: Oxford University Press, 1968.
Aiken, in his review of T. S. Eliot's verse play, *Murder in the Cathedral* (1935), commends the playwright for avoiding the "sham antique" and artiness that sometimes pervade verse plays based on historical subjects. He calls the play "a triumph of poetic genius that out of such actionless material—the mere conflict of a mind within itself—a play so deeply moving, so exciting, should have been written." He applauds the tenderness and humanity that permeate the play.

Fergusson, Francis. *The Idea of a Theater*. Princeton, N.J.: Princeton University Press, 1949.
Fergusson's assessment of T. S. Eliot's *Murder in the Cathedral* (1935) is one of the most respected in print. Fergusson considers the play unique, a work that has invented a new idea of theater. He traces the plot to ancient, ritualistic tragic forms. He claims that the first part of the play is devoted to building understandings, whereas the second part is reminiscent of the last act of a Shakespearean

tragedy, citing the catastrophe with its accompanying chorus. He calls the ending of the play "rhythmic, visual, exciting, and musical."

Gardner, Helen. *The Art of T. S. Eliot*. New York: E. P. Dutton, 1949, 1950, 1959; new ed., 1968.
The timeliness of T. S. Eliot's *Murder in the Cathedral* (1935) is not lost on Gardner. She notes the currency of the church-state conflict, on which Eliot has written considerably in prose. Gardner identifies the central theme of the play as "martyrdom in its strict, ancient sense." She thinks that Eliot's attempt to present Thomas as the martyr "in will and deed" is a bold stroke—perhaps too bold to succeed. She notes the play's lack of action and calls its protagonist "unconvincing." She finds the real drama of the play in the choruses.

Goldman, Michael. "Fear in the Way: The Design of Eliot's Drama." In *Eliot in His Time*, edited by A. Walton Litz. Princeton, N.J.: Princeton University Press, 1973.
Goldman discusses some of the misinterpretations of T. S. Eliot's *Murder in the Cathedral* (1935), contending that "Thomas is an easier dramatic subject for Eliot than his later heroes, because he remains active all the time he is on stage, aggressive even while he waits and watches." Goldman calls the dramatic force of the play "haunting."

Howarth, Herbert. *Notes on Some Figures Behind T. S. Eliot*. Boston: Houghton Mifflin, 1964.
Howarth, in a detailed essay about T. S. Eliot's *Murder in the Cathedral* (1935), notes that although it was not written with an eye toward commercial production, the play maintains the requisites of such theater. Howarth contends that the play "is exemplary in that it has spoken to Britain and won something like popularity without any surrender of elevation." He calls the play austere, its dialogue demanding, but commends the play for being truly dramatic.

Kenner, Hugh. *The Invisible Poet: T. S. Eliot*. New York: McDowell, Obolensky, 1959, 1965.
Kenner sees T. S. Eliot's *Murder in the Cathedral* (1935) as a study of the struggle between individual will and the will of God. By the time the play opens, Thomas has almost resolved that struggle. Kenner points out Eliot's problem, much like that found in detective fiction, of knowing how much step-by-step development to present and how much omniscient narration to permit. He comments that "Eliot's ingenious stratagem was to give the first telling the substantiality of dramatic exhibition, and produce the glib summing-up as a fatuous anticlimax."

Smith, Carol H. *T. S. Eliot's Dramatic Theory and Practice*. Princeton, N.J.: Princeton University Press, 1963.

Smith deals with T. S. Eliot's *Murder in the Cathedral* (1935) in an essay in which she also considers his earlier play, *The Rock* (1934). She approaches the play by saying that it "has often been called limited in its appeal" but goes on to say that it is the degree of religious commitment of audiences that determines the play's limitations; they are not inherent. The inability of the public to understand Eliot's message is therefore, in Smith's mind, at the heart of any devaluation of the play.

Spender, Stephen. *T. S. Eliot*. New York: Viking Press, 1975.
Spender contends that the theme of all of T. S. Eliot's plays "after his conversion is the discovery by heroes, and one heroine, of their religious vocation." In the case of Thomas, the task is not that he must prepare himself for martyrdom, but rather that he must "cleanse himself of all self-regarding motives for martyrdom." Spender credits the "magnificent series of choruses" with permitting Eliot to achieve his universal vision in the play.

The Elder Statesman

Headings, Philip R. *T. S. Eliot*. New York: Twayne, 1964; rev. ed., Boston: Twayne, 1982.
Noting that in *The Elder Statesman* (1958) T. S. Eliot continues the basic themes of his earlier plays, Headings comments on the greatest difference between this play and the others: Eliot here deals more warmly with love that people feel for each other than in any of his previous plays. Headings concludes that *The Elder Statesman*, "considered in conjunction with all of Eliot's other works, is one of unexpected and unearned grace, of liberation and restoration through the healing power of love."

Jones, David E. *The Plays of T. S. Eliot*. London: Routledge & Kegan Paul, 1960; Toronto: University of Toronto Press, 1971.
Like most critics of T. S. Eliot's *The Elder Statesman* (1958), Jones finds the play structured on the Sophoclean model in *Oedipus at Colonus*. Jones shows how Eliot continues to develop themes he pursued in *Sweeney Agonistes* (1926) and *The Family Reunion* (1939), but he notes differences in this play: "The extravagant humor and the social satire are tempered to the more elegant level of society and the melodrama no longer leans to the grotesque." Jones considers the play's construction to be considerably more advanced than those of its predecessors in the Eliot canon.

Smith, Carol H. *T. S. Eliot's Dramatic Theory and Practice*. Princeton, N.J.: Princeton University Press, 1963.
Smith's comments on T. S. Eliot's *The Elder Statesman* (1958) emphasize that "both the tone and structure . . . are carefully arranged to stress the importance of love in the process of self-knowledge." Identifying Eliot's classical source for

this play as Sophocles' *Oedipus at Colonus*, Eliot's play stresses "expiation by prolonged suffering and devotion to the will of the gods." Smith contends that in this play, Eliot showed the most positive side of his ritual symbolism.

Williams, Raymond. *Drama from Ibsen to Brecht*. London, Oxford University Press, 1968.
Williams calls T. S. Eliot's *The Elder Statesman* (1958) a dramatic epilogue. He points out that "it brings together the two themes of the epigraphs to *Sweeney Agonistes* [1926]: the relations between human and divine love; and the consciousness of the Furies." Williams sees the play as focusing on death, which offers to the dying another reality.

EDNA FERBER

Connelly, Marc. *Voices Offstage: A Book of Memoirs*. Chicago: Holt, Rinehart and Winston, 1968.
Marc Connelly has keen recollections of Edna Ferber, whose collaboration with George S. Kaufman began at about the time Connelly's collaboration with him was ending. Ferber's first collaborative work with Kaufman was *Minick* (1924). Connelly knew Ferber well in the 1920's and 1930's when she was included in many of the social activities of various members of the Algonquin "Round Table."

Ferber, Edna. *A Kind of Magic*. Garden City, N.Y.: Doubleday, 1963.
In this autobiographical work, Edna Ferber devotes considerable space to her development as a playwright, although she remained essentially a novelist throughout most of her life. She provides details about her collaborations on Broadway plays that can be found in no other source. Ferber was never quite so confident about her ability as a playwright as she was about her ability as a novelist.

Gilbert, Julie Goldsmith. *Ferber: A Biography*. Garden City, N.Y.: Doubleday, 1978.
Goldsmith, Edna Ferber's great-niece, has written a compassionate biography of the novelist and playwright. It is especially valuable for the insights it brings to Ferber's dramatic collaborations with Moss Hart and George S. Kaufman. The book is not so critically acute in assessing Ferber's work as a more disinterested study would have been, but it is factually accurate and is important in showing Ferber plunging into writing dramas that enjoyed a degree of commercial success. The illustrations are excellent and the index is reliable.

Hart, Moss. *Act One*. New York: Random House, 1959.
In this chatty, informal autobiography, Moss Hart tells much about his collaborations with Edna Ferber and about her collaborations with George S. Kaufman. He also makes illuminating comments about her involvement in the dramatic milieu of New York in the late 1920's and 1930's. Unfortunately, Hart's book, which was never intended as a reference item, lacks both a table of contents and an index, making it difficult to use if one is seeking information about specific people.

Miller, J. William. *Modern Playwrights at Work*. New York: Samuel French, 1968.
Miller notes that Edna Ferber went from high school into a job as a reporter for her hometown newspaper and thus got her start in writing. He quotes Ferber as saying of her collaboration with George S. Kaufman, "We did our arguing before anything was set on paper." Ferber tells of the fieldwork she did to make sure that *Stage-Door* (1936) was as authentic as she could make it.

SUSAN GLASPELL

Bigsby, C. W. E. "Introduction." In *Plays by Susan Glaspell*, edited by C. W. E. Bigsby. Cambridge, England: Cambridge University Press, 1987.
In his thirty-page introduction to this collection, Bigsby credits Glaspell with the founding of the Provincetown Players, saying that "without her there must be some doubt as to whether the Provincetown Players would ever have been established." He is even more lavish in his praise when he writes, "In her work, as in her life, she never settled for anything less than total commitment. Sometimes that took her where few others were willing or ready to follow. She chanced more than most of her contemporaries and achieved more than many of them." Bigsby compares Glaspell to Eugene O'Neill, noting that O'Neill's experimental work did not always succeed but that it pointed in significant directions. The book has a selected bibliography.

Dell, Floyd. *Homecoming*. New York: Farrar and Rinehart, 1933.
Dell knew Susan Glaspell and her husband, George Cram Cook, well and was himself much involved with the Provincetown Players and with the Playwright's Theatre, established by Cook in the 1916-1917 season as a winter home for the Provincetown Players. Dell provides an intimate view of theater in Greenwich Village in that era of great international unrest and social upheaval. He captures the essence of Greenwich Village and shows how Glaspell and Cook were prominent in the theater movement there.

Gelb, Arthur, and Barbara Gelb. *O'Neill*. New York: Harper & Row, 1960, 1962, 1973, 1987.
In one of the fullest biographies of Eugene O'Neill to date, the Gelbs frequently mention Glaspell and her professional relationship with O'Neill. It was Glaspell and O'Neill who began and helped to sustain the Provincetown Players. Glaspell's husband, George Cram Cook, established the Playwright's Theatre in Greenwich Village as a place where members of the Provincetown Players could produce their work during the winter season. The Gelbs' passing references to Glaspell throughout their book are extremely informative. Their full, comprehensive index will lead readers to these references easily.

Gould, Jean. *Modern American Playwrights*. New York: Dodd, Mead, 1966.
Gould devotes the second chapter of this fourteen-chapter book to Susan Glaspell, concentrating more on her role in founding the Provincetown Players than on her writing, although Gould does mention Glaspell's plays in passing. This illustrated volume has a useful index.

Krutch, Joseph Wood. *The American Drama Since 1918*. New York: Random House, 1939.
Krutch's treatment has more to do with the rise of little theater in the United

States than with Glaspell's plays. Krutch shows that Susan Glaspell was untiring in promoting the cause of theater both in Provincetown and, with her husband, in New York City.

Lewisohn, Ludwig. *Expression in America*. New York: Harper and Brothers, 1932.
In a nine-page section of this book, Lewisohn, who knew Glaspell well, offers extremely positive criticism of her work. He notes particularly her ability to capture the essence of America, particularly of the Midwest, in her plays.

Sheaffer, Louis. *O'Neill: Son and Artist*. Boston: Little, Brown, 1973.
Almost every book about O'Neill provides some information about Susan Glaspell and her husband, George "Jig" Cram Cook. In this book, however, Sheaffer mentions them frequently and appreciatively. The Cooks were among O'Neill's closest friends and most valuable professional associates. Sheaffer's extensive index will lead those interested in Glaspell to the numerous references Sheaffer made to her.

Waterman, Arthur R. *Susan Glaspell*. New York: Twayne, 1966.
Waterman's study, following the format of Twayne's United States Authors Series, begins with a chronology, has an initial biographical chapter, and four chapters analyzing Glaspell's work. A final summary chapter is followed by an annotated bibliography and a full index. He devotes chapters 3 and 4 to Glaspell's involvement in the Provincetown Players and the Playwright's Theatre—which her husband, George Cram Cook, founded—and to her plays. After Glaspell wrote *Allison's House* (1930), which won the 1931 Pulitzer Prize in Drama, she confined her writing to novels and short stories. A fifth chapter in Waterman's book, "Midwestern Perspectives," deals with the regional qualities in her novels. Waterman is not a sympathetic critic of Glaspell. He writes, "In her work we find all the defects of regional writing: Conservatism, unabashed sentiment, an overwhelming middle-class point of view, and reverence for tradition for its own sake."

78

PAUL GREEN

General Studies

Adams, Agatha Boyd. *Paul Green of Chapel Hill*. Chapel Hill, N.C.: University of North Carolina Press, 1951.
The book relates Paul Green to Chapel Hill, the town in which he really came of age and to which he always returned. In a way, his desire to live in Chapel Hill turned him from Broadway and resulted in his emphasizing symphonic dramas during his career after the 1930's. Green was inextricably involved with Chapel Hill, and Adam's book shows the depth and intricacy of that involvement.

Clark, Barrett. *Paul Green*. New York: Robert M. McBride, 1928.
This thin volume, the first book on Green, was published before he had made his most significant contributions to the theater, particularly through his regional plays, which he called symphonic dramas. Clark writes of a playwright who had, by 1928, written more than thirty plays, but whose finest work was still to come. Among the plays Clark comments on are *Blackbeard* (1922), *In Aunt Mahaly's Cabin: A Negro Melodrama* (1924), *The No 'Count Boy* (1924), *Quare Medicine* (1925), *In Abraham's Bosom* (1926), and the ambitious *Lonesome Road: Six Plays for the Negro Theatre* (1926).

Flora, Joseph M., and Robert Bain. *Fifty Southern Writers After 1900*. Westport, Conn.: Greenwood Press, 1987.
The information given about Paul Green is accurate and provides a fine overview of the author and his work. The section entitled "Studies of Paul Green" is helpful in leading readers to other sources on this playwright.

Isaacs, Edith J. R. *The Negro in American Theater*. New York: Theatre Arts, 1947.
Isaacs compares Green to Eugene O'Neill and is particularly impressed by his ability to bring black dialect onto the stage. She calls Green "unabashedly theatrical" and feels that he may be the playwright to write memorable American drama comparable to O'Neill's. Isaacs recognizes Green's poetic use of language and his sound depiction of characters from among the oppressed African Americans of his area.

Kenny, Vincent S. *Paul Green*. New York, Twayne, 1971.
This 186th volume in Twayne's United States Authors Series follows the pre-scribed format: chronology, critical analysis, annotated bibliography, and index. Kenny provides the remarkable statistic that more people have viewed plays or motion pictures whose scripts were written by Paul Green than have seen the plays of Arthur Miller and Edward Albee combined. One might question whether

such is currently the case, but Paul Green, through his long-running symphonic dramas, has brought theater to millions. Kenny identifies Green as the inventor of symphonic drama and thinks that he will be remembered for this contribution made through such plays as *The Lost Colony* (1937) and *The Common Glory* (1947), although he will also be remembered for his pacifist play, *Johnny Johnson* (1936), for such folk plays as *In Abraham's Bosom* (1926) and *Lonesome Road* (1926), and for *The House of Connelly* (1931).

Lower, Charles, and William Fee. *History into Drama*. New York: Odyssey, 1963.
This case book on the *Lost Colony* (1937) shows how Green took the facts of history and imbued them with the kind of dramatic content required for successful staging. The book reproduces many of the documents with which Green was working and shows how they were woven into the fabric that is the play. They provide materials from people intimately involved in the early productions of *The Lost Colony*, which has now run on the Outer Banks of North Carolina almost without interruption every summer since it was first offered in 1937.

McCalmon, George, and Christian Moe. *Creating Historical Drama*. Carbondale, Ill.: Southern Illinois University Press, 1965.
McCalmon and Moe present the most comprehensive study of outdoor drama in the United States up to 1965. They give considerable space to discussing and analyzing all of Paul Green's symphonic dramas up to *The Stephen Foster Story* (1959). Their study has a comprehensive bibliography that will be of help to scholars interested in this area of study.

Rabkin, Gerald. *Drama and Commitment*. Bloomington, Ind.: Indiana University Press, 1964.
Rabkin offers a strong, positive assessment of Paul Green's Broadway plays, in which he felt that a significant talent was being used to present serious drama that had deep social content. Rabkin is totally unsympathetic with the subsequent course that Green's career took, regarding his symphonic dramas as "showy pageants."

Selden, Samuel. *Frederick Henry Koch*. Chapel Hill, N.C.: University of North Carolina Press, 1954.
In his sympathetic biography of Frederick Koch, Paul Green's teacher at the University of North Carolina and the guiding spirit behind the Carolina Playmakers, Selden has much to say about Paul Green's development from a southern country boy who came to the University from Lillington into a playwright of note who held enormous sway on Broadway for almost twenty years. This well-documented biography has a useful bibliography.

The Lost Colony

Spearman, Walter, assisted by Samuel Selden. *The Carolina Playmakers: The First Fifty Years*. Chapel Hill, N.C.: University of North Carolina Press, 1970.
Chapter 3 of this book, with its focus on outdoor drama, provides interesting information about Paul Green's involvement with the Carolina Playmakers from the organization's inception. Green was a student at the University of North Carolina during this period, and his play *Raleigh, The Shepherd of the Ocean* (1920) was written for the Carolina Playmakers. This play was an immediate precursor to Green's symphonic drama *The Lost Colony* (1937). The book contains pictures of Green.

LORRAINE HANSBERRY

Abramson, Doris E. *Negro Playwrights in the American Theatre, 1925-1959*. New York: Columbia University Press, 1969.
References to Lorraine Hansberry abound in this book, which points out Hansberry's direct experience of the events related in *A Raisin in the Sun* (1959). Her own father bought a house in a white neighborhood and was prevented from occupying it until, in one of the most celebrated housing cases to come before the Illinois Supreme Court—*Hansberry* v. *Lee* (311 U.S. 32)—the court ruled that Carl Hansberry and his family could occupy the house they had purchased. This book's excellent index will direct one easily to the material in it that focuses on Hansberry. An extensive bibliography is also provided.

Baldwin, James. "Sweet Lorraine." In *To Be Young, Gifted and Black: Lorraine Hansberry in Her Own Words*, adapted by Robert Nemiroff. New York: New American Library, 1970.
Baldwin's remembrance of Lorraine Hansberry, written shortly after her death, is warm and filled with insight into her contributions as a dramatist. Baldwin clearly understands that Hansberry was a black artist trying to move toward universal themes, as can be seen in her plays *The Sign in Sidney Brustein's Window* (1964) and *Les Blancs* (1970).

Bigsby, C. W. E. *Confrontation and Commitment: A Study of Contemporary American Drama, 1959-1966*. Columbia, Mo.: University of Missouri Press, 1969.
In a seventeen-page segment devoted to Lorraine Hansberry and her work, Bigsby presents a thorough analysis of *A Raisin in the Sun* (1959), identifying its themes and commenting on Hansberry's style and on the ironic twists in the play. He identifies Joseph Asagai in the play as Hansberry's spokesperson on matters of integration, family structure, and philosophical position. This volume has a helpful index and is well documented.

Bond, Jean Gardey, ed. *Lorraine Hansberry: Art of Thunder, Vision of Light*. New York: Freedomways, 1979.
This commemoration of Lorraine Hansberry contains contributions by many of her friends and professional associates: James Baldwin, Nikki Giovanni, Alex Haley, Adrienne Rich, and John O. Killens. The volume contains an extensive bibliography that includes articles, theses and dissertations, reviews, and portions of books in which such scholars as Darwin T. Turner comment on the playwright and her plays.

Carter, Steven R. *Hansberry's Dream: Commitment and Complexity*. Urbana, Ill.: University of Illinois Press, 1991.

After presenting a detailed chronology, Carter begins with a chapter that presents an overview of Lorraine Hansberry's cultural milieux and their relation to her aims in writing. He moves from this chapter to a consideration of her dramas and screenplays, including some incomplete ones, interpreting them sensibly and skillfully. He ends the book with a chapter that considers Hansberry's literary achievement in the thirty-four years she lived. The book, unfortunately, has no bibliography, although it does have a comprehensive index.

Cheney, Anne. *Lorraine Hansberry*. Boston: Twayne, 1984.
Adhering to the format of Twayne's United States Authors Series, Cheney begins with a detailed chronology and proceeds to two biographical chapters. She then proceeds with her discussion and analysis of Lorraine Hansberry's writing, devoting her fourth chapter to *A Raisin in the Sun* (1959), which won the Drama Critics' Circle Award, the first time that award went to an African American; Hansberry was also the youngest person ever to receive the award. Chapter 5 is devoted to *The Sign in Sidney Brustein's Window* (1964), chapter 6 to Hansberry's collected last plays, and chapter 7 to *To Be Young, Gifted and Black* (1969), produced posthumously. This book has an outstandingly annotated bibliography and a comprehensive index.

Cruse, Harold. *The Crisis of the Negro Intellectual*. New York: William Morrow, 1967.
Cruse's chapter about Lorraine Hansberry's *A Raisin in the Sun* (1959) provides an important counterbalance to much that has been written about the playwright in that Cruse takes her severely to task for imposing a white, middle-class value system on an African-American family. He launches into a denunciation of those associated with *Freedom*, including Hansberry, for their sympathy toward communism and their wishy-washy attitude about integration. Later scholars have found this book to be flawed in some of its factual information, but most acknowledge it as a landmark volume on African-American literature and life.

Fabré, Genevieve. *Drumbeats, Masks, and Metaphor: Contemporary Afro-American Theatre*. Cambridge, Mass.: Harvard University Press, 1983.
Fabré interpreted *A Raisin in the Sun* (1959) as an integrationist play in that the family in it espoused many of the ideals of middle-class whites and was aspiring to the American Dream. This common criticism of the play has led to accusations that Hansberry lacked racial pride.

Hansberry, Lorraine. *A Raisin in the Sun (Expanded Twenty-fifth Anniversary Edition) and The Sign in Sidney Brustein's Window*, edited by Robert Nemiroff. New York: New American Library, 1987.
This edition is indispensable to scholars because it contains important material from Hansberry's drafts that was omitted from other published versions of *Raisin*.

The "American Playhouse" edition of the play contains one scene not in this original version.

_____. *To Be Young, Gifted and Black: Lorraine Hansberry in Her Own Words*, adapted by Robert Nemiroff. New York: New American Library, 1970. The autobiographical *To Be Young, Gifted and Black* (1969) was produced posthumously in 1969, and Nemiroff's adaptation is essentially Hansberry's autobiography. The presentation is honest and direct. Hansberry pinpoints the conflicts young people of her ability face as they grow further from their own roots, especially when what has given them the ability to escape those roots is work based upon them.

Keyssar, Helene. *The Curtain and the Veil: Strategies in Black Drama*. New York: Burt Franklin, 1981.
In chapter 5, "Sounding the Rumble of Dreams Deferred: Lorraine Hansberry's *A Raisin in the Sun*" (1959), a thirty-three-page chapter, Keyssar reviews Lorraine Hansberry's career briefly and then directs her attention to analyzing *A Raisin in the Sun*. Keyssar fears that the play may be best remembered by white audiences as "historical event rather than experience." She contends that at times, Hansberry's "characterizations and plot structure call into question the very nature of the values and opportunities being presented as shared."

Lewis, Emory. *Stages: The Fifty-Year Childhood of the American Theatre*. Englewood Cliffs, N.J.: Prentice-Hall, 1969.
Lewis assesses both *A Raisin in the Sun* (1959) and *The Sign in Sidney Brustein's Window* (1964), calling the former a milestone in drama that "honestly etched black people." He recognizes *Brustein*'s accurate portrayal of metropolitan intellectuals but finds the play unsatisfying. He accuses it of meandering and considers it an incomplete work. A comprehensive index is a great asset in this book.

Malpede, Karen, ed. *Women in Theatre: Compassion and Hope*. New York: Drama Books Publishers, 1983.
Malpede credits Lorraine Hansberry with creating an entire family as protagonist in *A Raisin in the Sun* (1959) and argues for the appropriateness of her doing so given the fact that "the black communal structure . . . is precisely what has kept black people alive through generations of abuse." This argument flies in the face of the way Hansberry herself viewed her play, but it is an interesting theory.

Scheader, Catherine. *They Found the Way: Lorraine Hansberry*. Chicago: Campus Publications of the Children's Press, 1978.
This is a hortatory book, part of the "They Found a Way" series, designed for the juvenile market. Its information is accurate, however, and its illustrations are

profuse. Scheader emphasizes that Hansberry was the first African American and the youngest person to win the Drama Critics' Award, for *A Raisin in the Sun* (1959), her most celebrated play. Information from extensive interviews with Hansberry's former husband, Robert Nemiroff, and with her sister Mamie is included, as is some of Hansberry's own artwork. This was the first book to focus on the playwright.

Schiff, Ellen. *From Stereotype to Metaphor: The Jew in Contemporary Drama.* Albany, N.Y.: State University of New York Press, 1982.
The consideration in this book focuses on *The Sign in Brustein's Window* (1964). The author comments less on the overall quality of the play than on Hansberry's ability to present Brustein not as a stereotype but as a "Jew who is neither wicked, nor crafty, nor even a good businessman." The presentation is well reasoned. The book's index is helpful.

Simon, John. *Uneasy Stages: A Chronicle of the New York Theater, 1963-1973.* New York: Random House, 1975.
Simon badly misinterprets *Les Blancs* (1970), contending that it "does its utmost to justify the slaughter of whites by blacks." Later critics have pointed out that one who sees the conscious parallels between *Les Blancs* and William Shakespeare's *Hamlet* will reach a different conclusion: The aim of the play is to end injustice, not to annihilate a race.

Weales, Gerald. *American Drama Since World War II.* New York: Harcourt, Brace & World, 1962.
Although Weales deals with Lorraine Hansberry in three pages and considers only *A Raisin in the Sun* (1959), his perceptions are well worth reading. He contends that the play's "strength is its chief character, Walter Lee Younger, whose problem is complicated by his being a Negro but is much more basic than that. He is a victim of the American dream of success in its most virulent form, the Willy Loman strain that suggests not that success is possible in America, but that it is inevitable." He commends Hansberry's use of the comic line, contending that she uses it "not in idiom but in emotional intention," much as Clifford Odets did in his early plays.

_____. *The Jumping-off Place: American Drama in the 1960's: From Broadway to Off-Off Broadway to Happenings.* New York: Macmillan, 1969.
Weales writes incisively of *The Sign in Sidney Brustein's Window* (1964) in this book, saying that it was difficult to separate the play from the context of Lorraine Hansberry's dying during the whole of its Broadway run. The critical reviews were favorable but audiences failed to materialize, and the play was kept on Broadway for 101 performances only because friends of the playwright put up the money to keep it going. Weales finds fault with the play: "Miss Hansberry

has drawn a hero more complicated than the commitment she demands of him."
He sees, nevertheless, some good in the play, writing, "I am attracted to her
desire to buck the pessimistic tide and to recognize that, although her ideational
desire may finally have marred the play, she succeeds in a number of ways,"
which he goes on to specify.

LILLIAN HELLMAN

Adler, Jacob H. *Lillian Hellman*. Austin, Tex.: Steck-Vaughn Publishing, 1969. This early critical biography was excellent in its time but has been superseded by more recent scholarly books on Hellman. The book has shrewd insights into the plays and into the effect that the House Committee on Un-American Activities controversy had on Hellman as both a writer and a person.

Bentley, Eric, ed. *Thirty Years of Treason: Excerpts from the Hearings before the House Committee on Un-American Activities*. New York: Viking Press, 1971. The material in this book that deals with Hellman's responses to the HUAC is indispensable to an understanding of her single-mindedness, her strength, and her political orientation. The bibliographical details will also lead the intrepid reader to the original sources that are now available to the public. They chronicle the HUAC hearings completely.

Bills, Steven H. *Lillian Hellman: An Annotated Bibliography*. New York: Garland, 1979. Although much Hellman scholarship has appeared since the publication of this bibliography, its listings are excellent for the time span they cover. Bills provides extensive listings of critical considerations of individual plays as well as a comprehensive list of biographical pieces that focus on Hellman. The list of published interviews with Hellman provides yet another significant facet of this useful work.

Block, Anita. *The Changing World in Plays and Theatre*. Boston: Little, Brown, 1939. Although Block devotes only five or six pages to Hellman, her comments on *The Children's Hour* (1934) and her recognition of it as a milepost in American drama that brought an overtly homosexual theme onto the Broadway stage make this section worth reading. Block identifies Hellman as the pioneer she was, a stature made more remarkable by the fact that the Broadway stage of her day was dominated by male authors, directors, and producers.

Dick, Bernard F. *Hellman in Hollywood*. Teaneck, N.J.: Fairleigh Dickinson University Press, 1982. Dick traces Hellman's move from Broadway to Hollywood and gives detailed analyses of the transition of her plays from vehicles for Broadway to screenplays directed at more general and diverse audiences than typically see Broadway productions. Dick goes into the effect Hellman's political troubles had on her Hollywood career. He discusses each of her screenplays in an individual chapter. He notes the screen adaptations that Hellman wrote herself: *The Children's Hour* (1934) as *We Three*, *The Little Foxes* (1939), and *The Searching Wind* (1944).

The final two chapters in the book are devoted to a discussion of *Julia*. Besides a selected bibliography and an index, the book contains a valuable four-page "filmography" section.

Estrin, Mark W., ed. *Critical Essays on Lillian Hellman*. Boston: G. K. Hall, 1989.
This collection of twenty-three critical essays on Hellman by such scholars and critics as Robert Brustein, Jacob H. Adler, Linda Wagner-Martin, Alfred Kazin, Sidney Hook, John Hersey, and Pauline Kael is divided into three sections. The first deals with Hellman's plays, the second with her memoirs, and the third with her persona. The range of these essays is diverse. They are well selected and create an interesting point-counterpoint effect.

Falk, Doris V. *Lillian Hellman*. New York: Frederick Ungar, 1978.
This contribution to Ungar's Modern Literature Monographs series follows a standard format that begins with a chronology and contains an extensive bibliography and an index. After a beginning biographical chapter entitled "Hellman in Her Time," Falk spends about seventy pages discussing Hellman's approach to drama and the individual plays. She then launches into an extensive discussion of the memoirs, and this sixty-five-page section is the most insightful part of the book. It is well worth reading.

Flora, Joseph M., and Robert Bain. *Fifty Southern Writers After 1900*. Westport, Conn.: Greenwood Press, 1987.
For anyone who wants a quick overview of Lillian Hellman and her career, this is the book. After an initial biographical section, it discusses the major themes in Hellman's work before going on to a section on her critical reception, a bibliography of her work, and a list of secondary sources. A good treatment for the beginner.

Gassner, John. *Theatre at the Crossroads: Plays and Playwrights of the Mid-Century American Stage*. New York: Holt, Rinehart and Winston, 1960.
Calling Lillian Hellman "the possessor of the most masculine mind among our native playwrights," Gassner shows how the playwright overcame the barriers of writing conventional plays for conventional theater and created a more fluid kind of drama than had previously been written. He commends her for having the energy to bring *Toys in the Attic* (1960) to Broadway after a nine-year hiatus. He notes that Hellman knows how "to write for actors."

Gelderman, Carol. *Mary McCarthy: A Life*. New York: St. Martin's Press, 1988.
Although the account of the Hellman-McCarthy controversy and the subsequent lawsuit are told more from McCarthy's perspective than from Hellman's, this version is necessary for readers who wish to know Hellman well and to under-

stand the controversy fully. Gelderman attempts impartiality but does not succeed fully in achieving it despite the overall excellence and readability of her work.

Gould, Jean. *Modern American Playwrights.* New York: Dodd, Mead, 1966.
Chapter 8 of this book is devoted to Lillian Hellman. Gould comments on Hellman's daring choice of subject material, particularly in *The Children's Hour* (1934), her first major play. Gould also notes Hellman's political fortitude during the McCarthyism of the 1950's. This book is illustrated and has a good index.

Hellman, Lillian. *Pentimento: A Book of Portraits.* Boston: Little, Brown, 1973.
Hellman's second memoir is essentially a collection of portraits of people who were important to her during her life. The book is centered on her cousin Bethe, her uncle Willy, her friend Julia, and her lover Arthur Cowan. The narrative, however, goes far beyond these four central characters and deals in some detail with her relationship with Dashiell Hammett. The book also contains extensive comments about each of Hellman's plays and the people associated with their production, including actors, directors, and producers. The book ends with the story entitled "Turtle," which is about a snapping turtle that Hellman and Hammett captured. The turtle's tenacious hold on life made Hellman assess her whole concept of life.

_____. *Scoundrel Time.* Boston: Little, Brown, 1976.
In her third memoir, Hellman focuses particularly on the period of her life when she was under investigation by the House Committee on Un-American Activities. This book evoked considerable controversy and led to Hellman's celebrated public battle with Mary McCarthy, which resulted in Hellman's lodging a lawsuit against McCarthy for more than two million dollars. Hellman's death in 1980 brought an end to the litigation.

_____. *Three.* Boston: Little, Brown, 1979.
Included in this single large volume are Lillian Hellman's three autobiographical works: *An Unfinished Woman* (see below, 1969), *Pentimento: A Book of Portraits* (see above, 1973), and *Scoundrel Time* (see above, 1976).

_____. *An Unfinished Woman.* Boston: Little, Brown, 1969.
Hellman's first memoir was a resounding success because of its frank revelation of what her life had been, especially her early life, and because of its incredible succinctness of expression. The book deals less with Hellman as playwright than *Pentimento* does. A thirty-four-page section on the Spanish Civil War is particularly interesting; it is charming because of the human interest Hellman brings into it by devoting five pages of narrative to a crazy old Spaniard whom she meets in a park with his keeper.

Johnson, Diane. *Dashiell Hammett: A Life*. New York: Random House, 1983.
Because of the inextricable connections between Hammett and Hellman, this book, along with Hellman's memoirs mentioned above, is necessary reading for anyone wishing to understand the relationship and its impact upon Hellman's writing. Hammett's financial and physical dependence on Hellman after he was destroyed in the witch-hunts of the early 1950's might well have destroyed their relationship, but it did not. This book demonstrates how a dissolution was avoided despite Hellman's sometimes feeling put upon by having to look after Hammett in his final years.

Lederer, Katherine. *Lillian Hellman*. Boston: Twayne, 1979.
Following the usual format of Twayne's United States Authors Series, Lederer presents a chronology of Hellman's life, an annotated bibliography, and an index. After an initial chapter dealing with Hellman's biography, Lederer discusses the plays chronologically in chapters 2, 3, and 4. Chapter 5 focuses on the playwright's nonfiction writing, and a final chapter is entitled "An Ironic Vision." Lederer considers Hellman's best plays "ironic and novelistic." A useful introductory book for beginners, although it is now somewhat dated.

Lewis, Allan. *American Plays and Playwrights of the Contemporary Theatre*. New York: Crown, 1965.
According to Lewis, the three most prominent playwrights to come out of the Depression of the 1930's were Lillian Hellman, Clifford Odets, and Irwin Shaw. He discusses the three of them in his chapter entitled "Survivors of the Depression," lumping them together because they all were fundamentally concerned with social justice. Lewis claims that Hellman was the most resilient of the three writers he discusses in this chapter, because, when the social problems the depression brought about had dissipated, she went on to write such plays as *Toys in the Attic* (1960) and *My Mother, My Father, and Me* (1963).

Lyons, Bonnie. "Lillian Hellman: 'The First Jewish Nun on Prytania Street.'" In *From Hester Street to Hollywood: The Jewish-American Stage and Screen*, edited by Sarah Blacher Cohen. Bloomington, Ind.: Indiana University Press, 1983.
Lyons deals with Hellman as both playwright and screenwriter. She notes the strongly moralistic code that surfaces in Hellman's work despite the writer's frankness in dealing with topics such as homosexuality at a time when the very word was hardly spoken in polite society.

Moody, Richard. *Lillian Hellman*. New York: Pegasus, 1972.
This compact critical-biographical treatment has some strong insights into Hellman's plays, particularly into *The Children's Hour* (1934) and *The Little Foxes* (1939). Moody shows Hellman as the unwilling but undaunted political activist who defied the House Committee on Un-American Activities despite the great personal sacrifices that such defiance required.

Newman, Robert P. *The Cold War Romance of Lillian Hellman and John Melby.*
Chapel Hill, N.C.: University of North Carolina Press, 1989.
Newman chronicles one of Hellman's most intense love affairs, which was only
hinted at before the publication of this book, with career diplomat John Melby.
She and Melby met during Hellman's 1944-1945 sojourn in Moscow, and their
association continued for many years. Melby's career came to an abrupt end in
1953, when the McCarthy witch-hunts, of which Hellman was also a victim,
resulted in his leaving the State Department. A forty-page appendix delves into
the question of whether Hellman was a communist. A fourteen-page appendix
reproduces a selection of FBI documents relating to her case and to Melby's.

Riordan, Mary Marguerite. *Lillian Hellman, A Bibliography: 1926-1978.* Metuchen,
N.J.: Scarecrow Press, 1980.
Riordan's contribution to Scarecrow's Author Bibliographies Series begins with
a detailed chronology, then proceeds to sections dealing with Lillian Hellman's
plays and adaptations, her screenplays, including collaborations, books written
or edited by Hellman, contributions by Hellman to magazines and newspapers,
and unpublished works, letters, and recordings. These items are covered in thirty-
two pages. Following them, Riordan has sections on books about Hellman or
references to her in books, theses and dissertations, articles and letters about
Hellman in newspapers and periodicals, and articles or other references about
her work. Riordan provides a workable index.

Rollyson, Carl. *Lillian Hellman: Her Legend and Her Legacy.* New York: St.
Martin's Press, 1988.
This book, which covers the whole of Hellman's life, is chatty, sometimes
gossipy, and always interesting. It is particularly penetrating in its discussions
of Hellman's on-and-off relationship with Dashiell Hammett, the Marxist mystery
writer with whom she had a continuing affair. Hellman's involvement with the
House Committee on Un-American Activities in the 1950's is detailed extensively, as is her move from Broadway to Hollywood. The reaction to Hellman's
introduction of homosexuality onto the Broadway stage in the 1930's with the
production of *The Children's Hour* (1934) is discussed fully.

Schwartz, Nancy Lynn, and Sheila Schwartz. *The Hollywood Writers' Wars.* New
York: Alfred A. Knopf, 1982.
This lively book shows Hellman as a moral, witty intellectual who demands the
rights granted her under the Constitution of the United States. The excesses of
the Hollywood witch-hunts are revealed in all their ugliness in this book, and
Hellman, as one of the leftist members of the Screen Writers Guild, is one of
the central players in the controversy.

Sievers, W. David. *Freud on Broadway: A History of Psychoanalysis and the American Drama*. New York: Hermitage House, 1955.

In the section about Lillian Hellman, Sievers focuses chiefly upon the sexual aspects of *The Children's Hour* (1934). He also reaches the conclusion that "the theme of latent inversion . . . is suggested in a number of her plays." He calls *The Little Foxes* (1939) "a somber study in the psychology of evil" and considers it one of her best plays. Of her play *The Autumn Garden* (1951), Sievers says that it "is at the same time her most ineffectual, her most baffling and her most psychoanalytical." He finds that the play has no clearly defined plot development but considers it an extremely interesting work that reveals a great deal about its author.

Triesch, Manfred. *The Lillian Hellman Collection at the University of Texas*. Austin, Tex.: University of Texas Press, 1967.

This bibliographical work is valuable although it is now much outdated. It does reflect what is in the basic manuscript collection, however, and that makes it useful to Hellman scholars despite its age.

Wright, William. *Lillian Hellman: The Image, The Woman*. New York: Simon & Schuster, 1986.

Wright's is one of the two most comprehensive biographies of Lillian Hellman—Rollyson's is the other. It is based on extensive research and on more than 150 interviews with people who knew the playwright. The author has a keen appreciation for Hellman's laconic style, although his book, which is not quite five hundred pages long, is far from laconic. The book is enhanced by excellent illustrations and by an extensive index and bibliography. There is no table of contents, which at times is inconvenient.

SIDNEY HOWARD

Behrman, S. N. *People in a Diary*. Boston: Little, Brown, 1972.
Behrman reflects significantly on the founding of the Playwrights' Company and on Howard's involvement in it from its inception. Behrman, who knew Howard well, offers a sympathetic view of him in this book.

Brown, John Mason. *Upstage: The American Theatre in Performance.* New York: W. W. Norton, 1930.
This book's age is its virtue. Brown gives a fresh appraisal of Howard's work during the 1920's, when his star was very much in the ascendant. Brown's reviews of his plays are detailed and incisive.

Herron, Ima Honaker. *The Small Town in American Drama*. Dallas, Tex.: Southern Methodist University Press, 1969.
Writing about Sidney Howard's *Ned McCobb's Daughter* (1926), Herron says that in it "truth of characterization and situation is made all the more credible by Howard's careful selection of Down East scenic details and authentic properties to suggest the Yankee nature of generations of McCobbs." Herron also comments on *The Late Christopher Bean* (1932), *Alien Corn* (1933), and Howard's adaptation of Sinclair Lewis' *Dodsworth* (1934). An accurate index makes this book easy to use as a reference source.

Krutch, Joseph Wood. *American Drama Since 1918: An Informal History*. New York: George Braziller, 1957.
Krutch offers a thoughtful analysis of Howard's major work. He discusses him in the context of the new realism, placing him in a class with Maxwell Anderson and George Kelly. This book, whose bibliography and index are both useful, contains some of the most fruitful analyses of Howard's plays thus far available. Krutch considers Howard the least intellectual of his fellow dramatists but admires his ability to tell a good story.

Lewis, Sinclair. "The Art of Dramatization." In *Dodsworth*. New York: Harcourt, Brace, 1934.
In his introductory chapter to this book, Sinclair Lewis tells about his close work with Howard, who turned Lewis' novel into dramatic form. He gives a detailed account of the problems he and Howard encountered in making the adaptation. The piece is accompanied by a companion piece written by Howard.

Toohey, John L. *A History of the Pulitzer Prize Plays*. New York: Citadel Press, 1967.
Toohey's well-illustrated book contains reviews of each Pulitzer Prize Play, including Howard's *They Knew What They Wanted* (1924). The play is recog-

nized for its excellent characterization and for its social impact. It is also considered a daring play for its time; some people thought that the immorality they pointed to in it should have precluded it from winning the Pulitzer. Certainly, *They Knew What They Wanted* represents a high point in the drama of the early 1920's.

White, Sidney Howard. *Sidney Howard*. Boston: Twayne, 1977.
Part of Twayne's United States Authors Series, White's critical biography of Sidney Howard begins with a chronology, an initial biographical chapter, and additional chapters that deal chronologically and selectively with Howard's twenty-seven stage plays and thirteen screenplays. The annotated bibliography is extensive, and the index is serviceable. White pays special attention to *They Knew What They Wanted* (1924), which dealt for the first time on Broadway with frankly sexual situations and was considered quite shocking in its time.

Young, Stark. *Immortal Shadows*. New York: Charles Scribner and Son, 1948.
This collection of reviews written by Stark Young contains a number of reviews of Howard's work. Young's review of *The Silver Chord* (1926) is especially strong. He comments on the play's potential but notes that the script needs "a deeper texture of life."

LANGSTON HUGHES

Berry, Faith. *Langston Hughes: Before and Beyond.* Westport, Conn.: L. Hill, 1983.
Before the publication of Arnold Rampersad's two-volume critical biography of Langston Hughes (see below), Faith Berry's biography was the most comprehensive. It is still serviceable and eminently readable. Berry discusses the various plays Hughes wrote or was involved in as a collaborator or lyricist, although her chief focus is on his poetry and fiction. The bibliography is useful, and the index is reliable.

Bloom, Harold, ed. *Langston Hughes.* New York: Chelsea House, 1990.
This collection of essays about Langston Hughes and his work is well chosen, although it replicates some of the items from O'Daniel's earlier collection (see below). As part of the Modern Critical Views Series, this book follows a prescribed format. The essays emphasize Hughes as a poet rather than a playwright.

Dickinson, Donald C. *Bio-Bibliography of Langston Hughes.* Hamden, Conn.: Archon Books, 1964; updated 1972.
The biographical section of this book is of general interest although it offers little for those interested specifically in Langston Hughes as a dramatist. The second section, however, lists all of Hughes's work and secondary sources relating to it, including drama. The 1972 edition has been updated, although not completely.

Emanuel, James A. *Langston Hughes.* New York: Twayne, 1967.
What little Emanuel has to say about Langston Hughes's dramatic writing leads one to the conclusion that his forte was not drama, although *Mulatto* (1935) and *Street Scene* (1947), for which Hughes wrote the lyrics, were reasonably successful commercially. The information given about the Simple stories is useful in terms of Hughes's dramatization of Jesse Semple's exploits, *Simply Heavenly* (1957). This book follows the usual format of Twayne's United States Authors Series, providing a chronology, an annotated bibliography, and a comprehensive index.

Jemie, Onwuchekwa. *Langston Hughes: An Introduction to the Poetry.* New York: Columbia University Press, 1976.
Jemie, although limiting this consideration to Hughes's poetry, provides an interesting framework from which to view the writer's dramatic writing. Jemie contends that Hughes's work should be viewed from the perspective of both the folk tradition and the tradition of struggle and protest. This combination is clearly evident in the plays as well as the poems. Jemie also identifies two basic character types, Boyd and Semple, who represent the realist and the dreamer, the

former closely related to the temper of the 1930's, the latter to the temper of the 1960's.

Keyssar, Helene. *The Curtain and the Veil: Strategies in Black Drama.* New York: Burt Franklin, 1981.
In chapter 3, "The Inner Life Once Removed: Langston Hughes's *Emperor of Haiti,*" Keyssar not only examines *Emperor of Haiti* (pr. as *Drums of Haiti,* 1935) but also comments on the author's seven other full-length dramas and on some of his shorter ones. She credits Hughes for his leadership in helping to establish three African-American theater groups: the Suitcase Theatre of Harlem, the Negro Art Theatre of Los Angeles, and the Skyloft Players of Chicago. Keyssar admits that the language of the play is uneven and inconsistent, but she argues that this is because of the "specific confusion of a playwright struggling to combine often opposing strategic gestures."

Meltzer, Milton. *Langston Hughes: A Biography.* New York: Thomas Y. Crowell, 1968.
Meltzer's biography of Langston Hughes is a serviceable early study, but it has been superseded by several others. The information about Hughes as playwright is minimal, but there are a few valuable insights about the themes that seemed to interest the writer most. The bibliography is helpful, and the index is reliable.

Mikolyzk, Thomas A., comp. *Langston Hughes: A Bio-Bibliography.* Westport, Conn.: Greenwood Press, 1990.
The bibliography in this book closes the gap between Miller's bibliography (see below) and the present. The biographical overview offers a reasonable starting point for someone who is not familiar with Hughes. The index is serviceable.

Miller, R. Baxter. *Langston Hughes and Gwendolyn Brooks: A Study Guide.* Boston: G. K. Hall, 1978.
Miller's bibliography is thorough up to 1977. It has more information about Hughes as a poet than as a playwright, although everything available on him as playwright is mentioned. The bibliography includes a checklist of Hughes's writing—unfortunately, indicating neither place of publication nor publisher—and then is arranged year by year, listing books first and articles or portions of books afterward. Miller provides separate indexes for his two subjects.

Myers, Elizabeth P. *Langston Hughes: Poet of His People.* Champaign, Ill.: Garrard Publishing, 1970.
This is a good book for the beginner. It sketches Hughes's life and shows his development as a writer who was much influenced by the writing of Paul Laurence Dunbar and Carl Sandburg as well as by his association with Countée Cullen. Hughes's earliest exposure to composing was in his early childhood,

when his grandmother told him stories. Many of her rhythms and locutions became a part of his poetic arsenal and are reflected in his poetry, prose fiction, and plays.

O'Daniel, Therman B. *Langston Hughes: Black Genius.* New York: William Morrow, 1971.
Most of the fourteen essays in this book concentrate on Langston Hughes as a poet or writer of short stories. The Darwin Turner essay (see below) is the only one that focuses specifically on drama. The other essays, however, provide a balanced view of Hughes's artistic development. O'Daniel offers a bibliography of Hughes's work and of secondary sources in which he is discussed.

Rampersad, Arnold. *The Life of Langston Hughes, Volume I: 1902-1941: I, Too, Sing America.* New York: Oxford University Press, 1986; *Volume II: 1941-1967: I Dream a World.* New York: Oxford University Press, 1988.
This massive, prize-winning, two-volume biography of Langston Hughes is the authoritative work on the author. It considers all of Hughes's work, including his dramas. Rampersad is the only scholar to date to have gained full access to the Langston Hughes papers at Yale University. As a result, his biography contains a great deal of information that previous ones, as good as they were, had no way of presenting. Although this work lacks a bibliography, it has profuse notes. Its index is one of the most comprehensive in print.

Rollins, Charlemae H. *Black Troubadour: Langston Hughes.* New York: Viking, 1970.
This is one of the most intimate presentations available of Langston Hughes as a person, showing his interest in the intellectual currents of his time, in Harlem in the 1920's, and in France, where he spent several years. A chapter by Gwendolyn Brooks shows Hughes in informal ways, telling how he devoted a great deal of his time to helping fledgling writers.

Smalley, Webster, ed. *Five Plays by Langston Hughes.* Bloomington, Ind.: Indiana University Press, 1963.
This anthology contains Langston Hughes's *Mulatto* (1935), his most commercially successful play with 373 performances; *Soul Gone Home* (n.d.); *Little Ham* (1935); *Simply Heavenly* (1957); and *Tambourines to Glory* (1963). This is the only anthology to date of Hughes's dramatic writing.

Taylor, Patricia E. "Langston Hughes and the Harlem Renaissance, 1921-1931: Major Events and Publications." In *Harlem Renaissance Remembered*, edited by Arna Bontemps. New York: Dodd, Mead, 1973.
The Harlem Renaissance was so much a part of Hughes's life and his development as an artist that this essay, which does not deal directly with his plays, is extremely important in establishing background.

Tracy, Steven C. *Langston Hughes and the Blues*. Urbana, Ill.: University of Illinois Press, 1988.
Tracy discusses in significant detail the development of Langston Hughes's poetic style, which carried over into his dramatic dialogue. She traces a considerable part of his style to the blues, which Hughes dearly loved. This book, with a useful index and valuable bibliographical information, has extremely pertinent information about the development of Hughes's unique way of using language.

Turner, Darwin T. *Afro-American Writers: Goldentree Bibliographies in Language and Literature*. New York: Appleton-Century-Crofts, 1970.
Although Turner devotes barely more than three pages to Langston Hughes in this bibliography, he does mention the most important resources up to 1969.

_____. "Langston Hughes as Playwright." In *Langston Hughes: Black Genius*, edited by Therman B. O'Daniel. New York: William Morrow, 1971.
Turner comments on Langston Hughes's drama with definite artistic reservation, contending that Hughes was much more successful as a poet than as a playwright. He points to *Don't You Want to Be Free?* (1938) as Hughes's most artistically successful play, despite the predictability of its progression. He identifies *Tambourines to Glory* (1950) as being among Hughes's most appealing plays. Turner calls many of Hughes's characters stereotypes upon whose dialogue great sentimentality is superimposed.

Williams, J. Kenny. *They Also Spoke: An Essay on Negro Literature in America, 1787-1930*. Nashville, Tenn.: Townsend Press, 1971.
This essay considers Hughes as a part of the Harlem Renaissance. Its most important contribution is in its perception that although he experimented with African-American dialect, Hughes ultimately used the verbal rhythms of the blues rather than those of African-American preachers. His writing did not have the hortatory quality of many African-American writers whose roots were in the South rather than in the Midwest, as Hughes's were. Williams identifies Hughes as a literary realist.

98

WILLIAM INGE

Broussard, Louis. *American Drama: Contemporary Allegory from Eugene O'Neill to Tennessee Williams*. Norman, Okla.: University of Oklahoma Press, 1962. Broussard advances the somewhat heterodox notion that William Inge shares a considerable literary kinship with T. S. Eliot in his fascination with the commonplace. He interprets Inge's plays allegorically and sheds light on some of the apparent paradoxes in them. This book has a useful index and a satisfactory bibliography.

Clurman, Harold. *Lies Like Truth*. New York: Macmillan, 1958. Harold Clurman, who directed *Bus Stop* (1955), focuses on William Inge's *Picnic* (1953) in this book. He considers *Picnic* a resounding success in its ability to capture the frustrations that small-town life can engender and the way in which those frustrations are vented in such situations.

Devlin, Albert J., ed. *Conversations with Tennessee Williams*. Jackson, Miss.: University of Mississippi Press, 1986. Among the items included in this collection of articles by and interviews with people who knew Tennessee Williams is William Inge's first article on the playwright, published in the St. Louis *Star-Times* on November 11, 1944. It was through his interview with Williams that Inge came to know the playwright well enough that Williams invited him to see *The Glass Menagerie* (1944) in Chicago during its initial run. It was this experience that made Inge realize that he, too, could write plays.

Diehl, Digby. "William Inge." In *Behind the Scenes: Theater and Film Interviews from the Transatlantic Review*, edited by Joseph F. McCrindle. New York: Holt, Rinehart and Winston, 1971. Diehl interviewed William Inge in 1967, seven years before the playwright's death and a year after his play *Where's Daddy?* (1966) closed on Broadway after twenty-one performances. Inge resisted being interviewed because he considered himself to be in a "transitional period." In the interview, he mentions the need to find himself anew. He mentions that he is working on a new play, *Bad Breath* (it did not materialize), in the absurdist mode. He strikes out at New York critics, who had reviewed his last three plays negatively, even—in Inge's eyes—vengefully. He says, "I think that the instant a person becomes famous in America a machine is set in motion to destroy him."

Donahue, Francis. *The Dramatic World of Tennessee Williams*. New York: Frederick Ungar, 1964. Donahue gives considerable information about Tennessee Williams' first meeting with William Inge, who interviewed him in 1944 for the St. Louis *Star-Times* and became a close friend. Donahue shows how Williams motivated Inge to write and how he helped him to market his first play. He does not go into some of the aspects of their relationship that Spoto (see below) covers in his biography of Williams.

Dusenbury, Winifred L. *The Theme of Loneliness in Modern American Drama.* Gainesville, Fla.: University of Florida Press, 1960.

Dusenbury is mostly concerned with William Inge's *Come Back, Little Sheba* (1950) in her study of loneliness in American drama. She focuses particularly on Lola and on the elements that isolate her, showing that as the play ends, Lola is forced to accept a new maturity, although Dusenbury offers little hope that this acceptance will dramatically change Lola's slovenly life. The book has a valuable bibliography and an inclusive index.

Freedman, Morris. *American Drama in Social Context.* Carbondale, Ill.: Southern Illinois University Press, 1971.

Freedman's assessment of William Inge's plays is quite positive. Freedman contends that Inge has delighted more audiences than Edward Albee and Tennessee Williams, which is very likely the case. The question, of course, is whether a playwright's function is to delight audiences. This book has a useful index and is well documented.

Gassner, John. *Theatre at the Crossroads.* New York: Holt, Rinehart and Winston, 1960.

Gassner identifies William Inge's *The Dark at the Top of the Stairs* (1958) as "a group play . . . excellently orchestrated," which is a fresh judgment of the play. He considers *Come Back, Little Sheba* (1950) to be William Inge's best play, an assessment that is shared by many scholars and critics.

Gould, Jean. *Modern American Playwrights.* New York: Dodd, Mead, 1966.

Gould devotes the thirteenth of this book's fourteen chapters to William Inge and his plays, commenting on the halcyon days of the 1950's that came to an end with *A Loss of Roses* (1959), a play that marked the beginning of Inge's retreat from Broadway. This volume is illustrated and has a serviceable index.

Herron, Ima Honaker. *The Small Town in American Drama.* Dallas, Tex.: Southern Methodist University Press, 1969.

Herron reviews Inge's plays from *Come Back, Little Sheba* (1950) to *A Loss of Roses* (1959), finding all of them to be extremely regional and most of them to be dependent upon a small-town milieu, particularly *Picnic* (1953) and *The Dark at the Top of the Stairs* (1957). She agrees with Tennessee Williams, quoting him: "[Inge] uncovered a world within a world, . . . a secret world that exists behind the screen of neighborly decorum . . . [the world beneath] the genial surface of common American life."

Inge, Luther C. *Travels in Search of the Past: The Ancestry of William Motter Inge, Playwright*. Oklahoma City, Okla.: Synder's Press, 1991.
In this book, Luther Inge, William Inge's nephew, who was nine years younger than the playwright, documents the history of the Inge family and offers interesting reminiscences of his uncle. He presents photocopies of interesting papers that trace some of the members of the Inge family back to the mid-1600's, when they came from England to the United States. The book has valuable illustrations of the Inge family, including the playwright at various stages of his development.

Kerr, Walter. "Albee, Miller, Williams." In *Thirty Plays Hath November: Pain and Pleasure in the Contemporary Theater*, edited by Walter Kerr. New York: Simon & Schuster, 1969.
In the portion of his essay that deals with Tennessee Williams, Walter Kerr makes trenchant observations about William Inge's *Natural Affection* (1963), which was a resounding failure on Broadway. He writes in the context of Tennessee Williams' later plays, which he considers self-parody; Kerr considers *Natural Affection* self-parody, but not quite the assertive self-parody that Williams' plays of the same period had become. He attributes this to the fact that William Inge was still writing vigorously, "whereas Mr. Williams was writing palely and more vulnerably."

Lewis, Allan. *American Plays and Playwrights of the Contemporary Theatre*. New York: Crown, 1965.
Looking back over William Inge's career and its most auspicious beginning, Lewis attempts to analyze what caused it to decline so precipitously after *The Dark at the Top of the Stairs* (1957), Inge's last commercially successful play, claiming that in the play, Inge popularizes Freudian analysis. In the play, Lewis contends, "Evil is clinically analyzed rather than dramatically presented." One of the most interesting aspects of Lewis' comments is in his comparison of Inge's *Bus Stop* (1955) and Maxim Gorki's *The Lower Depths* (1912). He calls *Come Back, Little Sheba* (1950) Inge's best play.

McClure, Arthur. *Memories of Splendor: The Midwestern World of William Inge*. Lawrence, Kans.: Kansas State Historical Association, 1989.
McClure, making use of the Inge Archive at Independence (Kansas) Community College and other sources, places William Inge artistically within the cultural milieu in which he grew up. He comments on Inge's attempts to have *Splendor in the Grass* (1961) filmed in his hometown, Independence. This book is brief—eighty-five pages—but it contains much valuable information.

_____. *William Inge: A Bibliography*. New York: Garland, 1982.
McClure has divided this bibliography, which is ninety-three pages long, into four parts: works by William Inge, bibliographical information, critical articles and reviews of Inge's work, and William Inge and film. The book needs updating but has been extremely valuable to Inge scholars, particularly for what it has to say about the materials in the William Inge Collection at Independence (Kansas) Community College, the chief repository of his papers.

Newquist, Roy. *Counterpoint*. Chicago: Rand McNally, 1964.
Newquist's ten-page interview with William Inge took place in New York in February, 1964. The first two and one-half pages are valuable because they are essentially autobiographical. Inge says that although he is considered a traditional writer, he is most interested in avant-garde writing, mentioning specifically Eugene Ionesco's *Rhinocéros* (*Rhinoceros*, 1960) and Edward Albee's *Who's Afraid of Virginia Woolf?* (1962). He contends that for three consecutive decades, dramatic criticism has been more destructive than constructive. Speaking of his motives in writing, Inge says, "I've always wanted to warm people more than to warn them."

Shuman, R. Baird. *William Inge*. New York: Twayne, 1965; rev. ed., Boston: Twayne, 1989.
This first full-length study of William Inge follows the format of Twayne's United States Authors Series, beginning with a detailed chronology and moving to an initial biographical chapter. The remaining chapters analyze Inge's published works in chronological order, and a final chapter assesses Inge's contribution. Both editions of this book have annotated bibliographies and comprehensive indexes. The revised edition is expanded to include Inge's work between 1964 and his death in 1973, including his two novels and several of his shorter plays.

Sievers, W. David. *Freud on Broadway*. New York: Hermitage House, 1955.
Sievers' insights into William Inge's *Come Back, Little Sheba* (1950) and *Picnic* (1953) are provocative, showing how pent-up frustrations often suggest sexual solutions. He writes, "*Picnic* illustrates the most mature level of American drama in the fifties, able to draw upon Freudian insights without succumbing to the obvious or the trite." Sievers labels both of the Inge plays he reviews naturalistic and supports the case for this classification with considerable evidence. He claims that Inge's psychoanalysis helped him in his plays to "utilize its insights without following outworn literary patterns." The book has a useful index and a chapter-by-chapter bibliography.

Spoto, Donald. *The Kindness of Strangers: The Life of Tennessee Williams*. Boston: Little, Brown, 1985.
Spoto's biography of Tennessee Williams contains innumerable references to

William Inge and his relationship with Williams. Their friendship collapsed dramatically at times, but Williams motivated Inge to write Broadway plays. It was Williams who arranged for Audrey Wood, his agent, to read *Come Back, Little Sheba* (1950) and other Inge plays. Through this contact, Inge was able to have his first Broadway production. As the popularity of Inge's plays surpassed that of Williams' in the late 1950's, Williams became jealous and vindictive. Considerable bitterness ensued. When Inge was nearing the end of his life, however, and was living in California, battling deep depression on a daily basis, Williams renewed their friendship.

Steen, Mike. *A Look at Tennessee Williams*. New York: Hawthorn Books, 1969. Steen's long interview (pages 93-125) with William Inge reveals much about the professional and personal relationship between the two. The interview is interesting for what it reveals about Inge's values and his view of play writing at a time when Inge was experiencing the personal humiliation that led to his suicide in 1973.

Voss, Ralph F. *A Life of William Inge: The Strains of Triumph*. Lawrence, Kan.: University of Kansas Press, 1989. Voss's book is the most comprehensive consideration of William Inge to date. Its organization is simultaneously chronological and geographical, dealing with Inge in Kansas, Missouri, New York, and California. Voss has a good feel for Inge's Kansas origins and their presence in much of his work. His study is informed by extensive interviews with those who knew Inge and by a careful perusal of materials in the William Inge Collection of Independence (Kansas) Community College, which has the most extensive collection of Inge papers in the country. The book has a comprehensive index but no bibliography.

Weales, Gerald. *American Drama Since World War II*. New York: Harcourt, Brace & World, 1962. Weales considers William Inge quite commonplace. He makes some important points regarding Inge's progression (and regression) as a playwright. He writes, "It may well have been *The Glass Menagerie*, which, as Inge has admitted, brought him to the writing of plays, that caused him to sprinkle *Sheba* with symbols that do not grow out of the drama, but are grafted onto it." Weales goes on to say that Inge overcame this problem in *Picnic* (1953) and *Bus Stop* (1955) but reverted to it heavy handedly in *The Dark at the Top of the Stairs* (1958). Weales comments on Inge's "talent for small, touching effects" in his early plays, but feels that he misplaced this talent in *Dark* and did not find it again.

Wood, Audrey, with Max Wilt. *Represented by Audrey Wood*. Garden City, N.Y.: Doubleday, 1981. Wood became William Inge's first agent when Tennessee Williams, who was also her client, asked her to read *Come Back, Little Sheba* (1950), which she succeeded in placing on Broadway. In this book, Wood reveals some of her insights into Inge's development as a playwright. She witnessed the deep uncertainties that led him into psychoanalysis even before *Sheba* was brought to Broadway and that kept him in psychoanalysis for the better part of the next two decades.

104

GEORGE S. KAUFMAN

Burrows, Abe. *Honest, Abe: Is There Really No Business Like Show Business?* Boston: Little, Brown, 1980.
Burrows presents candid impressions of George Kaufman and of his working relationship to him as a playwright. The presentation, brash and witty, demonstrates Burrows' appreciation of Kaufman's humor and satirical edge.

Connelly, Marc. *Voices Offstage: A Book of Memoirs.* Chicago: Holt, Rinehart and Winston, 1968.
This book is valuable for its overall memories of Connelly's association with Kaufman when he collaborated with him in the early 1920's. He verifies their continuing friendship and association during the years after their collaboration ended in 1924. Connelly sometimes misremembers details, but this book is valuable for its overview of Kaufman.

Ferber, Edna. *A Kind of Magic.* Garden City, N.Y.: Doubleday, 1963.
Ferber offers detailed accounts of her work with George S. Kaufman on two collaborations, *The Land Is Bright* (1941) and *Bravo!* (1948). The Ferber collaboration began in 1924 with *Minick* (1924) and continued for the next twenty-five years.

Gaines, James R. *Wit's End: Days and Nights at the Algonquin Round Table.* New York: Harcourt Brace Jovanovich, 1977.
In his interpretive essay, Gaines includes an excellent account of George S. Kaufman and his relation to the other members of the "Round Table." The material on Marc Connelly's relationship with Kaufman is especially useful.

Goldstein, Malcolm. *George S. Kaufman: His Life, His Theater.* New York: Oxford University Press, 1979.
This is one of the best books on Kaufman. It is especially valuable for its in-depth analyses of the more significant plays. The chapter on Edna Ferber as Kaufman's collaborator is intriguing, as is chapter 10, which deals with Kaufman's initial collaborations with Moss Hart. Goldstein presents sensitively some of the disappointments that George S. Kaufman endured in the late 1940's and 1950's when his health declined and his collaborations were not working out well. Chapter 22, "Tests of Endurance," is especially sensitive. Although the book has an index and notes, it has no bibliography.

Hart, Moss. *Act One.* New York: Random House, 1959.
It is unfortunate that Moss Hart's informal autobiography, lacking both a table of contents and an index, is so hard to use, because it is packed with important detailed information about the New York theater from 1920 almost to 1959. The

information Hart provides about George S. Kaufman and his continued collaboration with him is particularly pertinent and extremely interesting.

Mason, Jeffrey D. *Wise-Cracks: The Farces of George S. Kaufman*. Ann Arbor, Mich.: UMI Research Press, 1988.
Mason explores the sources of George S. Kaufman's humor. He demonstrates how Kaufman used his ear for dialect and for the typical speech patterns of New York Jews as the bases for his humor. This book presents important insights into Kaufman's method of achieving the kind of wit that permeated his plays. The study is part linguistic, part literary.

Miller, J. William. *Modern Playwrights at Work*. New York: Samuel French, 1968.
Miller offers valuable information about how George S. Kaufman conducted the many collaborations in which he was involved. He discusses Kaufman's work with Edna Ferber, Marc Connelly, Moss Hart, Katharine Dayton, Morrie Ryskind, and Leueen McGrath. Miller provides interesting details about Kaufman's work habits.

Nannes, Casper. *Politics in the American Drama as Revealed by Plays Produced on the New York Stage, 1890-1945*. Philadelphia: University of Pennsylvania Press, 1950; republished and expanded as *Politics in the American Drama*. Washington, D.C.: Catholic University of America Press, 1960.
Nannes shows the subtle changes that occurred in Kaufman's outlook from the 1920's until the rise of Hitler and the suppression of European Jews. Nannes shows how Kaufman's attitudes changed more sharply with the rise of Nazism in Germany and indicates how this change affected his writing.

Nolan, Paul T. *Marc Connelly*. New York: Twayne, 1969.
Following the prescribed format of Twayne's United States Authors Series, this compact volume begins with a chronology and ends with an annotated bibliography and index. The entire second chapter is devoted to the George S. Kaufman-Marc Connelly collaboration, which resulted in nine plays between 1920 and 1924. The most successful of these plays were *Merton of the Movies* (1922) and *Beggar on Horseback* (1924), which ran for 398 and 224 Broadway performances, respectively. The latter was one of the best-received expressionistic plays of its day on Broadway.

Pollack, Rhoda-Gale. *George S. Kaufman*. Boston: Twayne, 1988.
This volume, a part of Twayne's United States Authors Series, provides a chronology before the full text begins and both an annotated bibliography and a useful index. Pollack indicates the difficulty of writing a critical assessment of someone who frequently collaborated—Kaufman collaborated with more than a dozen other writers. The coverage is, nevertheless, comprehensive, and is

American Drama: 1918-1960

especially valuable for its discussion of the Marc Connelly-George Kaufman collaboration and for a later chapter that deals with Kaufman's collaboration with Moss Hart on *Merrily We Roll Along* (1934), *You Can't Take It with You* (1936), and *The Man Who Came to Dinner* (1939). Pollack identifies as Kaufman's special stylistic characteristics his quick wit, fast-paced dialogue, jibes at the establishment, use of wisecracks, close observation and presentation of details, and satiric tone.

Teichmann, Howard. *George S. Kaufman: An Intimate Portrait*. New York: Atheneum, 1972.

Teichmann, who collaborated with Kaufman on *The Solid Gold Cadillac* (1951), knew Kaufman well in his later years, and in this book he addresses such matters as Kaufman's reaction to McCarthyism and the witch-hunts of the early 1950's. Although this book is at times slightly one-sided, it has much valuable and interesting information about the playwright.

CARSON McCULLERS

Although Carson McCullers is known primarily as a novelist and short-story writer, she contributed to American drama through the adaptations for Broadway of a number of her pieces of prose fiction.

Carr, Virginia Spencer. "Carson McCullers." In *Contemporary Authors: Biblio-graphical Series, American Novelists*, volume 1, edited by James J. Martine. Detroit: Bruccoli-Clark/Gale Research, 1986.
This fifty-two page bibliography of both primary and secondary sources is a great addition to Carson McCullers research. It deals briefly with the plays.

_____. "Carson McCullers." In *Fifty Southern Writers After 1900: A Bio-Bibliographical Sourcebook*, edited by Robert Bain and Joseph M. Flora. West-port, Conn.: Greenwood Press, 1986.
Although this bibliography is only eleven pages long, it is packed with valuable information about both primary and secondary sources. It concentrates on the prose fiction.

_____. *The Lonely Hunter: A Biography of Carson McCullers*. Garden City, N.Y.: Doubleday, 1975; London: Peter Owen, 1976; New York: Carroll & Graf, 1985.
This is the authoritative biography of Carson McCullers. It is thorough, and it gives adequate attention to the two major plays, *The Member of the Wedding* (1950) and *The Square Root of Wonderful* (1957). Carr concludes that although the former was an American classic, the latter was a disaster, largely because McCullers, heady from the success of *The Member of the Wedding* and eager for another Broadway triumph, did not resist the pressures from directors, producers, and play doctors to strip it of the qualities that were her hallmark.

_____. *Understanding Carson McCullers*. Columbia, S.C.: University of South Carolina Press, 1990.
Carr deals with Carson McCullers essentially as a writer of prose fiction. Her sixth chapter, however, is entitled "The Plays: *The Member of the Wedding* and *The Square Root of Wonderful*." In its seventeen pages, it deals well with the two plays it considers and with McCullers' involvement in them, pointing out that only the encouragement of Tennessee Williams led McCullers to attempt play writing, although she had wanted to do it since early childhood. The initial biographical chapter of this book is interesting. The bibliography is selective but extremely well done. The index is reliable.

_____ and Joseph R. Millichip. "Carson McCullers." In *American Women Writers: Fifteen Bibliographical Essays*, edited by Maurice Duke, Jackson R. Bryer, and M. Thomas Inge. Westport, Conn.: Greenwood Press, 1981.
This bibliographical essay provides valuable suggestions and directions regarding both primary and secondary sources. Its biographical references will be more helpful to readers than what it has specifically to say about McCullers as a dramatist.

Clarke, Gerald. *Capote: A Biography*. New York: Simon & Schuster, 1988.
Clarke writes in depth about Truman Capote's friendship with Carson and Reeves McCullers, saying that when McCullers and Capote met, the two sensed instantly that they shared a great deal of the same background and outlook. Tensions arose in the relationship, however, and before long the two were archenemies, remaining so throughout their lives.

Evans, Oliver. *Carson McCullers: Her Life and Work*. London: Peter Owen, 1965; reissued as *The Ballad of Carson McCullers*. New York: Coward-McCann, 1966.
Evans' study is the first book-length treatment of Carson McCullers. It covers her work quite fully, analyzing each novel and many of her works of short fiction. It treats the dramas only tangentially. The book is valuable for showing the kind of critical reception McCullers was used to receiving at the time that she turned to drama.

Kiernan, Robert F. *Katherine Anne Porter and Carson McCullers: A Reference Guide*. Boston: G. K. Hall, 1976.
This dual bibliography, arranged chronologically, provides a bibliography not of Carson McCullers' own writings but rather of writings about her. The coverage is extensive, and the annotations are highly informative. The book has separate indexes for each of the two writers it covers.

McDowell, Margaret B. *Carson McCullers*. New York: Twayne, 1980.
McDowell's book is perceptive and thorough. Following the conventional format of Twayne's United States Authors Series, it provides a detailed chronology and an initial biographical chapter followed by chapters that analyze McCullers' work. The emphasis is on the prose fiction, but the two Broadway plays are also dealt with interestingly and productively. McDowell's perspective is decidedly, intelligently feminist. Her bibliography is well annotated, her index dependable.

Phillips, Louis. "The Novelist as Playwright: Baldwin, McCullers, and Bellow." In *Modern American Drama: Essays in Criticism*, edited by William E. Taylor. Deland, Fla.: Everett/Edwards, 1968.
Phillips generalizes on Carson McCullers' two attempts at drama by quoting a line that Berenice utters in *The Member of the Wedding* (1950): "When folks are

lonesome and left out, they turn so mean." He calls this the unifying theme in all of McCullers' work and shows how it pertains particularly to the two plays.

Shapiro, Adrian M., Jackson R. Bryer, and Kathleen Field. *Carson McCullers: A Descriptive Listing and Annotated Bibliography of Criticism*. New York: Garland Press, 1980.
This bibliography is the most complete one up to 1980, providing information about primary and secondary sources, with copious annotations. The listings are well arranged and easily accessible.

Westling, Louise. *Sacred Groves and Ravaged Gardens: The Fiction of Eudora Welty, Carson McCullers, and Flannery O'Connor*. Athens, Georgia: University of Georgia Press, 1985.
Although this feminist assessment of Carson McCullers' fiction says little about her dramas, Westling's identification of her female characters as "rebellious tomboys" can be carried over productively into an interpretation of *The Member of the Wedding* (1950). This book nicely combines feminist theory with regional interpretation.

Wikborg, Eleanor. *"The Member of the Wedding": Aspects of Structure and Style*. Atlantic Highlands, N.J.: Humanities Press, 1975.
Although Wikborg is concerned with the novels more than the plays, her study is valuable because it is the first linguistic analysis of Carson McCullers' work. It shows in detail how she manipulated symbols to her artistic advantage. Wikborg emphasizes the ways in which McCullers' symbols function at various levels of meaning.

ARTHUR MILLER

General Studies

Carson, Neil. *Arthur Miller*. New York: Grove Press, 1982.
Carson's volume in the Grove Press Modern Dramatists Series contains a biographical chapter followed by chapters on the major plays, from *The Man Who Had All the Luck* (1944) to *The Creation of the World and Other Business* (1972). The author, like all the contributors to this series, is concerned with Miller's plays as theater and focuses on such matters as performance, character interpretation, staging, themes, and contexts.

Cohn, Ruby. *Dialogue in American Drama*. Bloomington, Ind.: Indiana University Press, 1971.
Chapter 3 in this book is entitled "The Articulate Victims of Arthur Miller" (pages 68-96). Cohn emphasizes the effect that seeing Clifford Odets' *Awake and Sing!* (1935) had on Miller, claiming that just as Odets had taken "from John Howard Lawson a blend of lofty morality and city slang," Miller took these elements from Odets and gave them his own distinctive touch. She credits O'Neill with having produced the first dialogue in American drama that gave audiences a sense of life well observed, and she contends that Miller advanced that tradition, allowing "dignified uneducated characters [to] articulate functionally in dramatic context."

Corrigan, Robert W. *Arthur Miller: A Collection of Critical Essays*. Englewood Cliffs, N.J.: Prentice-Hall, 1969.
Among the more interesting essays in this collection are Harold Clurman's "Arthur Miller's Later Plays," Tom F. Driver's "Strength and Weakness in Arthur Miller," M. W. Steinberg's "Arthur Miller and the Idea of Modern Tragedy," and Gerald Weales' "Arthur Miller's Shifting Image of Man." See below for essays in this volume that discuss individual plays. The book contains a chronology of important dates and a selected bibliography.

Evans, Richard I. *Psychology and Arthur Miller*. New York: E. P. Dutton, 1969.
Evans' book begins with a preface by Robert Whitehead. It is divided into three parts: "The Writer as Creator," "The Writer and Psychology," and "The Writer and Society." One appendix is entitled "The Dialogue Format—An Innovation in Instruction," another, "Trends in Personality Psychology Relating to Dialogue." There is a list of recommended readings in place of a standard bibliography. It is followed by an index. Evans, fully aware of the role the subconscious assumes in the making of plays, approaches Miller from the standpoint of one who is well trained in psychology. He identifies elements in the works of which Miller was not fully conscious.

Ferres, John H. *Arthur Miller: A Reference Guide*. Boston: G. K. Hall, 1979.
This bibliography goes a decade beyond Hayashi's (see below) and updates it
well. After an eight-page introduction, Ferres lists Miller's major works and then
lists in 210 pages writings about Miller from 1944 to 1977. An index facilitates
the use of this book, which is an essential guide for anyone pursuing serious
research on Arthur Miller.

Hayashi, Tetsumaro. *Arthur Miller Criticism (1930-1967)*. Metuchen, N.J.: Scarecrow Press, 1969.
This comprehensive bibliography is divided into three parts. The first deals with
primary sources, both published and unpublished, about Miller. The second deals
with secondary sources, including biographies, book-length critical works,
dissertations, articles, essays in books, and book reviews. The third part presents
audiovisual materials, including movies, movie reviews, and phonograph records.
This is the best bibliography up to the date of its publication, although it is now
outdated. (See the Ferres entry above for another bibliography.)

Hayman, Ronald. *Arthur Miller*. New York: Frederick Ungar, 1972.
Following the format of Ungar's World Dramatic Series, this book is pleasingly
illustrated with halftone prints. The book begins with a chronology and follows
it with a nineteen-page interview with Miller. This is followed by extended
analytical discussions of every play from *All My Sons* (1947) to *The Price* (1968).
Hayman points to "Miller's solidly carpentered structures, the clear outlines he
draws around characters and incidents, and his repudiation of ambiguity." The
later pages of the book include a listing of stage productions of the plays under
discussion and the cast of characters for each of the original productions. A
bibliography and index further enhance the book's usefulness.

Kerr, Walter. "Albee, Miller, Williams." In *Thirty Plays Hath November: Pain and
Pleasure in the Contemporary Theater*, edited by Walter Kerr. New York: Simon
& Schuster, 1969.
Kerr claims that for the first half of his career, Arthur Miller was busy inventing
himself, but that after *The Price* (1968), Miller, "the master moralist[,] had
suddenly relaxed in two ways." The first of Miller's new faces was "an astonish-
ingly droll one"; the second face "was one of uncertainty."

Miller, Arthur. *Salesman in Beijing*. New York: Viking Press, 1984.
Enhanced with photographs by Miller's wife, photographer Inge Morath, this
book details the 1983 production of *Death of a Salesman* (1949) in Beijing. The
book is essentially a running notebook of all that led up to the production,
including the rehearsals, which were held daily, morning and evening. The book
is a significant social document about a China emerging with difficulty from the
Cultural Revolution, during which eight plays, most of them political propaganda,

were approved for production. Miller's talks with the Chinese began in 1978 and continued until approval was given for a production that he monitored closely and whose rehearsals he attended faithfully.

_____. *Timebends: A Life*. New York: Grove Press, 1987.
Miller's autobiography runs to more than six hundred pages and is of considerable psychological interest, although the early pages that chronicle his genealogy tend to lag and are not particularly relevant to the heart of the book—Miller's life. Miller comes through in this book as a superachiever with an overactive social conscience. Most of the book makes fascinating reading, and the index is extensive and accurate, making it useful for anyone who wishes to look for specific items relating to Miller.

Moss, Leonard. *Arthur Miller*. New York: Twayne, 1967; rev. ed., Boston: Twayne, 1980.
Following the prescribed format of Twayne's United States Author Series, this book begins with a chronology, proceeds to an initial biographical chapter, and then discusses the plays in chronological order. The selected annotated bibliography is extensive—thirty-six pages. The revised edition contains minor changes as well as an additional chapter that considers *The Price* (1968) and *The Creation of the World* (1972). Moss, acknowledging Miller's sociopolitical leanings, prefers in these books to approach him psychologically rather than from a sociopolitical perspective. The biographical chapter was updated for the revised edition, in which Moss included the text of an interview he had with Miller in 1979. This interview gives Miller's present perspective on drama and society. The index is helpful and accurate.

Murray, Edward. *Arthur Miller, Dramatist*. New York: Frederick Ungar, 1967.
Noting the fragmented nature of Miller criticism up to the date of this book, Murray promises an analytical discussion of all the major plays considered in terms of structure, character, dialogue, and theme. Murray does not pay close attention to Miller's language, which he labels unpoetic, viewing it only as a vehicle for moving the action forward, revealing character, and extending the thematic scope of the plays. He devotes chapters to *All My Sons* (1947), *Death of a Salesman* (1949), *The Crucible* (1953), *A Memory of Two Mondays* (1955), *After the Fall* (1964), and *Incident at Vichy* (1964). The book contains a bibliography but no index.

Nelson, Benjamin. *Arthur Miller: Portrait of a Playwright*. New York: David McKay, 1970.
Nelson discusses all the plays through the late 1960's under such whimsical titles—drawn from Miller's dialogue—as "To him they were all my sons, and I guess they were" (*All My Sons*, 1947) and "I am not a dime a dozen!" (*Death*

of a Salesman, 1949). The selected bibliography is a bit thin. The index is adequate. Essentially, Nelson seeks to show how Miller grew as an author, relating him to the temper and tensions of his time.

Roudane, Matthew, ed. *Conversations with Arthur Miller*. Jackson, Miss.: University Press of Mississippi, 1987.
In this volume, Roudane has gathered a number of interviews with Arthur Miller, touching on nearly all the aspects of his life and work and dealing with all of his major plays. The coverage is broad and valuable to readers who want to gain a balanced overview of this playwright.

Schlueter, June, and James K. Flanagan. *Arthur Miller*. New York: Frederick Ungar, 1987.
This volume in Ungar's Literature and Life: American Writers Series follows a prescribed format, with a chronology, a biographical chapter, a discussion of Miller's major dramas, and a summary chapter entitled "Contemporary—and Vintage—Miller." The selected bibliography is well chosen, and the index is accurate and reasonably complete. The documentation is thorough but not intrusive.

Tynan, Kenneth. "American Blues: The Plays of Arthur Miller and Tennessee Williams." In *American Theater: A Collection of Critical Essays*, edited by Alvin Kernan. Englewood Cliffs, N.J.: Prentice-Hall, 1967.
Although he finds fundamental differences between Arthur Miller and Tennessee Williams, one a playwright of action, the other a "poet *manqué*," Tynan sees a fundamental connection between the two: "Miller is a rebel against, Williams a refugee from the familiar ogre of commercialism, the killer of values and the leveller of men." He calls Miller's plays "patrist," Williams' "matrist." He concludes that Miller and Williams "have produced the most powerful body of dramatic prose in modern English," claiming that they write with equal power from antithetical points of view.

Welland, Dennis. *Arthur Miller*. New York: Grove Press, 1961.
Welland's volume is one of Grove Press's Evergreen Pilot Books. The coverage is selective rather than comprehensive, but the plays that are covered are dealt with well. Chapter 5, which focuses on *The Crucible* (1953), is filled with sensitive insights. The final chapter, "The Drama, the Family, and Society," brings the discussion to a satisfying, thought-provoking closure. Welland lists the New York productions of Miller's plays and provides a bibliography.

After the Fall

Lewis, Allan. *American Plays and Playwrights of the Contemporary Theatre*. New York: Crown, 1965.

Of particular value in Lewis' chapter on Arthur Miller, subtitled "Return to the Self," is a perceptive analysis of *After the Fall* (1964), a play that Miller brought to New York after a nine-year hiatus. Lewis' comments on Miller's use of the unidentified, unspecified Listener in the play, a figure similar to Sir Henry Harcourt-Reilly in T. S. Eliot's *The Cocktail Party* (1949), are particularly challenging.

All My Sons

Greenfield, Thomas Allen. *Work and the Work Ethic in American Drama, 1920-1970*. Columbia, Mo.: University of Missouri Press, 1982.
Greenfield identifies *All My Sons* (1947) as an early attempt "to evolve a view of working life as consuming the entirety of human experience." He likens Joe Keller to Willy Loman because both are totally consumed by their work, although they are on extremely different levels.

The Crucible

Budick, E. Miller. "History and Other Spectres in *The Crucible*." In *Arthur Miller*, edited and with an introduction by Harold Bloom. New York: Chelsea House, 1987.
In assessing *The Crucible* (1953), Budick contends that the play "forces a revolution in our perception and definition of reality." Miller realized that guilt is the major motivating force behind the play. The play, rather than revolving around "the courts and their oppression of the community," revolves around "the figure of Miller's goodman, John Proctor." The author discusses the paradoxes found in the play's protagonist.

Herron, Ima Honaker. *The Small Town in American Drama*. Dallas, Tex.: Southern Methodist University Press, 1969.
The Crucible (1955) is the Miller play most firmly rooted in small-town America. Herron devotes six pages to it in her chapter entitled "The Puritan Village and 'The Common Madness of the Time.'" She contends that Miller, in this play, suggests that any individual under the "yoke of an inhibitive Puritanism may well typify the threats that constantly endanger Everyman." For Miller, the small town is oppressive and threatening.

Kauffmann, Stanley. *Persons of the Drama: Theater Criticism and Comment*. New York: Harper & Row, 1976.
Kauffmann calls *The Crucible* (1955) Arthur Miller's best play. He says of it that the "first three acts have some motor force," but claims that it deals "exclusively with received liberal ideas. The best social dramatists, and many inferior ones, have usually dealt with dangerous ideas."

Porter, Thomas E. *Myth and Modern American Drama*. Detroit: Wayne State
University Press, 1969.
Porter finds in Arthur Miller's *The Crucible* (1955) a replaying of the ancient
myth of natural law versus human-made law, which he calls the Myth of the
Law. He notes that the expectation of a fair trial is a necessary component of this
myth. When this expectation is not met, one has a dramatic situation. Contending
that the emotional factor in the trial that takes place in *The Crucible* is not
accounted for by the rules, he shows how Miller creates the dramatic fabric of
his play.

Death of a Salesman

Eisinger, Chester E. "Focus on Arthur Miller's *Death of a Salesman*: The Wrong
Dreams." In *American Dreams, American Nightmares*, edited by David Madden.
Carbondale, Ill.: Southern Illinois University Press, 1970.
Eisinger identifies the basic conflict in Arthur Miller's *Death of a Salesman*
(1949) as the struggle between the dream and the reality. Eisinger contends that
Miller "romanticizes the rural-agrarian dream but does not make it genuinely
available to Willy." Miller, according to Eisinger, then uses this dream as an
excuse for sentimentality. Eisinger also discusses the business-success dream. He
does not consider Willy Loman a tragic hero, merely a silly, ineffectual man for
whom audiences feel pity. He also does not equate Willy's failure with a failure
of Willy's country.

Greenfield, Thomas Allen. *Work and the Work Ethic in American Drama, 1920-
1970*. Columbia, Mo.: University of Missouri Press, 1982.
Greenfield writes that Arthur Miller explores the spiritual aspects of Willy
Loman's crisis caused by such matters as "the recognition of one's own false
values, the regret and self-hatred caused by past errors, and the uncontrollable
urge to deceive oneself." In order to create a character to serve his purposes,
Miller had to create "not a realistic, photographic representation of a salesman
but an abstraction."

Hurrell, John D., ed. *Two Modern American Tragedies: Reviews and Criticism of
"Death of a Salesman" and "A Streetcar Named Desire."* New York: Charles
Scribner's Sons, 1961.
Hurrell has gathered a large number of early reviews of and articles about the
two plays under consideration here and, in doing so, has provided those interested in Arthur Miller and Tennessee Williams with a substantial resource. The
selection is representative and helpful.

Jackson, Esther Merle. "*Death of a Salesman*: Tragic Myth in the Modern Theatre."
In *Arthur Miller*, edited and with an introduction by Harold Bloom. New York:
Chelsea House, 1987.

Jackson's essay, which first appeared in the *College Language Association Journal*, contends that Arthur Miller "follows O'Neill in suggesting that suffering in the modern world is often deceptively masked, inasmuch as it has been clearly removed from the context of the purely physical." She claims that the situation in this play is tragic and that if it fails as tragedy, it is because of the choice of protagonist: Willy Loman does not have far enough to fall to seem classically tragic.

Kauffmann, Stanley. *Persons of the Drama: Theater Criticism and Comment.* New York: Harper & Row, 1976.
Kauffmann's penetrating analysis of *Death of a Salesman* (1949) is excellent, particularly when viewed in the light of what trust means in family relationships. Kauffmann calls the play "cloudy" thematically. He objects that "there is no anagnorisis for Willy, no moment of recognition: he dies believing in money—in fact, he kills himself for it, to give his son Biff the insurance benefit as a stake for more business." Kauffmann asks a pertinent question that few have asked: Why is Willy in such dire financial straits? He has almost paid off his mortgage and his house, around which high buildings are rising, must be on valuable land that Willy could sell at a decent profit, thereby creating a comfortable nest egg.

Koon, Helene Wickham, ed. *Twentieth Century Interpretations of Death of a Salesman.* Englewood Cliffs, N.J.: Prentice-Hall, 1983.
The ten essays in this collection are preceded by Koon's introduction and are followed by a chronology and a selected bibliography. Among the essays are Barclay W. Bates's "The Lost Past in *Death of a Salesman*," Sighle Kennedy's "Who Killed the Salesman?" and Paul N. Siegel's "Willy Loman and King Lear." The collection is appealingly varied.

Meserve, Walter J., ed. *The Merrill Studies in Death of a Salesman.* Columbus, Ohio: Charles E. Merrill Publishing, 1972.
Meserve divides this resource book into five sections that deal respectively with the reception of *Death of a Salesman* (1949), with the play as a social problem and as a tragedy, with Miller's characters in the play, and with his style. Among the contributors are John Gassner, Harold Clurman, Esther Merle Jackson, and Leonard Moss. Of particular interest is Sister M. Bettina's essay, "Willy Loman's Brother Ben: Tragic Insight in *Death of a Salesman*." Some of the sections (Characters and Style, for example) are thin, although the essays that constitute them are well done. The fullest section is on the reception of the play (six essays), and one might question whether this topic deserves the most extensive coverage.

Parker, Brian. "Point of View in Arthur Miller's *Death of a Salesman*." In *Arthur Miller: A Collection of Critical Essays*, edited by Robert W. Corrigan. Englewood Cliffs, N.J.: Prentice-Hall, 1969.

Parker shows in this essay how Miller manipulates and controls point of view. He shows how the protagonist emerges as a complete character because audiences see him from the perspectives of his two sons and his wife. His character is most fully developed through Linda's exchanges with her sons about their father.

Porter, Thomas E. *Myth and Modern American Drama*. Detroit: Wayne State University Press, 1969.
The salient myth that Porter discusses in Arthur Miller's *Death of a Salesman* (1949) is the success myth. He contends that Miller used it consciously "in depicting the plot-situation, in drawing the hero, [and] in arranging the events of the action." He claims that in the figure of Willy Loman, Miller adopted a Dale Carnegie approach to motivate a play intended for audiences who had come to look upon the Horatio Alger legend with derision, but that by building his play around the American Dream, Miller "strikes deep into the consciousness of the audience."

Weales, Gerald, ed. *Arthur Miller: Death of a Salesman, Text and Criticism*. New York: Viking Press, 1967.
One of the most extensive resource works on this play, this volume includes typescript facsimiles of parts of the play as well as fair text of it. The critical portion of the book includes Miller's comments on the play, drawn from many sources. Jo Mielziner's essay on designing the play follows Miller's comments. The next section consists of contemporary reviews of the play by such critics as Harold Clurman, John Mason Brown, and Eleanor Clark. The remainder of the book consists of essays by a variety of critics and scholars, including John Gassner, William Wiegand, Weales, Ivor Brown, and George Ross. Under a concluding section called "Analogues," Weales presents essays by Eudora Welty, Tennessee Williams, and Irwin Shaw. The bibliography is useful, as are Weales's suggestions for discussion and papers.

Welland, Dennis. "*Death of a Salesman*." In *Arthur Miller*, by Dennis Welland. New York: Grove Press, 1961.
Welland's twenty-three-page coverage of *Death of a Salesman* (1949) does an excellent job of identifying the tensions around which the play revolves. The inner dynamics of the family are presented directly and succinctly here.

A View from the Bridge

Carson, Neil. "*A View from the Bridge* and the Expansion of Vision." In *Arthur Miller*, edited and with an introduction by Harold Bloom. New York: Chelsea House, 1987.
A View from the Bridge (1955) proved to be one of Arthur Miller's most confusing plays. This is in part because, as Carson notes, "Miller's tragic aesthetic differs in many significant respects from traditional classical and Christian

theories." The play confounded Miller himself. Carson shows the learning process the playwright went through in revising the one-act version presented in New York for the two-act London presentation.

Rothenberg, Albert, and Eugene D. Shapiro. "A Defense of Psychoanalysis in Literature: *Long Day's Journey into Night* and *A View from the Bridge*." In *Critical Approaches to O'Neill*, edited by John H. Stroupe. New York: AMS Press, 1988.

Both writers are practicing psychologists who, with valuable insights, write comparatively about these plays by Eugene O'Neill and Arthur Miller. Especially interesting is their discussion of the defensive structures in the two plays, which demonstrates a great deal about the differing approaches of these two major playwrights.

CLIFFORD ODETS

General Studies

Bentley, Eric, ed. *Thirty Years of Treason: Excerpts from the Hearings before the House Committee on Un-American Activities.* New York: Viking Press, 1971. Readers can gain considerable insight into Odets' shattered self-image by reading the portions of this book that relate to him. When he was called before the House Un-American Activities Committee (HUAC), he tried to save himself by implicating others, an act of cowardice for which he never forgave himself. Bentley's bibliographical notes will lead ambitious readers to the original transcripts of Clifford Odets' testimony, which is available in full under the Freedom of Information Act.

Brenman-Gibson, Margaret. *Clifford Odets, American Playwright: The Years from 1906 to 1940.* New York: Atheneum, 1981.
This first volume of Margaret Brenman-Gibson's critical biography of Clifford Odets is the most comprehensive and ambitious book about him to date. The author, a psychologist, knew Odets well and understood him. She has full access to his papers, upon which the book is based. This volume is one that Odets scholars will refer to rather than read cover to cover in a single sitting. An excellent, comprehensive index directs one accurately to parts of the book relevant to one's research. Brenman-Gibson was tireless in seeking material and in interviewing those who knew Odets. She has organized in highly useful form the vast body of material with which she was working. An obvious limitation is that the book ends with *Night Music* (1940), which was followed by five more major Odets plays. A second volume is in preparation to complete the coverage.

Block, Anita. *The Changing World in Plays and Theatre.* Boston: Little, Brown, 1939.
Block's early assessment of Odets at the time when he was staking his claim to recognition as a major playwright shows how he spoke forcefully and artistically to the concerns of the 1930's and how he tweaked the public conscience in his plays, particularly in *Waiting for Lefty* (1935), in which the theater audience becomes directly and physically involved at the end of the play.

Cantor, Harold. *Clifford Odets: Playwright-Poet.* Metuchen, N.J.: Scarecrow Press, 1978.
After a review chapter that relates Odets to the 1930's, Cantor identifies pervasive themes in Odets' plays, devoting separate sections to the family trap, the sellout, and the crisis of love. His most noteworthy contributions in this study, however, are his comments on dialogue and on Odets' use of Yiddish English

in his plays. The whole thrust of this study is on Odets as poet, and part 3, which is directly devoted to this investigation, contains the most valuable material in the study. It deals with Odets' lyricism, with his use of the wisecrack, the epigram, and the cliché. The bibliography is helpful, and the excellent index will aid scholars.

Clurman, Harold. *The Fervent Years: The Story of the Group Theatre and the Thirties*. New York: Alfred A. Knopf, 1945. Also New York: Hill & Wang, 1957 (with a foreword and epilogue by Clurman); New York: Harcourt Brace, 1975 (with the 1957 foreword and a new epilogue by Clurman).
Because of Clifford Odets' intimate involvement with the Group Theatre from its founding in 1931 to its dissolution in 1941, this book is highly informative, an indispensable resource for anyone interested in this revolutionary playwright. Clurman, who knew Odets on a day-to-day basis and who, with other members of the company, often shared quarters with him, shows him first as a struggling actor and frustrated playwright. He tells about Odets' sudden rise to prominence with *Waiting for Lefty* (1935), an event that resulted in his bringing three other plays to Broadway in 1935 alone. Clurman depicts sensitively Odets' move to Hollywood to write for the film industry and to raise money for the foundering Group Theatre in the late 1930's and early 1940's. The book contains invaluable information about all of Odets' plays up to *Clash by Night* (1941) and about his theatrical associates during the thirties. Reliable index.

Cooperman, Robert. *Clifford Odets: An Annotated Bibliography, 1935-1989*. Metuchen, N.J., 1990.
Part 1 of this book is a bibliographical essay that contains valuable information about the location of manuscripts and research materials. Part 2 contains the most extensive list in print of Odets' own work. Part 3 is a well-annotated bibliography of works about Odets. The approach is direct, comprehensive, and accurate. The index is useful and reliable.

Cunningham, Frank. "Clifford Odets." In *American Writers: A Collection of Literary Biographies*, edited by A. Walton Litz. New York: Charles Scribner and Son, 1981.
Cunningham situates Odets in the social and economic context of the 1930's and shows how his cause dissipated before his creative anger was spent. The result was a dislocation from which the playwright, despite his material success—or perhaps because of it—never recovered.

Dusenbury, Winifred L. *The Theme of Loneliness in Modern American Drama*. Gainesville, Fla.: University of Florida Press, 1960.
Dusensbury traces the theme of loneliness through the works of many American playwrights but gives special attention to Odets, discussing ways in which this

theme pervades his plays through *Night Music* (1940). She also demonstrates how the question of personal isolation is much a part of Odets' work, as reflected particularly in *Awake and Sing!* (1935) and *Paradise Lost* (1935), in which the basic social unit, the family, becomes a trap for the younger generation in a time of great social and economic upheaval.

Gibson, William. Preface in *Golden Boy Musical* by Clifford Odets. New York: Bantam Books, 1966.
This appreciative recollection by playwright William Gibson, one of Odets' closest friends and associates, shows the human side of the playwright in his final years.

Gould, Jean. *Modern American Playwrights*. New York: Dodd, Mead, 1966.
Chapter 9 of this fourteen-chapter book focuses on Clifford Odets. Although the chapter contains nothing new about the playwright, it provides a useful overview for the beginner. It is clear and well written. The book is illustrated and has an index. Gould provides in compact form a sweeping view of American dramatists from the end of World War I to Edward Albee.

Griffin, Robert J. "On the Lovesongs of Clifford Odets." In *The Thirties: Fiction, Poetry, Drama*, edited by Warren G. French. Deland, Fla.: Everett/Edwards, 1967.
Griffin is mostly concerned in his seven-page essay with Clifford Odets' plays that center on the family, particularly *Awake and Sing!* (1935) and *Paradise Lost* (1935). He comments on Odets' lyrical use of language.

Krutch, Joseph Wood. *The American Drama Since 1918*. New York: Random House, 1939; New York: George Braziller, 1957.
Attributing elements of Clifford Odets' style to Ernest Hemingway and other writers of what he calls "the hard-boiled school," Krutch says that after *Awake and Sing!* (1935), Odets had to decide the direction he would take, the "definitely 'revolutionary'" or one in the "more broadly humanistic tradition." According to Krutch, Odets' characters, despite their frequent ignorance and crudeness, work dramatically because Odets makes it "clear that people like this are going to go right on demanding of life more than it will ever give them."

Lewis, Allan. *American Plays and Playwrights of the Contemporary Theatre*. New York: Crown, 1965.
Linking Clifford Odets with Lillian Hellman and Irwin Shaw, Lewis identifies them as the prominent playwrights to emerge from the 1930's depression. He says that all of them had genuine social concerns about which they wrote. Once the Depression ended and the nation returned to greater prosperity, Odets faded from view because he had lost his subject. He tried to broach it again in *The Big*

Knife (1949), but the play was hardly convincing in the way *Waiting for Lefty* (1935) and *Awake and Sing!* (1935) had been. Lewis likens *Waiting for Lefty* to a tribal war dance, pointing out that "the formula for proletarian plays prescribed a third-act resolution."

Mendelsohn, Michael J. *Clifford Odets: Humane Dramatist*. Deland, Fla.: Everett/ Edwards, 1969.
In a book that follows a conventional chronological development, Mendelsohn suggests that Odets' emergence as a playwright stems from his "vague, abstract, idealistic way" of loving humanity. Mendelsohn relates Odets to the liberal, leftist writers of the 1930's. He contends that Odets would never have written at all "had he not been motivated by the inequities of American society" as he observed it. The book's thesis may be questionable, but it is an interesting one to consider. A psychoanalytic reading of Odets would yield results much different from Mendelsohn's. The book has a bibliography and an index.

Miller, Gabriel. *Clifford Odets*. New York: Continuum, 1989.
One of the volumes of the literature and life series that Frederick Ungar is producing on American writers, this book is organized around themes rather than according to strict chronology. In the second chapter, it assesses the early self-portraits in two unpublished works, *910 Eden Street* (1931; the prototype for *Awake and Sing!*) and *Victory* (1932). The book then moves to "The Chekhovian Vision," in which Miller considers *Awake and Sing!* (1935) and *Paradise Lost* (1935). This organization, which delays the discussion of *Waiting for Lefty* (1935) until the seventh chapter, "The Political Vision," works remarkably well in a book that provides an eight-page bibliography and an accurate index.

_____, ed. *Critical Essays on Clifford Odets*. Boston: G. K. Hall, 1991.
After an insightful introduction by the editor, this book presents a pertinent review of each of Odets' plays by such critics as Joseph Wood Krutch, John Mason Brown, Brooks Atkinson, and Richard Lockridge. Miller then reproduces early assessments of Odets by John McCarten and Edith J. R. Isaacs, following this brief section with three interviews with Clifford Odets by Michael Mendelsohn, Arthur Wagner, and Armand Aulicino. The rest of the book is devoted to essays about Odets and about each of his plays. Three of these essays—those by George L. Groman, Malcolm Goldstein, and Norma Jenckes—were written specifically for this volume. The remainder are derived from previous works by such scholars as Winifred L. Dusenbury, Gerald Weales, Edward Murray, Harold Cantor, Margaret Brenman-Gibson, R. Baird Shuman, and the editor. A comprehensive index is useful to the researcher.

Murray, Edward. *Clifford Odets: The Thirties and After*. New York: Frederick Ungar, 1968.

Murray views Odets as a revolutionary who suddenly lost his cause and could not find a new one that might stir him into writing with the conviction he had in the 1930's. He chronicles the artistic decline of the playwright, who made his name by pointing out the hypocrisy of middle-class standards and then lived in fear that as he prospered, he was beginning to live by them. The Odets that emerges from Murray's study is inwardly divided by the opposing forces that are at work on him.

Nannes, Casper. *Politics in the American Drama as Revealed by Plays Produced on the New York Stage*. Philadelphia: University of Pennsylvania Press, 1950; republished and expanded as *Politics in the American Drama*. Washington, D.C.: Catholic University of America Press, 1960.
These books contain the most perceptive analysis of Odets' *Till the Day I Die* (1935), a play Odets wrote as a companion piece for the one-act *Waiting for Lefty* (1935) after it was taken to Broadway. All of Odets' early plays are political, but *Waiting for Lefty* and *Till the Day I Die*, as Nannes shows, are the most overtly political of all his work.

Odets, Clifford. *The Time Is Ripe: The 1940 Journal of Clifford Odets*. New York: Grove Press, 1988.
Published twenty-five years after Odets died of cancer, this journal, kept during one of the most crucial years of the playwright's life, provides insights into the turmoil he was enduring at the time. His marriage to Luise Rainer was collapsing, the Group Theatre was under threat of disbandment, and Odets feared he had sold out by going to Hollywood as a film writer, even though he did so primarily to help sustain the Group Theatre financially. This volume was readied for publication by Odets' only son, Walt, who wrote a preface. The volume also contains a valuable, intimate introduction by playwright William Gibson, husband of Odets' biographer, Margaret Brenman-Gibson (see above), who knew Odets well for many years.

Rabkin, Gerald. *Drama and Commitment: Politics in the American Theatre of the Thirties*. Bloomington, Ind.: Indiana University Press, 1964.
In one of the longest chapters in this book, Rabkin studies and interprets Clifford Odets in terms of his early social dramas such as like *Waiting for Lefty* (1935) and *Golden Boy* (1937), going on to discuss some of his later plays and show how Odets was still struggling to demonstrate commitment. In writing about *The Big Knife* (1949), Rabkin identifies the big knife as the social force that cuts off aspiration in people. He says of it, "But we must ask, in what precisely does this force reside? For the difficulty with the play is that we are never exactly sure what the playwright was railing about."

Shuman, R. Baird. *Clifford Odets*. New York: Twayne, 1962.
This earliest full-length study of Clifford Odets is outdated. Most of its factual errors have been corrected by later critics. The book follows the usual format of the Twayne United States Authors Series, including a chronology, an annotated bibliography, and an index. The first chapter is biographical, and the remaining chapters analyze Odets' published plays, dealing with them in chronological order.

_____. "Clifford Odets and the Jewish Context." In *From Hester Street to Hollywood: The Jewish-American Stage and Screen*, edited by Sarah Blacher Cohen. Bloomington, Ind.: Indiana University Press, 1983.
In this essay, Shuman considers the effect that Odets' Jewish background had on him and on his writing. Shuman discusses Odets' upbringing in Jewish-American neighborhoods in Philadelphia and New York, delving into his relationship with his parents and with his aunt and uncle, who were older than Odets' parents when they came from Russia to the United States and retained many more of the customs of the old world than did their younger relatives. The essay treats such topics as Odets' use of the Jewish-American dialect and Jewish humor in his plays.

_____. "Clifford Odets: From Influence to Affluence." In *Modern American Drama: Essays in Criticism*, edited by William E. Taylor. Deland, Fla.: Everett/Edwards, 1960.
This essay deals with Odets' psychological decline after he ceased to be an angry critic of the social ills of the 1930's as those ills began to disappear and as Odets, now a prosperous Hollywood film writer, came to be haunted by the feeling that he had sold out artistically. Odets felt a kinship with the destitute victims of the Great Depression. When they were pulled out of their poverty by the improving economy brought about by the entry of the United States into World War II, Odets lost his cause and found it difficult to find another one as compelling.

Weales, Gerald. *Clifford Odets: The Playwright*. Indianapolis, Ind.: Bobbs-Merrill, 1971; republished as *Odets: The Playwright*. New York: Methuen, 1985.
This is the best compact critical biography of Clifford Odets. The later edition is not significantly revised, so either version of the book will prove useful. Weales is particularly concerned with Odets as a relatively unknown actor and unsuccessful playwright who almost overnight found himself the toast of Broadway. Weales does a fine job of relating Odets to the sociopolitical currents of his time and produces shrewd assessments of one of the most influential and troubled playwrights of the twentieth century. A complete bibliography, following six pages of notes on sources, and an extensive index enhance the book's utility.

Awake and Sing!

Clurman, Harold. *The Fervent Years: The Story of the Group Theatre and the Thirties*. New York: Alfred A. Knopf, 1945. Also New York: Hill and Wang, 1957 (with a foreword and an epilogue by Clurman); New York: Harcourt Brace, 1975 (with the 1957 foreword and a new epilogue by Clurman).

Clurman devotes most of chapter 12 to an account of how Odets transformed the unproduced and unpublished *910 Eden Street* into *Awake and Sing!* (1935) after the resounding success of *Waiting for Lefty* (1935) in January, 1935. The Group—especially Luther Adler—had scorned the play, but after *Lefty* it was essential that it come forth with another Odets play; since this one was virtually complete, it was rushed into production.

Golden Boy

Clurman, Harold. *The Fervent Years: The Story of the Group Theatre and the Thirties*. New York: Alfred A. Knopf, 1945. Also New York: Hill & Wang, 1957 (with a foreword and an epilogue by Clurman); New York: Harcourt Brace, 1975 (with the 1957 foreword and a new epilogue by Clurman).

The Group Theatre, according to Harold Clurman, was beginning to run out of steam in 1937, but then Clifford Odets wrote *Golden Boy* (1937), which it produced for an overall outlay of $19,000. The play was a rousing success and helped revitalize the Group for a brief period. Odets, ever loyal to the organization, pumped a great deal of his income from the play and from his screenwriting in Hollywood into saving the Group, which finally disbanded in 1941.

126

EUGENE O'NEILL

General Studies

Ahuja, Chaman. *Tragedy, Modern Temper, and O'Neill*. Atlantic Highlands, N.J.: Humanities Press, 1984.
Ahuja begins with a discussion of O'Neill's quest for tragedy, then moves on to a chapter on the core of irony in his plays. The next chapter is entitled "Lessons in Tragedy," followed by "Infiltration of Modernism." The sixth chapter, "Freudian Sickness and American Tragedy," is quite biased in its views of the psychological presence in modern drama. A final word in chapter 9, "Psyche, Soul, and Irony," shows a similar closed-mindedness.

Alexander, Doris. *The Tempering of Eugene O'Neill*. New York: Harcourt, Brace & World, 1962.
Although later biographies have discounted some of the information in this Eugene O'Neill biography, the book is interesting and well written. The Gelbs' study (see below) offers a much fuller treatment based on materials to which Alexander did not have access. The bibliography is strong, the index useful.

Bentley, Eric. *Theatre of War: Modern Drama from Ibsen to Brecht*. New York: Viking Press, 1973.
In this book, Eric Bentley vents his long-standing hostility toward Eugene O'Neill. He gives a jaundiced evaluation of O'Neill's career, based more upon personal animosity than artistic analysis. Bentley moralizes considerably in his comments about the plays of O'Neill, and his comments are so obviously biased as to be highly questionable. This book is interesting to read as a minority assessment.

Berlin, Normand, ed. *Eugene O'Neill, Three Plays: Mourning Becomes Electra, The Iceman Cometh, Long Day's Journey into Night: A Casebook*. New York: Grove Press, 1982; London: Macmillan, 1989.
This book offers comments by O'Neill about each play under discussion, reviews and other comments on its first Broadway production, and critical studies by such O'Neill scholars as C. W. E. Bigsby, Egil Tornqvist, Robert B. Heilman, Raymond Williams, Eric Bentley, and Joseph Wood Krutch. The format is convenient for anyone wishing to study the three plays discussed.

Bloom, Harold, ed. *Eugene O'Neill*. New York: Chelsea House, 1987.
Bloom's collection contains nine essays about Eugene O'Neill as well as the editor's introduction. Among the contributors are Lionel Trilling, Michael Manheim, Doris Falk, Travis Bogard, Jean Chothia, and C. W. E. Bigsby. Each

of the essays has been published previously, but it is useful to have them brought together under one cover. The editor provides a chronology, a bibliography, and a reliable index.

Boulton, Agnes. *Part of a Long Story*. Garden City, N.Y.: Doubleday, 1958.
Agnes Boulton, Eugene O'Neill's second wife and the mother of two of his three children, attempts in this anecdotal book to explain some of the details of her life with O'Neill. This book takes her life with O'Neill only up to 1919, the year in which their son Shane was born. A promised second volume has not materialized. Although the book is highly subjective, it offers insights into O'Neill's creative process and into his insecurities and arrogance. The book is gossipy rather than scholarly, but the gossip is well grounded in fact and helps to illuminate some of the internal conflicts out of which both the playwright's work and personal agony grew. Interesting glimpses of Ella O'Neill, the playwright's mother.

Bowen, Croswell. *Curse of the Misbegotten: A Tale of the House of O'Neill*. New York: Ballantine Books, 1959.
Although Bowen claims that this book was written with the assistance of Eugene O'Neill's younger son, Shane, there is some doubt that such was actually the case. Bowen presents a sensational view of a family that was, admittedly, tormented. Somehow, Bowen does not go as far as he might in showing how a creative talent grew out of—and in some ways was nourished by—that torment.

Brustein, Robert. *The Theater of Revolt*. Boston: Little, Brown, 1964.
With characteristic acerbity, Robert Brustein calls Eugene O'Neill's early plays complete failures artistically. He admits, however, that O'Neill earned his place as a towering global figure among playwrights and that *Long Day's Journey into Night* (wr. 1941, pr. 1956) represents the playwright at his best. Brustein's overall assessment of O'Neill is detailed and intelligent, although one may quarrel with some of its contentions.

Cargill, Oscar, et al., eds. *O'Neill and His Plays*. New York: New York University Press, 1961.
This collection is a crucial item in O'Neill scholarship. It contains a remarkably far-ranging bibliography that lists all the major secondary sources relating to O'Neill up to 1960. The assessment of O'Neill's work is, as is inevitable in O'Neill scholarship, very much bound up with the facts of his life, which colored his output substantially. This book has, besides its excellent bibliography, an extensive index. The approaches to the plays are appealingly varied.

Carpenter, Frederic I. *Eugene O'Neill*. New York: Twayne, 1964.
Given the space limitations imposed by the prescribed format of Twayne's United States Authors Series, Carpenter has presented a fair picture of the playwright.

128   *American Drama 1918–1960*

This study is well suited to the beginning O'Neill scholar or enthusiast. Carpenter carefully sketches the dramatic context into which O'Neill emerged as a young playwright. He shows O'Neill's development and demonstrates well the ways in which he used the torments of his personal existence to create and inform his drama. The book has an annotated bibliography and a comprehensive index as well as a detailed chronology.

Chabrowe, Leonard. *Ritual and Pathos: The Theater of O'Neill.* Lewisburg, Penn.: Bucknell University Press, 1976.
Chabrowe supports quite impressively his thesis that Eugene O'Neill's work is in the tradition of ritualistic or religious theater. If one accepts the initial thesis, the book is excellent. If one rejects that thesis, however, as many critics have, Chabrowe may seem to be tailoring the facts with which he is working to support his basic contentions and suppressing facts that would fail to support it.

Chothia, Jean. *Forging a Language: A Study of the Plays of Eugene O'Neill.* Cambridge, England. Cambridge University Press, 1979.
Despite the excellent job Cohn did of assessing language in *Dialogue in American Drama* (1971, see below), Chothia has been able to press the study of O'Neill's use of language much further in this first full-length study of how the playwright used language and how he matured in its use through the years. This book is thorough and searching. It takes into account both sides of most of the arguments with which it deals. The index is useful.

Clark, Barrett H. *Eugene O'Neill: The Man and His Plays.* New York: Dover, 1947.
This expanded and revised edition of Clark's 1926 biography, the first full-length assessment of Eugene O'Neill, is based on interviews with O'Neill, letters, and other documents. It is at times anecdotal and not always 100-percent reliable, but it remains a valuable resource for those interested in the early career of this playwright.

Cohn, Ruby. *Dialogue in American Drama.* Bloomington, Ind.: Indiana University Press, 1971.
Cohn devotes the sixty-page second chapter of her book—"The Wet Sponge of Eugene O'Neill"—to a penetrating assessment of Eugene O'Neill's use of dialogue. Cohn calls dialogue O'Neill's "major theatrical instrument," noting that O'Neill's characters talk themselves through many of their quests. She demonstrates how O'Neill uses verbal repetition to great effect, especially in *Long Day's Journey into Night* (wr. 1941, pr. 1956) and *The Iceman Cometh* (1946). In *Long Day's Journey*, Cohn notes how O'Neill's choice of words—*blame* and *lie* are frequently on the characters' lips—builds the atmosphere and tension in the play. She claims that the "early plays oscillate between the stilted rhetoric of melodrama and the ungrammatical colloquialism of the realist novel." This book has a selected bibliography and a comprehensive index.

Dickinson, Thomas H. *Playwrights of the New American Theater.* New York: Macmillan, 1925.

Because this book was written when Eugene O'Neill's career was still developing, it provides interesting insights and predictions. Dickinson identifies two qualities that make O'Neill a consummate artist: "1. A rigorous selectiveness, an ability even brutal to discard his own work if it does not please him; 2. A diversity of formula in composition." Dickinson says that of the fifty plays O'Neill had written up to 1925, he had destroyed twenty. Chapter 2, on O'Neill, "The Playwright Unbounded," is sixty-eight pages long, about 20 percent of the total length of the book. The index is serviceable.

Downer, Alan S., ed. *American Drama and Its Critics: A Collection of Essays.* Chicago: University of Chicago Press, 1965.

George Jean Nathan's contribution to this collection focuses on Eugene O'Neill and his dramas. Nathan shows O'Neill's progression in both technique and ideas as he wrote increasingly complex and demanding drama.

Engel, Edwin. *The Haunted Heroes of Eugene O'Neill.* Cambridge, Mass.: Harvard University Press, 1953.

Despite its age, Engel's book remains indispensable to Eugene O'Neill scholars. Engel presents the first full assessment of O'Neill's intellectual background, giving a full account of the playwright's early readings in philosophy, psychology, and literature. Engel is not gentle in assessing O'Neill's early career, but his assessments are well reasoned.

Falk, Doris V. *Eugene O'Neill and the Tragic Tension.* New Brunswick, N.J.: Rutgers University Press, 1958.

Falk succeeds quite well in identifying Eugene O'Neill with the classical tragic tradition, showing how he adhered to the Aristotelian conventions of tragedy in his plays and informed them with his knowledge of Jungian psychology. Falk's comments on *Mourning Becomes Electra* (1931) are particularly informative. The basic thesis of this study has been supported by later scholars. The book's bibliography and index are useful.

Floyd, Virginia, ed. *Eugene O'Neill: A World View.* New York: Frederick Ungar, 1979.

The three divisions of this book view O'Neill from a European perspective, an American perspective, and from the perspective of some of those who acted in his plays. The foreign perspective represents O'Neill's reception in Britain, Scandinavia, Czechoslovakia, Poland, Hungary, Germany, and the Soviet Union and considers European influences upon O'Neill as well as his critical reception. The six essays in the section that deals with the American perspective consider

O'Neill's Catholicism, his puritanism, the poetry and mysticism in his plays, O'Neill as exile, and O'Neill as humanist. In the last section, Florence Eldridge, Arvin Brown, Geraldine Fitzgerald, and Ingrid Bergman tell of their associations with O'Neill. Among the academic contributors are Horst Frenz, Esther M. Jackson, Timo Tiusanen, Clifford Leech, and Egil Tornqvist.

_____. *The Plays of Eugene O'Neill*. New York: Frederick Ungar, 1985. Floyd is a historical critic who essentially uses biography to explain O'Neill's plays. The presentation is chronological and sensible, although its scope is limited by the author's critical stance. Nevertheless, Floyd understands the plays well. One can hardly deny that the biographical associations one can make between O'Neill and his plays are legitimate ones. The bibliography is useful, and the index is reliable.

Gassner, John, ed. *O'Neill: A Collection of Critical Essays*. Englewood Cliffs, N.J.: Prentice-Hall, 1964.
The fifteen essays in this book were contributed by such Eugene O'Neill scholars and critics as John Howard Lawson, Hugo von Hofmannsthal, Travis Bogard, Stark Young, Eric Bentley, Richard Hayes, and Tom Driver. Particularly informative are Robert F. Whitman's "O'Neill's Search for a 'Language of the Theatre'" and John Gassner's "The Nature of O'Neill's Achievement: A Summary and Appraisal." Gassner concludes that "O'Neill's interest and power as a playwright were derived, in fact, from his dividedness. . . . The alienation apparent in his dramatic talent commands respect for a writer who had the courage of his discontent."

Gelb, Arthur, and Barbara Gelb. *O'Neill*. New York: Harper & Row, 1960, 1962, 1973; enlarged ed., 1987.
Until Sheaffer's two-volume biography of O'Neill (see below) appeared, the Gelbs' extensive biography, which is approximately one thousand pages long, was the authoritative one. It is a pioneering work whose authors interviewed hundreds of people who knew O'Neill, many of them dead by the time Sheaffer was doing his research. They also had the complete cooperation of O'Neill's widow, Carlotta Monterey O'Neill, who gave them access to many unpublished resources that helped to explain a great deal about O'Neill's career. The book has a monumental, flawlessly accurate index and is illustrated. There is no bibliography.

Krutch, Joseph Wood. *American Drama Since 1918*. New York: George Braziller, 1957.
One of the seven chapters in Krutch's book is devoted to Eugene O'Neill and his plays. Krutch sets O'Neill apart from the other playwrights of his generation by pointing out O'Neill's consistent devotion to the principles of classical tragedy

in his work. Acknowledging the unevenness of O'Neill's writing, Krutch comments on his single-minded devotion to play writing. He claims that if O'Neill falls short of greatness, it will be because of his "failure to accept soon enough or fully enough any intellectual formula." Krutch discusses O'Neill's major plays in this chapter in their own context and in the context of works by such other writers as John Steinbeck and Lillian Hellman.

Lewis, Allan. *American Plays and Playwrights of the Contemporary Theatre*. New York: Crown, 1965.
The beginning chapter of Lewis' book is a twenty-page essay on Eugene O'Neill entitled "The Tragic Homecoming." Although this chapter deals with other O'Neill plays in detail, what Lewis says about *Mourning Becomes Electra* (1931) colors much of the rest of his commentary. He notes O'Neill's borrowing of the love-guilt complex from August Strindberg. He goes into the Freudian aspects of the incestuous overtones in much of O'Neill's work.

Manheim, Michael. *Eugene O'Neill's New Language of Kinship*. Syracuse, N.Y.: Syracuse University Press, 1982.
Manheim uses language as a key to the family relationships in Eugene O'Neill's later plays. The author claims that although O'Neill was steeped in the melodramatic tradition of his father, it was not being melodramatic that established his reputation. Rather, it is "that the great pity and terror his plays evoke begins in himself—in the guilt, the frenzy over his family." It was O'Neill's gift of establishing the elements of this pity and terror, as manifested in his language, that made him the playwright he was.

Martine, James J. *Critical Essays on Eugene O'Neill*. Boston: G. K. Hall, 1984.
Part of G. K. Hall's Critical Essays on American Literature Series, Martine's collection contains fourteen essays written specifically for this volume by such Eugene O'Neill scholars as Jackson Bryer, Peter Egri, June Schlueter, Carl E. Rollyson, Jr., Michael Manheim, and Lisa M. Schwerdt. The range of topics is impressive, and most of the major plays, as well as a number of the minor ones, receive incisive comment. The book has a reliable and useful index.

Miller, Jordan Y. "Eugene O'Neill." In *American Winners of the Nobel Literary Prize*, edited by Warren G. French and Walter E. Kidd. Norman, Okla.: University of Oklahoma Press, 1968.
Jordan Miller provides a thirty-page essay on O'Neill, indicating the playwright's surprise at being named the 1936 laureate in literature only five years after Sinclair Lewis had won the same prize. The essay reviews O'Neill's productive career and life accurately and succinctly.

_____. *Eugene O'Neill and the American Critic: A Bibliographical Checklist*. Hamden, Conn.: Archon Books, 1962; rev. ed., 1973.

Miller begins with a chronology of Eugene O'Neill's life, which is followed by a chronology of his publications and a list of his major productions with the names of the original cast members. He then moves to a fifty-three-page bibliography of general references in book form, followed by a sixty-one-page list of general references in periodicals. Miller devotes the next 253 pages to bibliographical references for specific O'Neill plays, including some quite obscure ones, such as *The Ancient Mariner* (1924), *The First Man* (1922), and *Exorcism* (1920). A concluding section lists thirteen pages of graduate-student research that has produced theses and dissertations. The bibliography is well indexed. The book is now obviously outdated, although it has some valuable information about resources.

Miller, J. William. *Modern Playwrights at Work*. New York: Samuel French, 1968.
Miller's fifty-three-page chapter on Eugene O'Neill focuses particularly on his background and work habits. Miller shows how O'Neill assessed his own writing and goes into considerable detail about the revisions he made in his work, particularly in *Mourning Becomes Electra* (1931). Miller says, "O'Neill could work at writing and rewriting for long periods like a man possessed by demons."

Moorton, Richard F., Jr., ed. *Eugene O'Neill's Century: Centennial Views on America's Foremost Tragic Dramatist*. Westport, Conn.: Greenwood Press, 1991.
This contribution to Greenwood Press's Drama and Theatre Studies Series contains twelve essays that consider O'Neill's stature as a writer of tragedy. In his essay, editor Richard F. Moorton defends O'Neill as a consummate tragedian, finding the genius of O'Neill's tragedy in the playwright's violation of intimate relationships, particularly family relationships. He points out that such an approach is necessary in the Aristotelian concept of tragedy. The book's essays range from S. Georgia Nugent's psychoanalytical feminist critique of *Mourning Becomes Electra* (1931) to Lowell Swortzell's essay about O'Neill's attitude toward children and adolescents as revealed in his plays. The book has an adequate index. Burton L. Cooper's essay on adapting O'Neill for film has a valuable appendix on television adaptations of his plays.

Quinn, Arthur Hobson. *A History of American Drama from the Civil War to the Present Day*. New York: F. S. Crofts, 1927, 1945, 1964.
Arthur Hobson Quinn was the first major scholarly critic to consider O'Neill and his work in depth, which he did in the first edition of his *History of American Drama* in 1927. Quinn recognizes O'Neill as the watershed of drama as it is known in the modern United States, clearly identifying him as the first modern American playwright. Quinn's account, although dated, is an extremely significant one. The book has a sound index.

Ranald, Margaret Loftus. *The Eugene O'Neill Companion*. Westport, Conn.: Greenwood Press, 1984.
Ranald's huge, alphabetically arranged compendium of Eugene O'Neill material deals with O'Neill, his family, his friends, his plays, his manuscripts, characters in his plays, directors and producers, and much else. Some of the entries are long, and some are quite short. Each play is synopsized fully. A cast of characters and production notes are provided for each play. The book has a complex but well-arranged bibliography and a comprehensive index.

Sarlos, Robert K. *Jig Cook and the Provincetown Players*. Amherst, Mass.: University of Massachusetts Press, 1982.
Sarlos recounts how George Cram "Jig" Cook and his wife, playwright Susan Glaspell, were involved with the Provincetown Players from the beginning. Eugene O'Neill was very much a part of the group that helped to establish the Players, and Sarlos provides the fullest overview in print of O'Neill's association with it.

Sanborn, Ralph, and Barrett H. Clark, comps. and eds. *A Bibliography of the Works of O'Neill Together with the Collected Poems of Eugene O'Neill*. Privately printed, 1931; New York: Benjamin Bloom, 1965.
Part 1 provides collations telling where O'Neill's poems can be found and full collations of his plays. Part 2 lists—without annotations—critical material about O'Neill, information about four unpublished plays, and notes on O'Neill plays found in anthologies. Part 3 is devoted to the poems, which take up fifty pages. They were published against O'Neill's will. This work, the 1965 reprinting of which is not updated, was superseded by Miller's (see above). Both are now outdated, although they are of some use to scholars.

Sheaffer, Louis. *O'Neill: Son and Artist*. Boston: Little, Brown, 1973.
This second volume in Louis Sheaffer's immense two-volume biography of Eugene O'Neill deals in detail with most of the major plays but is concerned primarily with trying to unravel the mystery of O'Neill's highly complicated psyche. This treatment deals with O'Neill as uncomfortable father, unnerving husband to three women, alcoholic, and finally as the tragic figure who, at the height of his creative powers, was rendered physically unable to write by the inroads that illness made upon his motor control. This extensive book has a splendid index and a sound bibliography. It is generously illustrated.

_____. *O'Neill: Son and Playwright*. Boston: Little, Brown, 1968.
The first volume of Louis Sheaffer's two-volume biography, the fullest in print, concentrates largely on Eugene O'Neill's life through 1919—especially his love-hate relationships with his parents and his only sibling, his brother James, ten years his senior. Sheaffer's detailed discussion of the plays of this first major American playwright in the light of his early life and of his paradoxical family

relationships is invaluable. The book has a strong bibliography and an impressive index. The illustrations are excellent.

Stroupe, John H., ed. *Critical Approaches to O'Neill.* New York: AMS Press, 1988.
The dozen essays in this book are contributed by such scholars as Michael Manheim, Louis Shaeffer, Thomas P. Adler, and Michael Hinden. Four of the essays focus narrowly on specific plays, although all the essays cover essentially O'Neill's major dramatic output. Especially pertinent are John Chioles' "Aeschylus and O'Neill: A Phenomenological View," Louis Sheaffer's "Correcting Some Errors in Annals of O'Neill," and Joseph J. Moleski's "Eugene O'Neill and the Cruelty of Theater." The book has a serviceable index.

Tiusanen, Timo. *O'Neill's Scenic Images.* Princeton, N.J.: Princeton University Press, 1968.
The major contribution of Tiusanen's work is that the author demonstrates how Eugene O'Neill communicates by nonverbal means. Several writers have focused their attention on O'Neill's language, which is of the utmost importance, but of almost equal importance is the means of communication that Tiusanen considers.

Ah, Wilderness!

Bogard, Travis. "The Historian: *Mourning Becomes Electra* and *Ah, Wilderness!.*" In *Eugene O'Neill,* edited and with an introduction by Harold Bloom. New York: Chelsea House, 1987.
It has long been thought that *Ah, Wilderness!* (1933) is pure autobiography, and Travis Bogard makes this contention official. He says categorically that "however masked, *Ah, Wilderness!* is direct autobiography, relating its characters to those who were to emerge in the admittedly autobiographical *Long Day's Journey into Night*" (wr. 1941, pr. 1956).

Kauffmann, Stanley. *Persons of the Drama: Theater Criticism and Comment.* New York: Harper & Row, 1976.
Kauffmann tells the interesting story of how "Eugene O'Neill dreamed this play one night in September 1932," wrote the entire scenario within the next twenty-four hours, and had the play on Broadway within six weeks of finishing the working script. Kauffmann calls the play "an exercise in wish-fulfillment," an image of what O'Neill conceived the perfect family to be.

Kimbel, Ellen. "Eugene O'Neill as Social Historian: Manners and Morals in *Ah, Wilderness!*" In *Eugene O'Neill,* edited by James J. Martine. Boston: G. K. Hall, 1984.
Kimbel identifies the central theme of the play as the relationship of parents to

their children. The play also represents the two-day period that was really the rite of passage of the son, Richard Miller. Kimbel concludes, "O'Neill knew from his lack of it, the advantages to the child of the kind of family he gives us in *Ah, Wilderness!*" (1933). She quotes him as saying that the play shows life as he wishes his had been.

Van Laan, Thomas F. "Singing in the Wilderness: The Dark Vision of O'Neill's Only Mature Comedy." In *Eugene O'Neill*, edited and with an introduction by Harold Bloom. New York: Chelsea House, 1987.
Van Laan approaches Eugene O'Neill's best-known comedy very seriously, questioning whether the play is as other critics have depicted it. He sets up his argument by writing, "The fundamental strategy of the play involves something comparable to altering the 'ah' of delight to one more suggestive of contempt." He then goes on to discuss the play in the light of the three typically middle-class American clichés the play sets up. He concludes that "*Ah, Wilderness!* is a much richer and more interesting play than it is generally taken to be."

Anna Christie

Bogard, Travis. "*Anna Christie*: Her Fall and Rise—." In *O'Neill: A Collection of Critical Essays*, edited by John Gassner. Englewood Cliffs, N.J.: Prentice-Hall, 1964.
Bogard relates *Anna Christie* (1921) to Eugene O'Neill's *Chris Christopherson* (unpublished, 1920), a one-act play that was its predecessor. Bogard claims that *Anna Christie* "was to set forth the positive basis for his later tragedies." He relates the play to O'Neill's study of Friedrich Nietzsche's philosophy of tragedy, which apparently had not proceeded as far when he wrote this play as it was to go later in his career.

Desire Under the Elms

Racey, Edgar F., Jr. "Myth as Tragic Structure in *Desire Under the Elms*." In *O'Neill: A Collection of Critical Essays*, edited by John Gassner. Englewood Cliffs, N.J.: Prentice-Hall, 1964.
Racey finds *Desire Under the Elms* (1924) to be directly related to the Hippolytus myth about which Euripides wrote his famous play by that name. Racey thinks that O'Neill was influenced by Jean Racine's adaptation of that tale. The author shows how O'Neill, using "the bare framework of a New England domestic tragedy . . . has grafted a religious symbology, almost an iconography," upon the play. He finds O'Neill dependent upon the classical myth for both plot and structure.

Schlueter, June, and Arthur Lewis. "Cabot's Conflict: The Stones and Cows in O'Neill's *Desire Under the Elms*." In *Eugene O'Neill*, edited by James J. Martine. Boston: G. K. Hall, 1984.
The authors quote Eugene O'Neill, who says that the "battle of moral forces in the New England scene [is] what I feel closest to as an artist." They discuss Ephraim Cabot in terms of this battle, pointing out that "in marked contrast to the hard, cold stones, the cows offer Cabot softness and warmth, perhaps even the satisfaction of a latent sexuality his Puritan ethic has denied." In setting fire to his house at the end of the play, Cabot is turning his back on all he has worked for, all that his Puritan work ethic has yielded.

Hughie

Porter, Laurin Roland. "*Hughie*: Pipe Dream for Two." In *Eugene O'Neill*, edited by James J. Martine. Boston: G. K. Hall, 1984.
Porter considers Eugene O'Neill's one-act play *Hughie* (wr. 1941, pr. 1959) a condensed version of *The Iceman Cometh* (wr. 1939, pr. 1956). Both plays are about a corrupt society. Porter finds that O'Neill's solution to dealing with this society is common to the two plays: "The common denominator in each case is the need for a pipe dream, since life cannot be endured without a protective shield of illusion." Porter does not believe that the resolution of *Hughie* communicates an optimistic message, as some other scholars have thought.

Raleigh, John Henry. *The Plays of Eugene O'Neill*. Carbondale, Ill.: Southern Illinois University Press, 1965.
Raleigh writes, "Historically considered, *The Iceman Cometh* (wr. 1939, pr. 1956) and *Hughie* (wr. 1941, pr. 1959) are companion pieces." He calls *Hughie* "one of the most optimistic plays that O'Neill ever wrote." This is not an uncommon view, although it has been challenged by later critics.

The Iceman Cometh

Bentley, Eric. "Trying to Like O'Neill." In *O'Neill: A Collection of Critical Essays*, edited by John Gassner. Englewood Cliffs, N.J.: Prentice-Hall, 1964.
Eric Bentley, never a Eugene O'Neill enthusiast, writes about his experience in codirecting a German presentation of *The Iceman Cometh* (wr. 1939, pr. 1946). He argues that "to get at the core of reality in *The Iceman*—which is also its artistic, its dramatic core—you have to cut away the rotten fruit of unreality around it." Bentley claims that the play's diffuseness robs it of its suspense, and in his version of the play in Germany, about an hour was cut out of the dialogue.

Carpenter, Frederic I. "Focus on Eugene O'Neill's *The Iceman Cometh*: The Iceman Hath Come." In *American Dreams, American Nightmares*, edited by David Madden. Carbondale, Ill.: Southern Illinois University Press, 1970.

Frederic Carpenter identifies the real subject of Eugene O'Neill's *The Iceman
Cometh* (wr. 1939, pr. 1946)—as many other critics have—as pipe dreams. He
explores the meaning of the play's title and O'Neill's choice of names for the
play's characters. Carpenter asserts that "the meaningful action of O'Neill's
tragedy does not take place on stage, but offstage, both physically and in the
reader's mind."

Frazer, Winifred Dusenbury. *Love as Death in "The Iceman Cometh."* Gainesville,
Fla: University of Florida Press, 1967.
Frazer explores the love-death perplex that is found in most of Eugene O'Neill's
work and in much literature generally. She relates elements in O'Neill's early,
seafaring days to the play convincingly and perceptively. She notes the characteristic way in which O'Neill intermixes the literal and the symbolic, and how his
use of a cast of characters who are all outcasts of society calls to mind Maxim
Gorki's *The Lower Depths* (1912).

Lee, Robert C. "Evangelism and Anarchy in *The Iceman Cometh.*" In *Eugene
O'Neill*, edited and with an introduction by Harold Bloom. New York: Chelsea
House, 1987.
Lee begins by saying that in considering Eugene O'Neill, "one must always go
back to *The Iceman Cometh* [wr. 1939, pr. 1946], for it is both his culmination
and his demise." Lee shows the intricacy of the love-hate relationships in the
play, demonstrating how they are interwoven and how they become the play's
most significant controlling devices.

Manheim, Michael. *Eugene O'Neill's New Language of Kinship.* Syracuse, N.Y.:
Syracuse University Press, 1982.
Addressing Eugene O'Neill's use of language in *The Iceman Cometh* (wr. 1939,
pr. 1946), Manheim says that all the hostility and goodwill in the play, the two
seemingly contradictory elements, grow out of "the illusions these characters are
striving to preserve, but that is not the main point. The main point is that the
emotions themselves are authentic and the continuing rhythm of their oscillation,
albeit with variations, is assured."

_____. "The Transcendence of Melodrama in O'Neill's *The Iceman Com-
eth.*" In *Eugene O'Neill*, edited by James J. Martine. Boston: G. K. Hall, 1984.
Manheim writes about the many contradictions in *The Iceman Cometh* (wr. 1939,
pr. 1946) and explains them in terms of the two conflicting melodramas that are
unfolding as the play's two leading characters' stories are revealed. Of Harry and
Larry, Manheim says, "They each seem caught between conflicting melodramas
in their lives." To Manheim, Larry seems the better-resolved figure: "He, like
the play he speaks for, in transcending the melodramatic view of existence, leaves
us with an image of existence in flux."

Long Day's Journey into Night

Adler, Thomas P. "'Daddy Spoke to Me!': Gods Lost and Found in *Long Day's Journey into Night* and *Through a Glass Darkly*." In *Critical Approaches to O'Neill*, edited by John H. Stroupe. New York: AMS Press, 1988.
Adler explores the affinity between Eugene O'Neill and Ingmar Bergman, quoting Bergman as saying, contrary to the common opinion that all art is political, "all art has to do with ethics." Adler relates this statement to O'Neill's contention that "drama that doesn't deal with man's relation to God is worthless." He sees in the figure of Mary Tyrone a statement that is a "rejection of the burden and responsibility of married sexuality [which] occurs frequently in O'Neill's plays."

Barlow, Judith E. *Final Acts: The Creation of Three Late O'Neill Plays*. Athens, Ga.: University of Georgia Press, 1985.
Barlow's scholarly study is valuable because it provides insights into Eugene O'Neill's creative processes by focusing on the revision he made in the manuscript of *Long Day's Journey into Night* (wr. 1941, pr. 1956). The book is based upon O'Neill's manuscripts in the library of Yale University.

Bloom, Steven F. "Empty Bottles, Empty Dreams: O'Neill's use of Drinking and Alcoholism in *Long Day's Journey into Night*." In *Critical Essays on Eugene O'Neill*, edited by James J. Martine. Boston: G. K. Hall, 1984.
After Bloom makes the point that the symptoms of alcoholism and drug addiction are frequently similar, he goes on to show how the Tyrone family has, within an environment intruded upon by both of these ills, "successfully created a façade of calm and pleasant normality." Tracing through a close reading of the play the deterioration that continued alcoholism causes, Bloom concludes that this deterioration "is the life of an alcoholic, and for O'Neill, this is the life of modern man."

Bryer, Jackson R. "Hell Is Other People: *Long Day's Journey into Night*." In *The Fifties: Fiction, Poetry, Drama*, edited by Warren G. French. Deland, Fla.: Everett/Edwards, 1970.
In his brief treatment of this play, Bryer presents a thoughtful interpretation based upon the tortured and alternating interactions of the Tyrone family. He contends that *Long Day's Journey into Night* (wr. 1941, pr. 1956) "is one of the few American plays which meets most of the measures of modern tragedy."

Chothia, Jean. "*Long Day's Journey into Night*: The Dramatic Effectiveness of Supposedly Neutral Dialogue." In *Eugene O'Neill*, edited and with an introduction by Harold Bloom. New York: Chelsea House, 1987.
Chothia demonstrates how O'Neill came to control dialogue in *Long Day's Journey into Night* (wr. 1941, pr. 1956) more fully than in any of his earlier

works. She cites the melodramatic clichés of his earlier work in his attempts to show strong emotion among his characters and says that if readers "compare the strategic use to which they are put here, we have some measure of the kind of control O'Neill is exerting."

Driver, Tom F. "On the Late Plays of Eugene O'Neill." In *O'Neill: A Collection of Critical Essays*, edited by John Gassner. Englewood Cliffs, N.J.: Prentice-Hall, 1964.
Driver cautions against *ad hominem* readings of Eugene O'Neill that may lead one to think that his later plays, including *Long Day's Journey into Night* (wr. 1941, pr.1956), are chiefly concerned with the struggle between life and death and exorcising the fear of death. Driver contends that the plays are concerned with the meaning of life. "His plays declare that the meaning of life is its inevitable progression toward death."

Hinden, Michael. *Long Day's Journey into Night: Native Eloquence.* Boston: Twayne, 1990.
This contribution to Twayne's Masterwork Studies Series, following the format of that series, in part 1 presents *Long Day's Journey into Night* (wr. 1941, pr. 1956) in its historical context, then discusses the importance of the work, and then discusses its composition and critical reception. Part 2 deals with such questions as whose play it is—the parents' or the sons'—how the play qualifies as tragedy, how the play can be viewed as autobiography, and production matters. Hinden touches on the universality of the play's major themes. The book has a selected bibliography and a comprehensive index.

Kauffmann, Stanley. *Persons of the Drama: Theater Criticism and Comment.* New York: Harper & Row, 1976.
Kauffmann categorically calls Eugene O'Neill's *Long Day's Journey into Night* (wr. 1941, pr. 1956) "the best play ever written on this side of the Atlantic." He identifies the controlling technique in the play as "outburst and apology," which is precisely what keeps the momentum of the play at a high level.

Manheim, Michael. *Eugene O'Neill's New Language of Kinship.* Syracuse, N.Y.: Syracuse University Press, 1982.
Manheim's most valuable service in his discussion of *Long Day's Journey into Night* (wr. 1941, pr. 1956) is dividing the language in the play into categories and showing how the four major members of the cast fit into such categories as "hostility subsides, replaced by self-pity," "Jamie parodies his father," and "Mary, 'shocked and amused,' is contributing to a harmony they will shortly lose." This ingenious categorizing helps to show exactly how each character uses language to serve his or her own ends and how O'Neill creates dramatic tensions and alternations by manipulating language brilliantly.

Moorton, Richard F., Jr. "The Author as Oedipus in *Mourning Becomes Electra*
and *Long Day's Journey into Night.*" In *Eugene O'Neill's Century: Centennial
Views on America's Foremost Tragic Dramatist*, edited by Richard F. Moorton,
Jr. Westport, Conn.: Greenwood Press, 1991.
Moorton examines closely the theme of patricide and its attendant desire for the
mother in *Long Day's Journey into Night* (wr. 1941, pr. 1956), showing how
carefully O'Neill develops the themes of patricide and matricide in the two plays
under consideration. This psychoanalytical approach works well and poses
thought-provoking questions.

Porter, Laurin Roland. *The Banished Prince: Time, Memory, and Ritual in the Late
Plays of Eugene O'Neill*. Ann Arbor, Mich.: UMI Research Press, 1988.
The chapter Porter devotes to *Long Day's Journey into Night* (wr. 1941, pr.
1956) demonstrates the play's existentialist bent. Porter explores the Tyrones'
imprisonment in a situation from which there is no escape. The restriction and
constriction of the set intensify this sense of enclosure and entrapment.

Raleigh, John Henry. "O'Neill's *Long Day's Journey into Night* and New England
Irish-Catholicism." In *O'Neill: A Collection of Critical Essays*, edited by John
Gassner. Englewood Cliffs, N.J.: Prentice-Hall, 1964.
Raleigh finds such Irish characteristics as mercurial natures, sexual chastity (or
at least the illusion of it), turbulence, the ne'er-do-well syndrome that afflicts
many Irish families, and sentimentality a large part of the structure of *Long Day's
Journey into Night* (wr. 1941, pr. 1956). Raleigh is perceptive in saying that
"they are all animated by a tremendous zest for this life that is so terrible for
them, whiskey and all." He goes on to say that what the Tyrones fear most is
madness and death, especially suicide. He notes trenchantly, "Drink then is a
form of suicide."

Rothenberg, Albert, and Eugene D. Shapiro. "A Defense of Psychoanalysis in
Literature: *Long Day's Journey into Night* and *A View from the Bridge.*" In
Critical Approaches to O'Neill, edited by John H. Stroupe. New York: AMS
Press, 1988.
Both writers are practicing psychologists who, with valuable insights, write
comparatively about these plays by Eugene O'Neill and Arthur Miller. Especially
interesting is their discussion of the defensive structures in the two plays, which
reveals much about the differing approaches of these two major playwrights.

Sheibler, Rolf. *The Late Plays of Eugene O'Neill*. Bern, Switzerland: Francke
Verlag, 1970.
Sheibler devotes considerable space to *Long Day's Journey into Night* (wr. 1941,
pr. 1956). He focuses his attention largely on the character of Mary Tyrone, the
mother in the family, and shows how, structurally, much of the play revolves

around her. It is her moods and problems that motivate the actions of most of the other characters.

A Moon for the Misbegotten

Falk, Doris V. "Fatal Balance: O'Neill's Last Plays." In *Eugene O'Neill*, edited and with an introduction by Harold Bloom. New York: Chelsea House, 1987.
Falk considers *A Moon for the Misbegotten* (wr. 1943, pr. 1947) as part of a series that began with *The Iceman Cometh* (wr. 1939, pr. 1956), included *A Moon for the Misbegotten* and *A Touch of the Poet* (1957), and ended with *Long Day's Journey into Night* (wr. 1941, pr. 1956). Her assessment of the play is that "pathos cannot save *A Moon for the Misbegotten* from the weakness of its outward situation—the theatrical cliché of clichés, for which there is no other word but corn." She also objects to the characterization, saying that the psychologies of the characters fit too perfectly.

Kauffmann, Stanley. *Persons of the Drama: Theater Criticism and Comment*. New York: Harper & Row, 1976.
According to Kauffmann, Eugene O'Neill's *A Moon for the Misbegotten* (wr. 1939, pr. 1947) is "a kind of postscript to *Long Day's Journey into Night*" (wr. 1941, pr. 1956). He claims that if one does not know *Long Day's Journey*, *Moon* "must seem only a drawn-out series of skits and areas, chiefly concerned with a sentimental Irish boozer."

Manheim, Michael. "O'Neill's Transcendence of Melodrama in *A Touch of the Poet* and *A Moon for the Misbegotten*." In *Critical Approaches to O'Neill*, edited by John H. Stroupe. New York: AMS Press, 1988.
Manheim discusses Eugene O'Neill's *A Touch of the Poet* (1957) and *A Moon for the Misbegotten* (wr. 1943, pr. 1947) together because he thinks "they are similar chiefly in that both begin with formulaic melodramatic intrigues which are spoofed or actually displaced as the plays develop." In *A Moon for the Misbegotten*, O'Neill, Manheim writes, "goes beyond the gentle mocking of melodrama in *A Touch of the Poet* to an actual displacement of it as the play's basis of construction." Manheim points to internal evidence in support of his claim that melodrama was much on O'Neill's mind as he wrote the play, including a reference in it to the melodramatic playwright David Belasco.

_____. *Eugene O'Neill's New Language of Kinship*. Syracuse, N.Y.: Syracuse University Press, 1982.
Manheim considers *A Moon for the Misbegotten* (wr. 1943, pr. 1947) as, essentially, a mellow play. In it, he finds the language of kinship falling into two basic categories: "the kinship of everyday conversation, and the deeper kinship which comes to exist between characters who are under great emotional stress." Both

of these categories, as he points out, are present in many O'Neill plays, especially in *Long Day's Journey into Night* (wr. 1941, pr. 1956).

Raleigh, John Henry. "The Irish Atavism of *A Moon for the Misbegotten.*" In *Eugene O'Neill: A World View*, edited by Virginia Floyd. New York: Frederick Ungar, 1979.
According to Raleigh, "a kind of racial or cultural memory" is alive in Eugene O'Neill's *A Moon for the Misbegotten* (wr. 1943, pr. 1947), the artist's last play. Raleigh considers this play one of O'Neill's most Irish, possibly the most Irish. He calls O'Neill a kind of Irish patriot who ended his career by setting the play in an Irish shanty like that in which his own father was born. Perhaps Raleigh's most salient point is that to O'Neill, "suffering is a secular equivalent to the notion of Original Sin, the inescapable outcome of the human condition."

Mourning Becomes Electra

Bogard, Travis. "The Historian: *Mourning Becomes Electra* and *Ah, Wilderness!*" In *Eugene O'Neill*, edited and with an introduction by Harold Bloom. New York: Chelsea House, 1987.
Bogard discusses the great secrecy that Eugene O'Neill observed as he was writing *Mourning Becomes Electra* (1931), a play that O'Neill often referred to as "unreal realism." This essay shows the mood shifts that O'Neill underwent as he wrote this play and demonstrates the changes in the basic idea of the trilogy that these mood changes helped to motivate. Only when he decided to use the *Oresteia* of Aeschylus as his model did the play begin to take its final form, although, according to Bogard, it ended up being closer to Euripides than to Aeschylus as it developed.

Manheim, Michael. *Eugene O'Neill's New Language of Kinship*. Syracuse, N.Y.: Syracuse University Press, 1982.
Manheim devotes his fifth chapter to *Mourning Becomes Electra* (1931) and in it notes that Eugene O'Neill was not at his best when he was inventing plots; this play, whose plot was taken from classical literature, does not burden him with that task. Manheim says that the dialogue in this play, "like that in the plays most recently preceding it, is enveloped by deception, scheming, and back-biting, and taken together with the other plays . . . constitutes a kind of 'No Exit' period for O'Neill, his true dark night of the soul, his vision of Hell."

Moorton, Richard F., Jr. "The Author as Oedipus in *Mourning Becomes Electra* and *Long Day's Journey into Night*." In *Eugene O'Neill's Century: Centennial Views on America's Foremost Tragic Dramatist*, edited by Richard F. Moorton, Jr. Westport, Conn.: Greenwood Press, 1991.
The Electra theme, which permeates *Mourning Becomes Electra* (1931), is

carefully presented in this thoughtful and thought-provoking essay. Lavinia Mannon's obvious desire for her father and her subsequent murder of her mother's lover are discussed fully in a psychoanalytical context. Moorton's interpretation is both classical and formalistic.

Nugent, S. Georgia. "Masking Becomes Electra: O'Neill, Freud, and the Feminine." In *Eugene O'Neill's Century: Centennial Views on America's Foremost Tragic Dramatist*, edited by Richard F. Moorton, Jr. Westport, Conn.: Greenwood Press, 1991.
Nugent's analysis of *Mourning Becomes Electra* (1931) from a psychoanalytical-feminist perspective reveals a whole area of interpretation that has heretofore lurked in the shadows. Nugent, using modern critical techniques, probes into O'Neill's subconscious and arrives at some amazing conclusions and at a reinterpretation of the play.

Porter, Thomas E. *Myth and Modern American Drama*. Detroit: Wayne State University Press, 1969.
Claiming that Eugene O'Neill's *Mourning Becomes Electra* (1931) deals with the experience of its characters on three levels—the individual, the societal, and the transcendental—Porter shows that "these levels are presented by the playwright as interpenetrating so that the history of the House becomes the history of the tribe and ultimately part of the history of the human race and its relationship with the gods." Porter seeks to demonstrate how O'Neill experimented with the conventional mythic, tragic forms of drama, and created a unique form in this play.

Young, Stark. "Eugene O'Neill's New Play [*Mourning Becomes Electra*]." In *O'Neill: A Collection of Critical Essays*, edited by John Gassner. Englewood Cliffs, N.J.: Prentice-Hall, 1964.
Young performs a valuable service in comparing Eugene O'Neill's trilogy with its classical Greek sources, showing how O'Neill molded the classical story to his own artistic purposes. Addressing the frequent accusation that the play is depressing, Young shows why to him the play is "exhilarating."

Strange Interlude

Manheim, Michael. *Eugene O'Neill's New Language of Kinship*. Syracuse, N.Y.: Syracuse University Press, 1982.
Manheim, discussing *Strange Interlude* (1928) and *Dynamo* (1929) in the same chapter, says that if O'Neill had been possessed by death in his earlier plays, "he was absolutely obsessed with it in *Strange Interlude*." He contends that the great problem in this play is that people say very little, communicating only marginally. In O'Neill's later plays, whatever the characters "feel is spoken aloud, and

the result is a good deal of hurt and resentment but also a good deal of enlightenment." In *Strange Interlude*, the opportunity for such enlightenment is denied by a lack of communication.

A Touch of the Poet

Manheim, Michael. "O'Neill's Transcendence of Melodrama in *A Touch of the Poet* and *A Moon for the Misbegotten*." In *Critical Approaches to O'Neill*, edited by John H. Stroupe. New York: AMS Press, 1988.
Manheim discusses Eugene O'Neill's *A Touch of the Poet* (1957) and *A Moon for the Misbegotten* (wr. 1943, pr. 1947) together because he thinks "they are similar chiefly in that both begin with formulaic melodramatic intrigues which are spoofed or actually displaced as the plays develop." Manheim notes that other critics have found strong echoes of Alexandre Dumas' *The Count of Monte Cristo* (1844), the play that made the reputation of O'Neill's father but also destroyed him as an actor.

_____. "Remnants of a Cycle: *A Touch of the Poet* and *More Stately Mansions*." In *Eugene O'Neill*, edited and with an introduction by Harold Bloom. New York: Chelsea House, 1987.
Through discussing Eugene O'Neill's language of kinship, Manheim explains some of the ambiguities in *A Touch of the Poet* (1957). Manheim notes that this O'Neill play is "deceptively simple on the surface [but] is actually among O'Neill's more complex plays and must be approached from a variety of directions." Manheim approaches it from three directions: characters, plot, and dialogue. He concludes that the play has two plots, that "autobiography is central to the work," and that the play's more important action "relates to O'Neill's complex of feelings associated with his mother."

ELMER RICE

Durham, Frank. *Elmer Rice*. New York: Twayne, 1970.
Following the usual format of Twayne's United States Authors Series, Durham presents a detailed chronology followed by a biographical chapter. He then analyzes Elmer Rice's major works. Durham points out that Rice had the longest productive career in American theater, writing from 1914 until 1963. The author approaches Rice's career chronologically, showing its development through the years, showing that as American theater developed, so did Rice. Durham is honest in identifying Rice's many potboilers for what they were, but he demonstrates Rice's conscious artistry and artistic contribution as well. A selected bibliography is followed by a comprehensive index.

Greenfield, Thomas Allen. *Work and the Work Ethic in American Drama, 1920-1970*. Columbia, Mo.: University of Missouri Press, 1982.
Although Greenfield thinks that Elmer Rice allowed his technical innovations to detract from the "overall impact of his plays," he contends that "Rice's social plays, and his dramatic presentation of the theme of work in particular, are collectively the most varied, the most thoughtful, and the most innovative American social dramas of the century." This eighteen-page chapter is one of the most thoughtful assessments in print of Rice as a social dramatist.

Hogan, Robert. *The Independence of Elmer Rice*. Carbondale, Ill.: Southern Illinois University Press, 1965.
After discussing Rice's manner of writing, Hogan presents chapters on him as the writer of potboilers, the experimenter, the realist, the social conscience, the patriot, the loser, the lost, and the saved. In the final chapter, Hogan lists productions of Rice's plays between 1958 and 1963, showing that *The Adding Machine* (1923) remained his most popular, followed by *Dream Girl* (1945). He notes that Rice published forty of his plays and had another thirteen that were either unproduced or unfinished. The book, whose preface is by Harry T. Moore, has a fine bibliography and a workable index.

Newquist, Roy. *Counterpoint*. Chicago: Rand McNally, 1964.
Newquist interviewed Elmer Rice in New York in August, 1963. Rice speaks about shrinkage in the American theater, from seventy theaters offering 250 productions in the 1926-1927 season to thirty theaters offering between fifty and sixty productions in the 1962-1963 season. He blames this shrinkage on economic factors and points to its implications for playwrights, especially newcomers. He considers the period from 1919 to 1934 the "Golden Age of American Theater." He warns of the problems and frustrations that playwrights endure, especially new playwrights, noting that of every hundred plays that are written, only one is ever produced. He notes that even Off-Broadway productions have become inordinately expensive to stage.

Palmieri, Anthony F. R. *Elmer Rice: A Playwright's Vision of America*. Teaneck, N.J.: Associated University Presses, 1980.
In this study, Palmieri deals chronologically with Elmer Rice's plays. He concludes that Rice remained an innovator throughout a career that spanned four decades. He notes the playwright's early experiments with expressionism, which was relatively new to the New York stage when *The Adding Machine* (1923) came to Broadway. Eugene O'Neill's *The Emperor Jones* (1920) and *The Hairy Ape* (1922) had been the only expressionist dramas on Broadway up to that time. Palmieri notes Rice's advanced psychological dramas, which were both Freudian and Jungian in their orientations. Rice's pacifism was obvious, but with the rise of Nazism in the mid 1930's, Rice moderated his views, as did many other intellectuals of his time.

Rabkin, Gerald. *Drama and Commitment: Politics in the American Theatre of the Thirties*. Bloomington, Ind.: Indiana University Press, 1964.
Rabkin acknowledges that Elmer Rice was "acutely attuned to the intellectual vibrations of his age" but concludes that his dramas have survived because of their social content rather than their artistic excellence. He contends that only *The Adding Machine* (1923) "has been successful in fully integrating form and idea." Rabkin reviews Rice's major dramatic writing and shows how the playwright was influenced intellectually by Marxism although he distrusted its dogmatism.

Rice, Elmer. *Minority Report: An Autobiography*. New York: Simon & Schuster, 1963.
The twenty-two chapters of this long book cover most of Rice's life, but chapter 10, which tells about his Hollywood experience and his disenchantment with it, is among the most interesting. In chapters 8, 19, and 21, Rice tells how he rebounded from recurrent losses in popularity. He also provides valuable information about the early days of the Dramatists' Guild. The lack of an index is a definite limitation.

LYNN RIGGS

Braunlich, Phyllis Cole. *Haunted by Home: The Life and Letters of Lynn Riggs*. Norman, Okla.: University of Oklahoma Press, 1988.
Braunlich's is the only full biography of Riggs. It begins with his life in Santa Fe, where he lived after he grew up, then returns to Oklahoma, his original home. This is essentially the story of a gifted playwright who never quite made the mark except tangentially when his play *Green Grow the Lilacs* (1931) was transformed into the long-running musical *Oklahoma!* (1943). Braunlich's book is well documented and illustrated. It contains informative excerpts from Riggs's letters. The bibliography and index are useful.

Clark, Barrett H. *An Hour of American Drama*. Philadelphia: J. B. Lippincott, 1930.
Clark, much impressed by regional and folk drama, claims that Eugene O'Neill, Paul Green, and Lynn Riggs are the equals of any European playwrights who were writing in the post-World War I years. When Clark wrote this, Riggs's best work was still to come, so his praise is particularly impressive.

Erhard, Thomas A. *Lynn Riggs: Southwest Playwright*. Austin, Tex.: Steck-Vaughn, 1970.
Erhard's slim pamphlet (forty-four pages all told) is a contribution to the Southwest Writers Series. It has no index, but its bibliography is the best on Riggs up to 1970. Riggs had four plays produced on Broadway. His *Green Grow the Lilacs* (1931) was the archetype for *Oklahoma!* (1943), which, until *My Fair Lady* (1956), held a record with 2,248 Broadway performances. Erhard calls Riggs "the greatest playwright to come out of the Southwest," a claim that one might challenge. He contends that had regional theater been more active during Riggs's lifetime, Riggs's reputation would have been much more widespread.

Green, Paul. *Dramatic Heritage*. New York: Samuel French, 1953.
Green, who was well acquainted with Riggs's work and respected it, views the playwright as a regionalist whose ability was never fully developed and who was not recognized for the substantial contribution he made in *Green Grow the Lilacs* (1931).

Marable, Mary Hays, and Elaine Boylan. *A Handbook of Oklahoma Writers*. Norman, Okla.: University of Oklahoma Press, 1939.
This early treatment is sympathetic. It emphasizes Riggs as a regional writer who captured the essence of the area about which he was writing.

Miller, J. William. *Modern Playwrights at Work*. New York: Samuel French, 1968.
Miller presents some minimal details about Lynn Riggs's life—his place of birth,

the university he attended, where he preferred to live, and how he earned a living before he became a playwright.

Waite, Marjorie Peabody. *Yaddo, Yesterday and Today.* Albany, N.Y.: Argus Press, 1933.

Lynn Riggs was in residence from June until October, 1927, at Yaddo, the artists' colony established in 1926 on the Spencer Trask estate in Saratoga Springs, New York. He was joined there by his University of Oklahoma professor, Walter Campbell, and Campbell's wife Isabel. Riggs's residence at Yaddo resulted in his making lasting friendships with such writers as George O'Neil and in his writing *Reckless* (1928), which later became a full-length play, *Roadside* (1930).

WILLIAM SAROYAN

Calonne, David Stephen. *William Saroyan: My Real Work Is Being*. Chapel Hill, N.C.: University of North Carolina Press, 1983.
Calonne writes about a William Saroyan who was introverted, shy around people, and sensitive to the point of feeling deeply any unkindness directed toward him. For those interested in Saroyan as a dramatist, the heart of this book will be chapters 5, 6, and 7, although the rest of the book makes excellent reading. Calonne sums Saroyan up best, perhaps, in saying, "Saroyan seeks the experience of being; he wants to go straight to the core of things—energetically, immediately, passionately." Calonne shows how Saroyan sought to explore "humanity's deepest spiritual aspirations," and how he did so by concentrating on individuals "struggling to live with grace and meaning." The bibliography is impressive, the index useful.

Floan, Howard. *William Saroyan*. New York: Twayne, 1966.
Following the prescribed format of the Twayne United States Authors Series, Floan provides a detailed chronology and an initial biographical chapter. He devotes the rest of the book to analyzing Saroyan's work. In writing about the plays, he notes Saroyan's singular imagination and his ability to interweave factual reality and fantasy. He acknowledges that Saroyan, as the artist himself felt, was undeservedly neglected as a writer. This book has a selected bibliography, which is annotated, and a reliable index.

Foard, Elisabeth C. *William Saroyan: A Reference Guide*. Boston: G. K. Hall, 1989.
Foard's bibliography brings up to date Kheridan's work (see below), which was published more than two decades earlier. Her book is comprehensive, seeking "to cover all secondary materials written about author/playwright William Saroyan." After a detailed chronology, Foard lists all of Saroyan's works and, in the latter three-quarters of the book, all of the significant writings about him, including books, portions of books, articles, reviews, and interviews. The book has a detailed index.

Gassner, John. *Theatre at the Crossroads: Plays and Playwrights of the Mid-Century American Stage*. New York: Holt, Rinehart and Winston, 1960.
Gassner presents a sensitive review of William Saroyan's *The Cave Dwellers* (1957), which he calls a "symbolist-surrealist fantasy on the unity and love of mankind." He notes the generosity of the critics toward a play that could not draw audiences and that finally closed prematurely from lack of patronage.

Gelb, Arthur, and Barbara Gelb. *O'Neill*. New York: Harper & Row, Publishers, 1960, 1962, 1973, revised and expanded, 1987.
The Gelbs tell the interesting story of how seventeen-year-old Oona O'Neill, in

the year before she married Charlie Chaplin, came to California with Carol Marcus, also seventeen, to be near Carol's boyfriend, William Saroyan, who had been inducted into the army. Oona wrote love letters to Saroyan for Carol, who was unsure of her epistolary accomplishments, but Oona cribbed much that was in these letters from ones her boyfriend, Jerry, was sending her. Saroyan did not like the glib tone of the letters he supposed to be from Carol. He later found out that they originated with Jerry, otherwise known as J. D. Salinger.

Justus, James H. "William Saroyan and the Theatre of Transformation." In *The Thirties: Fiction, Poetry, Drama*, edited by Warren G. French. Deland, Fla.: Everett/Edwards, 1967.
Justus focuses essentially on how William Saroyan's vision pressed through the boundaries of reality. His plays, which made their major contributions by dealing with illusions, are philosophically concerned with the tensions between reality and illusion in the quest to find the meaning in life.

Kauffmann, Stanley. *Persons of the Drama: Theater Criticism and Comment*. New York: Harper & Row, 1976.
Writing about a 1969 revival of William Saroyan's *The Time of Your Life* (1939), Kauffmann calls it "a Well-Patched Play." He comments on the trite theme: "In the time of your life, live." He notes that the play has only one "bad" character in it—Blick, the vice-squad detective, who is on stage for so short a time that there is no real tension between good and bad in the play.

Kheridan, David. *A Bibliography of William Saroyan: 1934-1964*. San Francisco: R. Beacham, 1965.
This bibliography was much needed when it appeared. As is inevitable, it has become dated and has been replaced by Elisabeth Foard's reference guide (see above). Saroyan lived and continued to produce until 1981. Kheridan lists all of Saroyan's work as well as all the secondary materials about him up to 1964. The book is still serviceable for people who are interested in the first half of the writer's career.

Krutch, Joseph Wood. *The American Drama Since 1918*. New York: Random House, 1939; New York: George Braziller, 1957.
Krutch admires William Saroyan for his optimism and naïveté, but he speculates that the decline in his later plays is perhaps in part because of "a simple exhaustion of the vein but is probably due also to an increasing slackness in construction, and what seems to be a failure to move in any discernible direction." He mentions Saroyan's casualness about his writing, his lack of discipline. He points to "diffuse meanderings" in some of the later plays.

Lee, Lawrence, and Barry Gifford. *Saroyan: A Biography*. New York: Harper &
Row, Publishers, 1984.
Lee and Gifford have examined much material about William Saroyan and have
been tireless in interviewing members of his family and others who were associated with him professionally. Their book is filled with detail and with long
quotations from their interviews. It is concerned more with Saroyan's intriguing
life than with presenting critical analyses of his work, although the authors
comment intelligently on his plays, stories, and novels. The authors write
understandingly and trenchantly of Saroyan's reaction to his declining popularity
during the last decade of his life. The book is well illustrated and, toward the
end, has a detailed chronology. It has a thin bibliography and a comprehensive
index.

Lewis, Allan. *American Plays and Playwrights of the Contemporary Theatre*. New
York: Crown, 1965.
With the Group Theatre's presentation of *My Heart's in the Highlands* (1939),
a play that bewildered many critics, William Saroyan began the public high jinks
that made him a newsworthy playwright. Lewis comments on his "casual,
explorative improvisation in dramatic writing." He notes Saroyan's speed of
composition. In his discussion of *My Heart's in the Highlands* (1939), *Hello, Out
There* (1941), *The Cave Dwellers* (1957), and other plays, Lewis shows that
Saroyan is gifted in impulsive outbursts but is not a steady, disciplined playwright.

Saroyan, Aram. *Last Rites: The Death of William Saroyan*. New York: William
Morrow, 1982.
Aram Saroyan, William Saroyan's only son, began a journal on April 14, 1981,
when he learned that his father was dying of prostate cancer. He kept the journal
through the weeks until his father's death on May 18, 1981. In this reflective
journal, Aram reveals a great deal about his relationship to his father and about
his father's relationship to members of his immediate family. He also details how
his father in essence disinherited him and Lucy, Saroyan's only daughter, by
leaving all of his money to the William Saroyan Foundation, providing only
provisional trust accounts for his family to tap in the case of dire necessity. The
book, which has neither bibliography nor index, provides valuable insights into
the mind of a deeply troubled, highly sensitive artist who never received his due.

Sievers, W. David. *Freud on Broadway: A History of Psychoanalysis and the
American Drama*. New York: Hermitage House, 1955.
Considering William Saroyan in a section devoted to him and to Gertrude Stein,
Sievers comments on the surrealism in the work of both. He comments that
Saroyan's "early one-act plays tended to have the surrealistic, free-associational
quality of a dream." As he traces Saroyan's career and his retreat into excessive

subjectivism, Siever comments that the "passive-dependency and infantile resent-ment of the material world" that he states whimsically in his early plays had, by the time of his *Sweeney in the Trees* (1946), grown "humorless and perilously close to psychotic."

Weales, Gerald. *American Drama Since World War II.* New York: Harcourt, Brace & World, 1962.
Weales comments sparingly on William Saroyan because he had only one play, *The Cave Dwellers* (1957), on Broadway after World War II. He makes a trenchant comment, however, in saying, "The inescapable suspicion is that pessimism and optimism have no relation to objective reality for Saroyan, that they are simply projections of personal moods." He cites the lightness of *My Heart's in the Highlands* (1939) and the blackness of *Hello, Out There* (1941) to illustrate his contention.

ROBERT E. SHERWOOD

Brown, John Mason. *The Ordeal of a Playwright: Robert E. Sherwood and the Challenge of War.* New York: Harper & Row, 1970.
This second volume of Brown's two-volume biography of Robert E. Sherwood covers the years from 1937 until his death in 1955. At the beginning of the period covered, Sherwood's pacifism was severely tested by the rise of the fascists in Germany and Italy. His *Abe Lincoln in Illinois* (1938) addresses the question of peace at any cost, a decision that Lincoln had to make. *There Shall Be No Night* (1940) goes one step further toward outlining the conditions under which war is the only viable option. Brown deals with a playwright who had to cope with the problems of this inner conflict. The book has an index.

_____. *The Worlds of Robert E. Sherwood: Mirror to His Times, 1896-1936.* New York: Harper & Row, 1965.
This first volume of Brown's two-volume biography of Robert E. Sherwood traces the playwright's development from childhood up to the mid-1930's and the Depression era. A veteran of World War I, Sherwood, as a result of his wartime experience, was a committed pacifist, as is revealed in plays such as *The Road to Rome* (1927), *Acropolis* (1933), and *Idiot's Delight* (1936). Brown, who devotes chapters 16 to 28 of the book to Sherwood specifically as a playwright, shows him as a developing playwright who frequently selected pacifist themes for his plays. This pacifism and Sherwood's romantic liberalism, however, did not work philosophically for the playwright in the face of what was going on in Hitler's Germany, and Sherwood's pacifist posture was changing by the end of the period this book covers.

Meserve, Walter J. *Robert E. Sherwood: Reluctant Moralist.* New York: Pegasus, 1970.
Meserve considers the moral dilemmas and ethical considerations with which Sherwood dealt in his plays. He sees Sherwood as a man of convictions, but one who was not inherently an activist in promoting them. In plays such as *Abe Lincoln in Illinois* (1938) and most particularly in *There Shall Be No Night* (1940), however, Sherwood is drawn into making a political statement. In the latter case, he had to renounce his long-held pacifism and admit that war is necessary in some situations. Sherwood's Lincoln play was also a step in this development.

Sahu, N. S. *Theatre of Protest and Anger: Studies in the Dramatic Works of Maxwell Anderson and Robert E. Sherwood.* Delhi, India: Amar Prakashan, 1988.
Sahu perhaps overstates the case when he talks about protest and anger in the plays of Robert E. Sherwood, whose transition from committed pacifist to

someone who realized that war is sometimes necessary is reflected in such plays as *The Road to Rome* (1927), *Waterloo Bridge* (1930), *Abe Lincoln in Illinois* (1938), and finally in *There Shall Be No Night* (1940) and *Small War on Murray Hill* (1957). Sahu defends his thesis, nevertheless, somewhat more convincingly in his comments about Sherwood than he does in those he makes about Maxwell Anderson. The book has a selected bibliography and an index.

Shuman, R. Baird. *Robert E. Sherwood*. New York: Twayne, 1964.
Following the format of Twayne's United States Authors Series, Shuman provides a detailed chronology and an initial biographical chapter, followed by chapters arranged in chronological order that analyze Robert E. Sherwood's works. Shuman notes Sherwood's leadership in founding the Playwrights' Producing Company and his presidency of the American National Theatre and Academy. The annotated bibliography is useful, and the index is comprehensive.

Sievers, W. David. *Freud on Broadway: A History of Psychoanalysis and the American Drama*. New York: Hermitage House, 1955.
In his seven-page section that focuses on Robert E. Sherwood, Sievers states that in the playwright's answer to a questionnaire Sievers distributed as he was preparing this book, Sherwood said that *Reunion in Vienna* (1931) and *The Petrified Forest* (1935) are his most Freudian plays. Sievers, however, finds strong Freudian overtones in most of Sherwood's dramas and presents compelling information in support of his contention. This book has an index of names and titles. It has a chapter-by-chapter bibliography and is well documented.

THORNTON WILDER

General Studies

Burbank, Rex J. *Thornton Wilder*. New York: Twayne, 1961; rev. ed., Boston: Twayne, 1978.
Burbank's *Thornton Wilder* is the first full-length study of this dramatist. The original edition deals with all the plays except *Plays for Bleecker Street* (1962), a group of three one-act plays designed to be an evening's entertainment. The final chapter on limitations and achievement, although quite brief, makes some valuable generalizations. Following the usual format of Twayne's United States Authors Series, Burbank provides a detailed chronology, an initial biographical chapter, chapters that analyze Wilder's works, an annotated bibliography, and a comprehensive index. Biographical details are updated in the revised edition of this book.

Broussard, Louis. *American Drama: Contemporary Allegory from Eugene O'Neill to Tennessee Williams*. Norman, Okla.: University of Oklahoma Press, 1962.
Broussard devotes chapter 6 of his eight-chapter book to a consideration of Thornton Wilder. He is especially appreciative of *Our Town* (1938) as an important vehicle for bringing expressionism to the popular American stage. He notes how Wilder was reaching toward expressionism in his early career, as is quite evident in his *The Happy Journey to Trenton and Camden* (1931) and *The Long Christmas Dinner* (1931), which experiment with handling generational time as Wilder was later to use it so well in *Our Town*. Broussard's illustrated volume has an interesting bibliography and an accurate index.

Edelstein, J. M. *A Bibliographical Checklist of the Writings of Thornton Wilder*. New Haven, Conn.: Yale University Press, 1959.
This early bibliography of Thornton Wilder's work was extremely useful in its day and is still of limited use to Wilder scholars.

Goldstein, Malcolm. *The Art of Thornton Wilder*. Lincoln, Nebr.: University of Nebraska Press, 1965.
Goldstein's book follows a conventional format, with one biographical chapter followed by several chapters that analyze Wilder's plays and seek to identify pervasive themes in them. Chapter 2, which focuses on Wilder's undergraduate plays, is particularly interesting as a means of seeing how the playwright developed. The volume contains a bibliographical note and an index.

Goldstone, Richard H. *Thornton Wilder: An Intimate Portrait*. New York: Saturday Review Press/Dutton, 1975.

One of the more perceptive books on Thornton Wilder, this volume presents accurate and cogent biographical information along with shrewd analyses of all of Wilder's major works. The book recognizes Wilder's personal insecurities and their effects upon his work. Goldstone has a fine sense of Wilder's expansiveness and his considerable humaneness.

_____, and Gary Anderson. *Thornton Wilder: An Annotated Bibliography of Works by and about Thornton Wilder.* New York: AMS Press, 1982.
The first part of this Wilder bibliography lists Wilder's works, interviews, homages, published letters, and so forth. The second part lists critical material about Wilder and reviews. It contains a section of dissertations. The final part, entitled "Indices," contains a name index and title indexes for Wilder's work and for secondary materials relating to him.

Gould, Jean. *Modern American Playwrights.* New York: Dodd, Mead, 1966.
Chapter 10 of this fourteen-chapter book is devoted to Thornton Wilder. The author points to both his erudition and his encompassing humanity. Wilder's plays demonstrate an unusual interest in the family. Wilder is concerned broadly with the family of humankind, with a generalized family that has a great deal to do with the fellowship of all human beings.

Guthrie, Tyrone. "The World of Thornton Wilder." In *American Theater: A Collection of Critical Essays,* edited by Alvin Kernan. Englewood Cliffs, N.J.: Prentice-Hall, 1967.
Recognizing Thornton Wilder's conscious use of symbols, Guthrie goes on to say that the essence of the playwright's theatrical creed is "that the theater is a place where actors and audience meet in a game." He says that Wilder does not use the stage to imitate nature but rather to bring forth, as economically as possible, a series of images. He likes bare stages because they demand more imagination of audiences than full sets do. Guthrie presents extremely telling personal insights into Wilder.

Haberman, Donald. *The Plays of Thornton Wilder.* Middletown, Conn.: Wesleyan University Press, 1967.
Haberman covers essential biographical details but focuses his major attention on the identification of Wilder's themes, which provided much of the impetus for his writing. Haberman understands well Wilder's psychological makeup and is able to use this knowledge as a key to interpreting the plays. The book's individual chapters consider such topics as religious implications in the plays (chapter 2), questions of universality (chapter 3), characterization and narration (chapter 4), the use of language (chapter 5), and the uses of myth (chapter 6). The book is well researched and thoughtfully presented.

Lewis, Allan. *American Plays and Playwrights of the Contemporary Theatre*. New York: Crown, 1965.
In chapter 4, Lewis considers Thornton Wilder and William Saroyan in tandem, concluding that Wilder is the more careful and deliberate craftsman. Of Wilder he says that "after painful analysis, he arrives at the awe and wonder of the simple things in life," pinpointing exactly what it is that makes Wilder the successful playwright he is. He notes that the musical *Hello, Dolly* (1963) is based on Wilder's *The Matchmaker* (1954). Lewis discusses *Our Town* (1938), *The Skin of Our Teeth* (1942), and *Plays for Bleecker Street* (1962) in some detail. He notes Wilder's expressionism and his innovative use of the narrator, which several later playwrights, including T. S. Eliot and Langston Hughes, adopted.

Papajewski, Helmut. *Thornton Wilder*. Translated by John Conway. New York: Frederick Ungar, 1968.
This compact volume is aimed essentially at European readers of Wilder's work. It offers a biographical overview, analyses of Wilder's major works, a bibliography, and an index. Papajewski synopsizes, but not at the expense of analysis. He understands the themes with which Wilder works and deals with them well, considering the book's brevity. Papajewski explains that European audiences think of Wilder as a traditionalist, which is not the way he is viewed in his own country.

Simon, Linda. *Thornton Wilder: His World*. Garden City, N.Y.: Doubleday, 1979.
Simon's book concentrates more on Wilder's life than on his work, and her presentation is fascinating. She traces his development from his early years in Wisconsin through his years in China, where his father was a diplomat, to his incredibly rapid rise to celebrity status with the production of *The Trumpet Shall Sound* (1927). Simon deals in passing with Wilder's homosexuality, which was of considerable concern to him, accounting in part perhaps for the bouts of self-doubt he endured and for his lack of self-confidence, which resulted in his having a quite modest demeanor. This illustrated book has an extensive bibliography and a reliable index.

Our Town

Atkinson, Brooks. "Mrs. Roosevelt on *Our Town*." In *The Passionate Playgoer*, edited by G. Oppenheimer. New York: Viking Press, 1958.
Atkinson, reporting on Eleanor Roosevelt's reaction to *Our Town* (1938), commented that the play had "moved her and depressed her beyond words." He reports that she said, "*Our Town* is interesting and original and I am glad I saw it, but I did not have a pleasant evening." Wilder's mother and sister were reported to have had similar reactions.

Atkinson, Brooks, and Albert Hirschfeld. *The Lively Years: 1920-1973*. New York: Association Press, 1973.
The authors devote three pages to *Our Town* (1938), commenting on Wilder's experimental technique, his handling of time, his use of language, and his social awareness.

Cohn, Ruby. *Dialogue in American Drama*. Bloomington, Ind.: Indiana University Press, 1971.
Cohn comments on the simplicity of Wilder's dialogue in *Our Town* (1938). She notes Wilder's debt to Gertrude Stein in his minimalist, essentialist approach to using language.

Downer, Alan S. *Fifty Years of American Drama, 1900-1950*. Chicago: Henry Regnery, 1951.
Downer, in a book that is largely a broad overview, comments that *Our Town* (1938) "is totally void of sensationalism, yet it took its place at once in the standard repertory of the American theater, as a kind of celebration of the humble."

Haberman, Donald. *Our Town: An American Play*. Boston: Twayne, 1989.
This contribution to Twayne's Masterwork Studies Series first considers *Our Town* (1938) in its historical context, then discusses the play's importance and its critical reception. It then considers the play in the light of four general topics: daily life, love and marriage, questions of the eternal, and the play on stage. Haberman considers *Our Town* to be a quintessential play depicting American life. He provides a well-selected bibliography and a useful index.

Herron, Ima Honaker. *The Small Town in American Drama*. Dallas, Tex.: Southern Methodist University Press, 1969.
Herron applauds Wilder for his refusal to write the kind of pseudorealistic, sentimental play that a work like *Our Town* (1938) might have become. She calls the play original, its drama stylized. She captures Wilder's method by simply saying, "*Our Town* presents the life ritual—the plain, uneventful life in a New Hampshire town—through relatively simple action." It is his mastery of this relatively simple action that gave Wilder his greatest impact. Herron compares *Our Town* to *Everyman*.

Hagopian, John V., and Martin Dolch. *Insight I: Analysis of American Literature*. Frankfurt, Germany: Hirschgraben-Verlag, 1971.
This six-page presentation is aimed at presenting Wilder's play to European audiences. The authors make a great deal of his expressionistic techniques, which were a mainstay of German theater when Wilder's *Our Town* (1938) was first making its impact.

McCarthy, Mary. *Sights and Spectacles, 1937-1956*. New York: Farrar, Straus and
Cudahy, 1956.
The usually acerb Mary McCarthy thought the play was "essentially lyric, not
dramatic." She concludes that "Mr. Wilder, in attempting to give [his] themes
theatrical form, was obliged, paradoxically, to abandon almost all conventions
of the theatre." She accuses the play itself of being "a refutation of its own
thesis."

Porter, Thomas E. *Myth and Modern Drama*. Detroit: Wayne State University
Press, 1969.
Porter devotes twenty-four pages to his discussion of Wilder's *Our Town* (1938),
pointing out the strong ritualistic elements of the play. He claims that Wilder
"canonizes . . .[an] indefatigable American optimism." He contends that by the
end of the play, "the mode of presentation and the content mesh inextricably
together." This is one of the more challenging extended essays on Wilder's most
celebrated play.

The Skin of Our Teeth

Atkinson, Brooks, and Albert Hirschfeld. *The Lively Years: 1920-1973*. New York:
Association Press, 1973.
In the four pages they devote to *The Skin of Our Teeth* (1942), the authors
comment on the timeliness of the play and on Wilder's unique use of his time
frame. They note basic structural changes that have occurred in his writing as
it has progressed.

Bauland, Peter. *The Hooded Eagle*. Syracuse, N.Y.: Syracuse University Press,
1968.
The brief portion of this book that is devoted to *The Skin of Our Teeth* (1942)
recognizes its experimental techniques as well as its ability to reach audiences
and succeed commercially. The play was right for its time.

Cohn, Ruby. *Dialogue in American Drama*. Bloomington, Ind.: Indiana University
Press, 1971.
Cohn notes Wilder's debt to James Joyce's *Finnegans Wake* (1939) in *The Skin
of Our Teeth* (1942). She also mentions his debt to Pirandello, noting that
Pirandello suggested in his theater trilogy "that the flux of reality will always
intrude into the conventions of theater."

Gilder, Rosamond. *Theatre Arts Anthology*. New York: Theatre Arts, 1950.
Gilder's was one of the most ecstatic reviews of *The Skin of Our Teeth* (1942).
She effused, "When the breath of creative imagination blows through the theatre,
what exhilaration to the lungs, what refreshment to the spirit!" She goes on to
call the play Wilder's tribute "to the indestructibility of the human race."

Herron, Ima Honaker. *The Small Town in American Drama*. Dallas, Tex.: Southern
   Methodist University Press, 1969.
   Recognizing Wilder's experimental technique in *The Skin of Our Teeth* (1942),
   Herron notes the timeliness of the play, which was completed shortly after the
   United States had entered World War II. It deals with humanity's "conflict with
   ignorance, folly, and [with] the general malaise through which our civilization
   was passing at the time the play was written." Herron is especially interested in
   Wilder's use of time.

TENNESSEE WILLIAMS

General Studies

Arnott, Catherine M., comp. *Tennessee Williams on File*. New York: Methuen, 1985.
This eighty-page book is part of Methuen's Writers on File Series. It lists short excerpts from key reviews of Williams' work, including a brief section on his nondramatic writing, a six-page segment on Williams' own comments about his work, and a selected bibliography.

Bigsby, C. W. E. *A Critical Introduction to Twentieth Century American Drama 2: Williams/Miller/Albee*. Cambridge, England: Cambridge University Press, 1984.
Bigsby examines Williams' plays carefully, paying particular attention to Williams' naturalism and determinism. He emphasizes the role of ambiguity in Williams' writing. This volume, which is presumably aimed at a sophisticated world audience rather than one that is narrowly American, is penetrating. Its bibliography is helpful, its index dependable.

Bock, Hedwig. "Tennessee Williams: Southern Playwright." In *Essays on Contemporary American Drama*, edited by Hedwig Bock and Albert Wertheim. Munich, Germany: Max Hüber Verlag, 1981.
Bock examines Williams' use of the southern myth and relates it to the psychological development of the plays and the neuroses associated with them. She is reasonably effective in penetrating Williams' subconscious through her interpretations of recurrent symbols and images in his plays.

Clarke, Gerald. *Capote: A Biography*. New York: Simon & Schuster, 1988.
Truman Capote's friendship with Tennessee Williams was a most tempestuous one but one on which Capote came to depend. Clarke goes into the interesting dynamics of Carson McCullers' attempt to turn Williams against Capote after her friendship with Williams turned to enmity, citing letters from McCullers to Williams. Clarke's excellent index will easily lead readers to his comments about the Capote-Williams friendship.

Cohn, Ruby. *Dialogue in American Drama*. Bloomington, Ind.: Indiana University Press, 1971.
The fourth chapter of this book (pages 97-129) is entitled "The Garrulous Grotesques of Tennessee Williams." Cohn shows how Williams, in reshaping his own work, in turning short plays and short stories into full-blown dramas, achieves what she calls his "dialogue of pathos." She attributes his dialogue, not

surprisingly, to his southern background. She points out that Williams moves beyond Eugene O'Neill in his use of "colloquial rhythms and idiom" and reacts against O'Neill "in his profuse images and relatively complicated syntax." This well-documented book has a bibliography and an index.

Courtney, Marguerite. *Laurette*. New York: Rinehart, 1955.
This biography of Laurette Taylor, whose portrayal of the mother in the original production of *The Glass Menagerie* (1944) helped to establish that play as a rousing success, contains valuable insights about Williams as well as about Taylor, who almost scuttled *The Glass Menagerie* by appearing for the dress rehearsal almost too drunk to stand. Williams' career and Taylor's are intricately interwoven, and this book provides reliable information about this interweaving.

Devlin, Albert J., ed. *Conversations with Tennessee Williams*. Jackson, Miss.: University of Mississippi Press, 1986.
This valuable collection contains articles by and interviews with people who knew and had worked closely with Williams. One of the pieces is William Inge's first article on Tennessee Williams, which was published in the St. Louis *Star-Times* in 1944, shortly before *The Glass Menagerie* (1944) opened in Chicago. Among those included in the volume are Rex Reed, Henry Hewes, Edward R. Murrow, Mike Wallace, Studs Terkel, David Frost, and Arthur Gelb. A chronology of Williams' life and work provides a useful resource; the index is full and accurate.

Donahue, Francis. *The Dramatic World of Tennessee Williams*. New York: Frederick Ungar, 1964.
Donahue bases his book on a series of articles Robert Rice wrote on Williams for the *New York Post* in April and May, 1958. He considers Williams' chaotic personal life, his difficult relationships, and his ability to draw on the painful elements in his life to create his dramas. Donahue also identifies Williams' basic themes as sex, especially homosexuality; violence; and neuroticism. He probes into Williams' psyche as deeply as he can to try to understand the sources of Williams' self-doubt and how this self-doubt is reflected in the works. It is self-doubt, too, that kept Williams writing, trying to prove his ability long after he had quite convincingly done so.

Falk, Signi. *Tennessee Williams*. New York: Twayne, 1968; 2d ed., Boston: Twayne, 1978.
Both editions of Falk's biography are among the most significant books published in Twayne's United States Authors Series. Both volumes provide a chronology of Williams' life, an annotated bibliography, and an index. Falk pays closest attention to Williams' use of character types in his plays, concentrating on how his characters relate to other characters within the plays, using these connections as clues to understanding "what that relationship says of [Williams'] view of the

world." The first four chapters pay particular attention to the effect that the South had on Williams as a writer.

Fedder, Norman J. *The Influence of D. H. Lawrence on Tennessee Williams.* The Hague: Mouton, 1966.
Fedder makes an effort (that at times seems a bit contrived) to prove that Williams was influenced substantially by D. H. Lawrence. Certainly, in his emphasis on sensuality, Williams seems to be Lawrence's heir, but the question of whether a direct influence exists is not answered authoritatively in this book.

Gunn, Drewey Wayne. *Tennessee Williams: A Bibliography.* Metuchen, N.J.: Scarecrow Press, 1980.
Gunn lists fifty theses or dissertations, more than four hundred critical articles or chapters in books, eighty interviews, and thirty-three volumes of collected reviews of Tennessee Williams' work. This book is somewhat outdated but is still immensely valuable to researchers.

Hirsch, Foster. *A Portrait of the Artist: The Plays of Tennessee Williams.* Port Washington, N.Y.: Kennikat Press, 1979.
After an initial biographical chapter, Foster delves into the plays, beginning with *Battle of Angels* (1940) and considering the other plays up to 1978 under such chapter titles as "Three Dark Plays" and "Two 'Affirmative' Plays." Hirsch stresses Williams' similarity to Joyce, sometimes straining to make his points, although his ideas regarding this similarity are thought provoking. The book has solid documentation, a selected bibliography, and an accurate index.

Jackson, Esther Merle. *The Broken World of Tennessee Williams.* Madison, Wis.: University of Wisconsin Press, 1966.
The most compelling chapter in this book is chapter 4, "The Anti-Hero." It is followed by "The Plastic Theatre" and by a chapter that provides shrewd interpretations of Williams' *Camino Real* (1953). Jackson contends that in Williams' plays "a whole art of writing, staging, acting, and design has resulted which has synthesized elements drawn from European drama with purely native forms." She claims that up to the date of her writing, Williams had not achieved an organic unity in his plays, attributing this to a "fundamental internal antagonism, an inner conflict between experience and meaning, poetry and logic, appearance and reality." Nevertheless, she lauds his poetic technique, claiming that it has helped him to develop a new form of writing.

Kerr, Walter. "Albee, Miller, Williams." In *Thirty Plays Hath November: Pain and Pleasure in the Contemporary Theater,* edited by Walter Kerr. New York: Simon & Schuster, 1969.
Kerr laments the passing of the vigorous Tennessee Williams who gave the public

The Glass Menagerie (1944) and *A Streetcar Named Desire* (1947), citing his *The Milk Train Doesn't Stop Here Anymore* (1967) as an exercise in self-parody. He compares this Williams failure with William Inge's *Natural Affection* (1963), also a failure, and *Natural Affection* comes off as not quite so assertive a self-parody as *Milk Train*, because Inge still writes with vigor, "whereas Mr. Williams is writing palely and more vulnerably."

Kauffmann, Stanley. *Persons of the Drama: Theater Criticism and Comment*. New York: Harper & Row, 1976.
Kauffmann has interesting comments on several Tennessee Williams plays, including the revival of *Cat on a Hot Tin Roof* (1955), *Out Cry* (1973), *Slapstick Tragedy* (1966), and *Small Craft Warnings* (1972). This critic regards Williams as one of the two most significant American playwrights but acknowledges the limitations of some of his plays.

Lewis, Allan. *American Plays and Playwrights of the Contemporary Theatre*. New York: Crown, 1965.
In his retrospective look at Tennessee Williams, Allan Lewis concludes that this once-talented playwright "either has reached the point of exhaustion or has grown submissive to commercial demands." Lewis reviews many of Williams' plays in his essay and points out that although the times have changed drastically since the 1940's, Williams has not changed with the times. He claims that Williams' fault is not that he has pursued the same theme for so many years but that he has not expanded and enriched it.

Londre, Felicia Hardison. *Tennessee Williams*. New York: Frederick Ungar, 1979.
This book, part of Ungar's World Dramatists Series, essentially considers Williams' early one-act plays and early full-length plays (from *Battle of Angels*, 1940, to *Night of the Iguana*, 1961) in the first and second sections and his later one-act plays and full-length plays (from *The Milk Train Doesn't Stop Here Anymore*, 1963, to *The Two Character Play*,1967) in the third and fourth sections. The book has halftone illustrations, a bibliography, and an index.

McCann, John S. *The Critical Reputation of Tennessee Williams: A Reference Guide*. Boston, G. K. Hall, 1983.
This comprehensive guide updates Gunn's bibliography (see above) somewhat. McCann lists more than 2,500 articles written on Tennessee Williams between 1939 and 1981. McCann works hard to be exhaustive and neutral in his approach to Williams' work.

Miller, J. William. *Modern Playwrights at Work*. New York: Samuel French, 1968.
Miller, in a fifty-one-page chapter on Tennessee Williams, gives considerable background information. He then launches into a valuable discussion of Williams'

work habits culled from interviews with and articles about the playwright. He discusses the three phases Williams thinks a playwright goes through in the creation of a play.

Nelson, Benjamin. *Tennessee Williams: The Man and His Work*. New York: Obolensky, 1961.
Nelson focuses on Williams' output during the 1940's and 1950's, giving accurate readings and reasonable interpretations of them. His book has been superseded by later appraisals of the playwright, although it made a significant contribution in its day.

Phillips, Gene D. *The Films of Tennessee Williams*. East Brunswick, N.J.: Associated University Presses, 1980.
This detailed book shows how Williams' plays, often much against his wishes, were altered for filming. Williams was involved in some of the film adaptations, but even when he was involved, his wishes were often ignored.

Rader, Dotson. *Tennessee: Cry of the Heart*. Garden City, N.Y.: Doubleday, 1985.
Rader presents an intimate, sometimes sentimental, sometimes gossipy informal view of his longtime friend Tennessee Williams, whom he saw regularly until the playwright's death in 1983. The book is based on Rader's diaries and on notes he took during his long association with Williams. Dotson provides insightful information about audience reaction to Williams' plays and Williams' reactions to his audiences. Those who wish to know more about Williams' sexual orientation can glean a great deal from this book, although other sources are equally informative on this matter, particularly Spoto's biography (see the entry below).

St. Just, Maria. *Five O'clock Angel: Letters of Tennessee Williams to Maria St. Just, 1948-1982*. New York: Alfred A. Knopf, 1990.
Williams met Maria St. Just on June 11, 1948, in London at a party given by John Gielgud. From that time until shortly before his death, he wrote scores of letters to her, and they are the substance of this book. The two had some common elements in their backgrounds—both were raised by their grandmothers—and they had a genuine fondness for each other, although their association was platonic. The letters provide a look at Williams during many unguarded moments and are interesting from that standpoint.

Shaland, Irene. *Tennessee Williams on the Soviet Stage*. New York: University Press of America, 1987.
In this slender volume's five chapters, Shaland writes about the earliest performances of Tennessee Williams' plays in Moscow, where *The Glass Menagerie* (1944) was first presented in 1969, followed by performances of *A Streetcar*

Named Desire (1947) in 1971. Shaland notes ways in which both plays were altered to conform with political requirements. When the latter play was performed in Leningrad in 1982, however, it was changed much less than it had been a decade earlier. Shaland comments on the Moscow and Leningrad performances of *Kingdom of Earth* (1968) in 1977 and 1978, respectively. *Orpheus Descending* (1957) and *Sweet Bird of Youth* (1959) were among the most heavily censored Williams plays to be presented in the Soviet Union.

Smith, Bruce. *Costly Performances: Tennessee Williams, The Last Stage.* New York: Paragon House, 1990.
In this illustrated volume, Smith considers what he calls the "Janus" key to understanding Tennessee Williams; the personal life is one face, and the dramatic side is the other. Smith traces the origins and names of Williams' protagonists. Smith, a longtime friend of Williams, had an intimate insight into Williams' relationship with his family. He writes, "What he couldn't find in the family, he made from the stuff and personalities of the life about him."

Spoto, Donald. *The Kindness of Strangers: The Life of Tennessee Williams.* Boston: Little, Brown, 1985.
Spoto's biography is the most comprehensive one on Tennessee Williams to date, yet it is not wholly satisfying, and it does not deal with the individual plays analytically. Instead, it details Williams' life and treats the plays in relation to his life. It is thorough yet frequently bland. It is well documented but often lifeless. Its bibliography is extensive, and its index is full and reliable.

Stanton, Stephen S. *Tennessee Williams: A Collection of Critical Essays.* Englewood Cliffs, N.J.: Prentice-Hall, 1977.
The first section of this book of fifteen essays deals with Williams' plays and contains essays by Robert Heilman, Gerald Weales, Harold Clurman, Thomas Adler, and Ruby Cohn—Cohn's contribution is the chapter on Williams from her book listed above. Section 2 deals with thematic matters such as the antihero, the predicament of women, fugitives, the search for God, and self-portraits, with essays by Thomas Adler, Nancy Tischler, Arthur Ganz, Esther Merle Jackson, and others. A very short final section considers work in progress. The book has a chronology and a selected bibliography but no index.

Steen, Mike. *A Look at Tennessee Williams.* New York: Hawthorn Books, 1969.
Steen, a friend of Williams, has presented a book that he freely admits is one-sided. It is, nevertheless, revealing because Steen has included extensive interviews with many of the people who knew the playwright best. Among those interviewed are William Inge, Rip Torn, Jessica Tandy, Hume Cronyn, Hal Wallis, Shelley Winters, Karl Malden, Paul Bowles, and George Cukor. The book is well illustrated and has a comprehensive index.

Tharpe, Jac, ed. *Tennessee Williams: 13 Essays*. Jackson, Miss.: University Press of Mississippi, 1980.
The most challenging essays in this collection, which has a solid bibliography and an excellent index, are Norman J. Fedders' "Tennessee Williams' Dramatic Technique," Leonard Casper's "Triangles of Transaction in Tennessee Williams," George N. Niesen's "The Artist Against Reality in the Plays of Tennessee Williams," and Peggy W. Prenshaw's "The Paradoxical Southern World of Tennessee Williams."

_____, ed. *Tennessee Williams: A Tribute*. Jackson, Miss.: University of Mississippi Press, 1977.
Tharpe has collected fifty-three essays about Tennessee Williams and his work for this varied volume. Among the contributors are Jacob H. Adler, Esther M. Jackson, Normand Berlin, Philip C. Kolin, Charles E. May, Nancy M. Tischler, Philip M. Armato, and William E. Taylor. The book is divided into a section on *A Streetcar Named Desire* (1947) and one section each on the other plays, the European contexts, themes, prose and poetry, techniques, and final assessments. The bibliography is well selected, and the index is dependable.

Thompson, Judith J. *Tennessee Williams's Plays: Memory, Myth, and Symbol*. New York: Peter Lang, 1987.
This volume in the University of Kansas' Humanistic Series provides a valuable modern reading of Williams' plays, placing them in the existential tradition. Thompson searches for Williams' archetypes, finding them by examining closely his classical allusions. This is one of the most sophisticated and intelligent readings of Williams' plays. The book is highly recommended.

Tischler, Nancy M. *Tennessee Williams: Rebellious Puritan*. New York: Citadel Press, 1965.
Tischler perhaps strains too hard to substantiate her thesis that Williams is at heart a puritan in rebellion. His short story "The Yellow Bird" (1944), however, from which *Summer and Smoke* (1947) was derived, would make one suspect that such was the case. This book presents interesting questions about Williams' romanticism. It shows how he uses autobiographical elements in his plays. Its bibliography and index are helpful.

Tynan, Kenneth. "American Blues: The Plays of Arthur Miller and Tennessee Williams." In *American Theater: A Collection of Critical Essays*, edited by Alvin Kernan. Englewood Cliffs, N.J.: Prentice-Hall, 1967.
Although he finds fundamental differences between Arthur Miller and Tennessee Williams, one a playwright of action, the other a "poet *manqué*," Tynan sees a fundamental connection between the two: "Miller is a rebel against, Williams a refugee from the familiar ogre of commercialism, the killer of values and the

168   *American Drama: 1918–1960*

leveller of men." He calls Miller's plays "patrist," Williams' "matrist." He concludes that Miller and Williams "have produced the most powerful body of dramatic prose in modern English," claiming that they write with equal power from two antithetical points of view.

Williams, Dakin, and Shepherd Mead. *Tennessee Williams: An Intimate Biography.* New York: Arbor House, 1983.
In this biography, published shortly after Tennessee Williams' death, his brother shares reminiscences of the playwright from what appears at times to be a somewhat faulty memory base. That Dakin did not understand his brother or his sexual orientation is evident from this book, which is intended to be a sympathetic presentation but which, when read closely, turns out to be neither sympathetic nor objective.

Williams, Edwina Dakin, as told to Lucy Freeman. *Remember Me to Tom.* New York: G. P. Putnam's Sons, 1963.
Tennessee Williams' mother, Edwina, kept a full file of materials relating to her son from the time he was a struggling playwright through his years of celebrity. This book is a memoir of her son based sometimes on the facts of his life, sometimes on a mother's reconstruction of a son to fit her specifications. The book is not always factually dependable, but it is full of insights with which any serious scholar of Williams must be familiar. Especially interesting are the portions of many of Williams' letters that are reproduced in the book and the extensive illustrations.

Camino Real

Miller, Jordan Y. "*Camino Real.*" In *The Fifties: Fiction, Poetry, Drama*, edited by Warren G. French. Deland, Fla.: Everett/Edwards, 1970.
Miller deals in eight pages with one of Tennessee Williams' most perplexing plays. He realizes its shortcomings but also sees it as an important indication of the way in which Williams' career was moving, getting further and further away from realism and escaping increasingly into fantasy.

Cat on a Hot Tin Roof

Kauffmann, Stanley. *Persons of the Drama: Theater Criticism and Comment.* New York: Harper & Row, 1976.
Kauffmann's analysis of Williams' meaning in a 1974 revival of *Cat on a Hot Tin Roof* (1955) is impressive. This play, surging with homosexual overtones, reflected many of the sexual tensions that Williams dealt with throughout his life. Kauffman's insights regarding Brick's sexuality are useful, but his interpretation of Big Daddy is especially impressive. Kauffmann calls Williams "one of the two

American dramatists of substance" but contends that this is not one of his best plays.

The Glass Menagerie

Greenfield, Thomas Allen. *Work and the Work Ethic in American Drama, 1920-1970*. Columbia, Mo.: University of Missouri Press, 1982.
Discussing *The Glass Menagerie* (1944) in the context of a chapter that also considers two Arthur Miller plays, Greenfield calls Amanda Wingfield a representative of "the dying but not quite dead pre-industrial work values of rural America." Her son Tom's problem is that warring within him is his desire for adventure and the need to conform to traditional values related to the work ethic. He calls Laura a hopeless prisoner of a system that adheres to that ethic.

Presley, Delma E. *The Glass Menagerie: An American Memory*. Boston: Twayne, 1990.
Following the format of the Twayne Masterwork Studies Series, Presley presents a chronology followed by a chapter that establishes the historical context of the play. This is followed by a chapter on the critical reception of the play. The author provides lists of primary and secondary sources relating to this drama. The book has a reliable index.

A Streetcar Named Desire

Adler, Thomas P. *A Streetcar Named Desire: The Moth and the Lantern*. Boston: Twayne, 1990.
In his contribution to Twayne's Masterwork Series, Adler provides a chronology, then presents the play in its historical context. He goes on to discuss the importance of the work and its critical reception in separate chapters. His final eight chapters are devoted to a reading of the play, considering in separate chapters its structure, style, four of its characters (Blanche, Stanley, Stella, and Mitch), further perspectives, and themes. The bibliography is well selected, and the index is comprehensive.

Clurman, Harold. "Tennessee Williams." In *The Divine Pastime: Theatre Essays*. New York: Macmillan, 1974.
Although Clurman's essay is only seven pages long, it is one of the most comprehensive reviews in print of *A Streetcar Named Desire*'s (1947) production. Clurman views the play from the production standpoint, and his observations are astute.

Hurrell, John D., ed. *Two Modern American Tragedies: Reviews and Criticism of "Death of a Salesman" and "A Streetcar Named Desire."* New York: Charles Scribner's Sons, 1961.

Hurrell has gathered many early reviews of and articles about the two plays under consideration here and, in doing so, has provided those interested in Arthur Miller and Tennessee Williams a substantial service. The selection is representative and helpful.

Jones, David Richard. *Great Directors at Work: Stanislavsky, Brecht, Kazan, Brook.* Berkeley: University of California Press, 1986.
Aside from Elia Kazan's own account of directing *A Streetcar Named Desire* (1947, see below), this is one of the most perceptive accounts of Kazan's approach to directing the original production of the play. It carefully examines the changes the play underwent from the original script to the initial performance.

Kazan, Elia. "Notebook for *A Streetcar Named Desire.*" In *Directors on Directing: A Source Book of the Modern Theatre*, edited by Toby Cole and Helen Krich Chinoy. Indianapolis, Ind.: Bobbs-Merrill, 1976.
This is one of the most insightful accounts of the way in which a play reaches the stage, of what happens from the time a director sees the original script until the curtain finally goes up on the performance. Kazan's comments on the reinterpretation of characters as the play moved toward production are especially trenchant.

Miller, Jordan Y., ed. *Twentieth Century Interpretations of "A Streetcar Named Desire": A Collection of Critical Essays.* Englewood Cliffs, N.J.: Prentice-Hall, 1971.
Although many of the essays in this book are beginning to be dated, they still raise interesting questions and offer valuable interpretations. The collection is truly representative for its time.

Porter, Thomas E. *Myth and Modern American Drama.* Detroit: Wayne State University Press, 1969.
Porter demonstrates how Tennessee Williams uses the "myth of the South" in *A Streetcar Named Desire* (1947). Much of Williams' view of the South was as romanticized and sentimentalized as the views of some of his characters, notably Amanda Wingfield and Blanche DuBois. Porter notes Williams' recognition of the fact that "the old ideals still draw sustenance from that subterranean cavern where emotional prejudices linger." It is on these subterranean emotions that he builds his play. Porter's comparisons of this play with Arthur Miller's *Death of a Salesman* (1949) are particularly apt.

Quarino, Leonard. "The Cards Indicate a Voyage on *A Streetcar Named Desire.*" In *Tennessee Williams: 13 Essays*, edited by Jac Tharpe. Jackson, Miss.: University of Mississippi Press, 1980.
Quarino's focus is on Blanche DuBois. He considers her trip to New Orleans in *A Streetcar Named Desire* (1947) to be a fast-forward vision of what her whole

life has been. He explicates some of the meanings of the poker game and other games of chance in the play.

Schvey, Henry I. "Madonna at the Poker Night: Pictorial Elements in Tennessee Williams' *A Street Car Named Desire.*" In *From Cooper to Philip Roth: Essays on American Literature*, edited by J. Bakker and D. R. M. Wilkinson. Amsterdam: Rodopi, 1980.
A Streetcar Named Desire (1947) is a remarkably visual play. Schvey considers its pictorial aspects and relates them to Williams' building of atmosphere and characterization. He considers Blanche to be, if not virginal, certainly innocent. Schvey is writing essentially for a European audience. He does a fine job of dealing with the play's ambiguities and apparent contradictions.

—————————. *Tennessee Williams: A Tribute.* Jackson, Miss.: University of Mississippi Press, 1977.
This collection devotes one hundred pages to essays that focus on *A Streetcar Named Desire* (1947). The authors are Leonard Quirino, Normand Berlin, Britton J. Harwood, John M. Roderick, Alan Ehrlich, Bert Cardullo, and Vivienne Dickson. They deal with such matters as the use of cards in the play, dramatic space, a study of the play's development through studying the manuscripts, and "complementarity." *Streetcar* is also mentioned extensively in other essays in the collection. The volume has a sensibly selected bibliography and a serviceable index.

Sievers, W. David. *Freud on Broadway: A History of Psychoanalysis and the American Dream.* New York: Hermitage House, 1955.
Of all the plays and playwrights Sievers considers in this book, *A Streetcar Named Desire* (1947) and Tennessee Williams are more germane to his arguments than any other except Eugene O'Neill. Sievers' extremely penetrating consideration of *Streetcar* is essential reading for anyone interested in viewing the play psychoanalytically.

Von Szeliski, John. *Tragedy and Fear: Why Modern Tragic Drama Fails.* Chapel Hill, N.C.: University of North Carolina Press, 1962, 1971.
In support of his argument that most modern tragedy is really "high melodrama," von Szeliski points to *A Streetcar Named Desire* (1947), contending that Blanche (like Willy Loman, Amanda Wingfield, and even Mary Tyrone) is weak. He writes, "Blanche knows bitterly that softness is not allowed in the survival pattern, but Williams prefers and defends softness. The weak are thus destined to become weaker and the strong stronger." This claim has been made by other critics who decry the decline of drama in American literature.

INDEX

Haberman, Donald 156, 158
Hagopian, John V., and Martin Dolch 158
Halperen, Max 43
Hanau, Stella, and Helen Deutsch 27
Hansberry, Lorraine 82, 83
Hart, James D., ed. 6
Hart, Moss 75, 104
Hartnoll, Phyllis, ed. 6
Hayashi, Tetsumaro 111
Hayman, Ronald 36, 111
Headings, Philip R. 64, 68, 70
Heilman, Robert 49
Hellman, Lillian 88
Herron, Ima Honaker 19, 43, 50, 62, 92, 99,
   114, 158, 160
Hilfer, Anthony C. 37
Hill, Linda M. 19, 40
Hinchliffe, Arnold P., ed. 65
Hinden, Michael 139
Hirsch, Foster 163
Hirschfeld, Albert, and Brooks Atkinson 13,
   158, 159
Hochman, Stanley, ed. 6
Hogan, Robert 145
Houghton, Norris 29
Howarth, Herbert 41, 65, 68, 72
Hurrell, John D., ed. 115, 169

Inge, Luther C. 100
Isaacs, Edith J. R. 19, 29, 78

Jackson, Esther Merle 115, 163
Jemie, Onwuchekwa 94
Johnson, Diane 89
Jones, David E. 65, 68, 70, 73
Jones, David Richard 170
Justus, James H. 150

Kanellos, Nicolas 29
Kauffmann, Stanley 19, 42, 114, 116, 134,
   139, 141, 150, 164, 168
Kazan, Elia 170
Keller, Dean H., ed. 7
Kenner, Hugh 65, 68, 71, 72
Kenny, Vincent S. 78
Kernan, Alvin, ed. 20
Kerr, Walter 20, 29, 37, 51, 100, 111, 163
Keyssar, Helene 20, 52, 83, 95
Kheridan, David 150
Kidd, Walter E., and Warren G French, eds. 6
Kiernan, Robert F. 108
Kimbel, Ellen 134
Kinnamon, Keneth, ed. 52
Kitchen, Laurence 20
Klink, William R. 47, 59

Kojecky, Roger 68
Kolin, Philip C., ed. 37
Kolin, Philip C., and J. Madison Davis 37
Koon, Helene Wickham, ed. 116
Kramer, Elaine Fialka, Dorothy Nyren Curley,
   Maurice Kramer, comps. and eds. 4
Kramer, Jerome A., Julian N. Wasserman, Joy
   L. Linsley, eds. 39
Kramer, Maurice, Dorothy Nyren Curley,
   Elaine Fialka Kramer, comps. and eds. 4
Krutch, Joseph Wood 21, 47, 56, 59, 76, 92,
   121, 130, 150
Kullman, Colby H., and William C. Young,
   eds. 7

Lederer, Katherine 89
Lee, Lawrence, and Barry Gifford 151
Lee, Robert C. 137
Lester, Eleanor 29
Lewis, Allan 21, 38, 59, 89, 100, 113, 121,
   131, 151, 157, 164
Lewis, Arthur, and June Schlueter 136
Lewis, Emory 83
Lewis, Sinclair 92
Lewisohn, Ludwig 77
Linsley, Joy L., Julian N. Wasserman, Jerome
   A. Kramer, eds. 39
Little, Stuart W. 30
Litz, A. Walton, ed. 65
Loeffler, Donald L. 38
Londre, Felicia Hardison 164
Loney, Glenn, ed. 7
Lovell, James, Jr., ed. 7
Lower, Charles, and William Fee 79
Lyons, Bonnie 89

McCalmon, George, and Christian Moe 79
McCann, John S. 164
McCarthy, Mary 159
McClure, Arthur 100, 101
McCrindle, Joseph F., ed. 21
McDowell, Margaret B. 108
Macebuh, Stanley 52
MacNicholas, John 7
Madden, David, ed. 21
Magill, Frank N., ed. 8
Malpede, Karen, ed. 83
Manheim, Michael 131, 137, 139, 141-144
Mantle, Burns 22
Mapp, Edward, ed. 8
Marable, Mary Hays, and Elaine Boylan 54,
   147
Martine, James J. 131
Mason, Jeffrey D. 105
Matthews, T. S. 66

INDEX

Sheaffer, Louis 77, 133
Sheibler, Rolf 140
Shivers, Alfred S. 48
Shuman, R. Baird 101, 124, 154
Sievers, W. David 24, 51, 57, 91, 101, 151,
    154, 171
Simon, John 84
Simon, Linda 157
Skinner, Richard Dana 60
Slide, Anthony, ed. 10
Smalley, Webster, ed. 96
Smith, Bruce 166
Smith, Carol H. 66, 69-72
Smith, Grover, Jr. 67
Smith, Wendy 31
Spearman, Walter, assisted by Samuel Selden
    32, 80
Spender, Stephen 69, 73
Spiller, Robert E., ed. 10
Spoto, Donald 101, 166
St. Just, Maria 165
Standley, Fred L., and Nancy V. Burt 53
Stanton, Stephen S. 166
Steen, Mike 102, 166
Stenz, Anita Maria 39
Stott, William, with Jane Stott 24
Stroupe, John H., ed. 134

Taylor, Patricia E. 96
Taylor, William E. 48
Teichmann, Howard 106
Tharpe, Jac, ed. 167
Thompson, Judith J. 167
Tischler, Nancy M. 167
Tiusanen, Timo 134
Toohey, John L. 92
Tracy, Steven C. 97
Triesch, Manfred 91
Turner, Darwin T. 97

Twentieth-Century Literary Criticism 10
Tyce, Richard 39
Tynan, Kenneth 113, 167

Van Laan, Thomas F. 135
Von Szeliski, John 24, 171
Vos, Melvin 39
Voss, Ralph F. 102

Waite, Marjorie Peabody 148
Wasserman, Julian N., Joy L. Linsley, Jerome
    A. Kramer, eds. 39
Wasson, Tyler, ed. 10
Waterman, Arthur R. 77
Weales, Gerald 25, 32, 45, 51, 84, 102, 117,
    124, 152
Welland, Dennis 113, 117
Westling, Louise 109
Wharton, James F. 51
White, Sidney Howard 93
Wikborg, Eleanor 109
Williams, Dakin, and Shepherd Mead 168
Williams, Edwina Dakin, as told to Lucy
    Freeman 168
Williams, J. Kenny 97
Williams, Jay 25
Williams, Raymond 69, 74
Willis, Kendall J. 10
Wood, Audrey, with Max Wilt 102
Wright, William 91

Yaakov, Juliette, and John Greenfield, eds. 10
Young, Stark 93, 143
Young, William C., ed. 11
Young, William C., and Colby H. Kullman,
    eds. 7

Zeigler, Joseph Wesley 32